Writing about Literature

AN INTRODUCTORY GUIDE

Writing about Literature

AN INTRODUCTORY GUIDE

PETER MELVILLE

University of Winnipeg

NELSON / EDUCATION

NELSON / E D U C A T I O N

Writing about Literature
by Peter Melville

**Vice President,
Editorial Director:**
Evelyn Veitch

**Editor-in-Chief,
Higher Education:**
Anne Williams

Executive Editor:
Laura Macleod

**Senior Marketing
Manager:**
Amanda Henry

Developmental Editor:
Theresa Fitzgerald

Permissions Coordinator:
Natalie Russell

**Content Production
Manager:**
Claire Horsnell

Production Service:
KnowledgeWorks Global
Limited

Copy Editor:
Margaret Crammond

Proofreader:
Jayaprakash

Indexer:
Kevin Broccoli

**Senior Production
Coordinator:**
Ferial Suleman

Design Director:
Ken Phipps

Managing Designer:
Franca Amore

Interior Design:
Sharon Lucas

Cover Design:
Sharon Lucas

Cover Image:
Ikon Images/Corbis

Compositor:
KnowledgeWorks Global
Limited

Printer:
RR Donnelly

**Library and Archives Canada
Cataloguing in Publication
Data**

Melville, Peter, 1973-
    Writing about literature:
    an introductory guide /
    Peter Melville.–1st ed.

Includes bibliographical
references and index.
ISBN 978-0-17-650105-1

    1. English language–
Rhetoric. 2. Literature–
History and criticism–Theory,
etc. 3. Criticism–Authorship.
4. Academic writing. I. Title.
PE1479.C7M44 2011 808'.042
C2010-904851-2

ISBN 13: 978-0-17-650105-1
ISBN 10: 0-17-650105-3

CONTENTS

PREFACE   viii

PART ONE: WHERE TO BEGIN   1

CHAPTER ONE: WHAT IS LITERATURE?   2
What Is Literature?   2
Writing about Literature (An Overview)   11
Works Cited   12

CHAPTER TWO: DIFFERENT WAYS OF WRITING ABOUT LITERATURE   13
What a Writing Assignment Is Asking You to Do   13
What to Do When You Are Given a Writing Topic   16
What to Do When You Are *Not* Given a Writing Topic   18
Building a Thesis   22
Journal Entries and Response Papers   26
Non-research Essays (Comparative and Non-comparative)   27
Research Essays   29
Sample Research Paper   30
Works Cited   35

CHAPTER THREE: DIFFERENT CRITICAL APPROACHES   36
Formalism/New Criticism   36
Structuralist Criticism   38
Deconstruction (Poststructuralist Criticism)   40
Reader-Response Criticism   42
Psychoanalytic Criticism   43
Marxist Criticism   45
Feminist Criticism   46
Gender Criticism and Queer Theory   48
New Historicism   50
Postcolonial Criticism and Critical Race Theory   51
Works Cited and Consulted   53
Suggested Further Reading   54

PART TWO: WRITING ABOUT LITERARY GENRES AND FILM   57

CHAPTER FOUR: WRITING ABOUT POETRY   58
What Is Poetry?   58
Who Is Speaking in a Poem and How?   59

What Is Happening? Where Does It Happen? And When?   62
Poetic Language   63
Prosody: Scanning for Sound   67
Poetic Form and Structure   70
Reading Demonstration: Poetry and New Criticism   73
Student Writing   74
Works Cited   78
Appendix: "Ode to a Nightingale" by John Keats   79

CHAPTER FIVE: WRITING ABOUT FICTION   83

What Is Fiction?   83
Plot   84
Narration and Point of View   87
Fictional Characterization   89
Setting   91
Symbolism and Theme   93
Reading Demonstration: Short Fiction and Feminism   95
Student Writing   97
Works Cited   102

CHAPTER SIX: WRITING ABOUT DRAMA   104

What Is Drama?   104
Character and Characterization   105
Structure and Plot   108
Setting . . . the Stage   110
Language and Style   111
Theme   113
Dramatic Type: Tragedy vs. Comedy   115
Reading Demonstration: *Hamlet* and New Historicism   117
Student Writing   119
Works Cited   123

CHAPTER SEVEN: WRITING ABOUT FILM   124

What is (Narrative) Film?   124
A Quick Note on Taking Notes   125
Narrative, Character, and Point of View   125
Mise-en-scène: Staging the Scene   127
Cinematography: Composing and Framing the Shot   128
Editing the Image   130
Reading Demonstration: *Trainspotting* and Kristevan Psychoanalysis   132
Works Cited   135

PART THREE: FOLLOWING THROUGH ON THE WRITING PROCESS   137

CHAPTER EIGHT: OUTLINES, DRAFTS, AND REVISIONS   138

Stage 1: From Thesis to Outline   138
Stage 2: The First Draft   142
Stage 3: Revising the First Draft   147
Stage 4: Proofreading and Peer Review   153
Stage 5: Reworking the Final Draft   154

PART FOUR: DOCUMENTING YOUR SOURCES AND FORMATTING YOUR PAPER   157

CHAPTER NINE: DOCUMENTING YOUR SOURCES AND FORMATTING YOUR PAPER   158

Citing Literary Works   159
Secondary Sources: How to Find Them   163
Secondary Sources: How to Cite and Reference Them   164
Preparing a List of Works Cited   167
Formatting: What Your Paper Should Look Like   172

APPENDIX: GLOSSARY OF CRITICAL TERMS   174

INDEX   181

PREFACE

This guide is designed as an accessible introduction to and future reference guide for writing about literature in the university or college classroom. It offers a comprehensive, step-by-step account of the writing process, from crafting a thesis statement and building an outline to revising drafts and producing a polished essay. In addition to offering strategies for different kinds of writing assignments (including journal entries, response papers, and research and non-research essays), the guide consistently underscores the importance of critical approaches to thinking and writing about literature. At each stage in the process, students are encouraged to consider not only the literary structures of a text, but also the ways that texts are shaped ideologically by the cultures in which they are produced and consumed. Accordingly, chapters on major genres attempt to integrate formal approaches to poetry, fiction, drama, and film with the insights of critical schools such as deconstruction, feminism, New Historicism, and psychoanalysis. While this combined focus on formal and critical approaches to literature and film forms a significant part of the guide's import and value, the guide is equally committed to providing a wide variety of student writing samples and reading demonstrations that reinforce basic writing skills and proper documentation methods.

The first part of the guide discusses what literature is, what sort of writing is typically assigned in first-year English courses, and what kind of theoretical approaches students may be asked to consider when writing about literature. Part 2 gives students an idea of what to look for when writing about different literary genres and/or film. Part 3 offers an example of an essay that has undergone much revision from its outline stage through its various draft stages, while Part 4 acts as a reference guide for formatting an essay and documenting different kinds of primary and secondary sources. Finally, a glossary of terms appears in the Appendix. While this book offers guidance throughout the different stages of the writing process, it is important to keep in mind that writing, like any other skill, requires practice. With a bit of patience and a willingness to revise and rewrite, your skills are bound to improve.

ACKNOWLEDGMENTS

I am indebted to my friend Richard Almonte for giving me the idea of writing this book and to Laura Macleod of Nelson Education for helping me to envision its overall concept and design. I would like to thank several members of the University of Winnipeg's Department of English for offering suggestions and sound advice (and allowing me to bend their ears), including Andrew Burke, Brandon Christopher, Murray Evans, Candida Rifkind, Heather Snell, and

Deborah Schnitzer. I am especially grateful to my developmental editor, Theresa Fitzgerald, for her friendly guidance and editorial assistance. I would also like to thank my research assistant Rebecca Widdicombe for her excellent work on the glossary that appears at the end of this book. For their invaluable insight and helpful suggestions, I am indebted to my manuscript reviewers: Majero Bouman, York University; Julie Cairnie, University of Guelph; Kathy Cawsey, Dalhousie University; Claudia Clausius, University of Western Ontario; Susanne Marshall, Dalhousie University; and Linda Rodenburg, Lakehead University. I am likewise grateful to everyone at Nelson Education who helped bring this work into print. As always, thanks go to Kerry Feeney for her generous encouragement and support. This book is dedicated to her and to Kate and Ben.

Part 1

WHERE TO BEGIN

Pocket watch and trees © IDC/amanaimagesRF/Getty Images.
Vintage script © Imagezoo/Images.com/Getty Images

What Is Literature?

WHAT IS LITERATURE?

As a general category of writing, "literature" can be remarkably difficult to define without at some point resorting to clichés about so-called literary excellence. What is excellence exactly, and how is it measured? According to literary historians, many people's assumptions about the exemplary nature of literature are indebted to the ideas of a nineteenth-century Oxford professor and poet by the name of Matthew Arnold. Best known for a kind of writing that blends literary criticism and cultural critique, Arnold believed that "culture" (his favourite example being literature) referred to humanity's "pursuit of [its] total perfection by means of getting to know . . . the best which has been thought and said in the world" (6). More specifically, he believed that by celebrating and making known the ideals and values embodied by literature and other "good" cultural pursuits such as art and architecture, English society would be able to triumph over and transcend what he called its "present difficulties" (6), which was his way of referring to the escalating conflict between the working and middle classes that eventually led to London's Hyde Park riots in 1866. According to Arnold, this sort of conflict might have been avoided were everyone given a well-rounded education in literature and culture. Members of both the working and middle classes would then have been prepared to put aside their differences and work toward the nation's more dignified quest for moral and intellectual refinement.

Arnold's recommendations for the ends of culture have since been the object of much suspicion, not least for his cavalier treatment of the concerns of a disenfranchised group such as England's nineteenth-century working classes. His ideas about literature nevertheless entrenched themselves within England's twentieth-century popular consciousness with the help of his best-known disciple F.R. Leavis, who is often credited for being the architect of the modern-day English department. Troubled by what he believed was a harmfully pervasive culture of standardization and levelling down that emerged in England and abroad in the years following the First World War, Leavis proposed that society might be saved by an elite "minority" of professors and academics who could not only appreciate the great literary works of the past and present, but also impart the values contained in these texts to future generations (4). His plan, which he first implemented at Cambridge University, was to instruct this minority to combat the powers of standardization by training the masses in the art of "close reading"—a very specific technique of reading literature discussed in Chapter 3. For Leavis, in other words, the "slow climb back" to civilized society that his colleague I.A. Richards thought was still possible began with the meticulous consideration of literary structures (qtd. in Leavis 30).

Leavis's lofty pretensions about the soul-saving power of literary study (widely accepted throughout the first half of the twentieth century) remain a source of some embarrassment for those whose profession it is to teach literature today, which is perhaps why his story is rarely discussed outside (or even within) academic circles.[1] It is nevertheless possible to sense an implicit awareness of his elitist ideals in the cynical objection of a person who, after being told that his or her favourite work of fiction can hardly be called literature, retorts, "What is literature, anyway? Who decides these things?" Such questions draw attention to the tendency of the word "literature" to privilege not only certain texts thought to be exemplary or even timeless, but also anyone who claims to be in a position to judge good writing from bad, literature from "trash." This is not to say that the category of literature should be abandoned simply because it continues to be used (or *abused*) at times to single out an "enlightened few" from the rest of the populace. Rather, we should keep in mind that thinking and writing about literature often involve thinking and writing about the *politics* of literature. As a professor of mine once told me, always ask yourself "*cui bono?*"—who benefits? Whose value systems are confirmed—and whose are denied—when a text is deemed worthy or unworthy of the name "literature"?

More than just a matter of politics, however, literature is also a matter of what academics call "aesthetics," which is to say, it is also a matter of *form*. When the question "What is literature?" arises out of a genuine sense of perplexity, particularly when a person is confronted by something that claims the title of literature but at the same time challenges his or her understanding of what literature is, then what that person is really asking is "What constitutes literary form? How is a work of literature recognized *as literature* and not something else?" The feeling of being puzzled before an aesthetic object with high aspirations is perhaps more common within the context of the art world, where one regularly

---

1 For more on the history of Arnold's and Leavis's ideas, see Eagleton.

hears passionate objections to the validity of certain kinds of abstract painting, performance art, or what controversial artist duo Christo and Jeanne-Claude call environmental installation art. While there are enough paint-splattered canvases and fabric-wrapped monuments to keep the art world guessing about the nature of art, there are likewise works of literature that may confound a person's literary sensibilities. The same person who denies the artistic merit of a Jackson Pollock painting, for example, might also deny, because of its apparent simplicity, the literariness of a work such as Ezra Pound's* most widely anthologized poem, "In a Station at the Metro," which is short enough to recite in a single breath: "The apparition of these faces in the crowd; / Petals on a wet, black bough" (1003). Most people accept the idea that poetry, especially modern or contemporary poetry, is shorter than other kinds of writing, but students often complain that some poems are simply too short and that Pound's haiku-like couplet, being a prime example, lacks enough substance to be taken seriously.

If Pound's little poem challenges one's sense of the *magnitude* of literature, then what is a person to think when confronted by the aggressive vulgarity of language in a novel such as Kathy Acker's *Empire of the Senseless*, where expletives (far too graphic to reprint here) are as common as punctuation? Acker's relentless use of obscene language does have a sophisticated purpose to it—namely, to expose and dismantle the hierarchies of sexual difference that she believed were embedded in literary convention and everyday speech. Still, a person might just as well disagree and call it pornography. The same could be said of the novels of Henry Miller. Lauded by some as groundbreaking and brilliant, Miller's writing is also criticized for being crass and deeply chauvinistic. Who is to judge such matters? At what point is it safe to say that one work is innovative or avant-garde while another is exploitative or sexist or just plain bad?

Once again, we return to the political question of who decides what literature is and what it is not. We should hardly be surprised by such a return, since this question has haunted literary studies for decades, if not centuries. We will revisit this line of inquiry at various points throughout this guide, particularly when discussing what some literary scholars call "the **canon**"—a term that refers to the collection of widely recognized "major" works and "classic" authors that make up a given culture's literary history. When asked to define literature, a person might simply say, "It's the canon." That person, especially if they are English-speaking, might then point to the works of Chaucer, Spenser, Shakespeare, Milton, Dryden, Pope, Wordsworth, Coleridge, Tennyson, Browning, Yeats, T.S. Eliot, and so on. Again we must ask ourselves, "*Cui bono?*" Who benefits from the canonization of such writers? A feminist might say the answer is simple: men benefit from the canon. Notice that the list of writers provided

---

*By Ezra Pound, from *Personae,* copyright © 1926 by Ezra Pound. Reprinted by permission of New Directions Publishing Corp.

is entirely composed of men. It could easily have included women writers such as Mary Shelley, Jane Austen, the Brontë sisters, and Virginia Woolf, but even these widely known women have had difficulty over the years securing a place in the English canon.[2] An important strategy of feminist literary criticism has been to revise or "Re-vision" a canon that has been historically biased toward men's writing (Rich 537). A Marxist literary scholar, on the other hand, might argue that the formation of the canon has disregarded the value of working-class literary production and therefore benefits the bourgeoisie. It is also worth pointing out that the canon tends to be predominantly white, British, and/or American. The presence of such biases have led some critics to prefer the term "selective tradition" when speaking about the "great works" of literary history. Emphasis falls on the word "selective" to show that the tradition, not unlike a person with "selective hearing," tends to remember only the texts it wants to.

As you can see, arriving at a definitive understanding of literature is a difficult business. Nevertheless, there are ways of thinking broadly about literature that can allow us to focus on the task of developing our writing skills. Taking into consideration many of the things mentioned above, we can identify the following general properties of literature.

1. Literature is literary.

To say that literature is literary sounds redundant, but this is more or less how the *Oxford English Dictionary* defines literature:* "1. [L]iterary culture," "2. [L]iterary work or production," and "3. Literary productions as a whole" (1638). Dictionaries often provide synonyms or related words in their definitions that send the reader on a circular journey from one word to the next and back again. As a case in point, the *OED*'s third definition for "[L]iterary"** merely returns us to where we began: "3. Of or pertaining to, or of the nature of, literature" (1638). Fortunately, the *OED* does say something about the word "literary" that corresponds with the way literary theorists occasionally understand the term: "1. Pertaining to the letters of the alphabet" (1638). In this instance, the term "literary" sounds rather uncomplicated and threatens to make anything that involves the use of letters a work of literature. The important thing to consider is that literature is literary in as much as it is *about* language (letters, words, etc.). More precisely, it is about certain *uses* of language that draw attention to language itself.

Consider Robert Burns's most famous line of poetry: "O, my luve's like a red, red rose" (1). A number of things are happening in this line that draw our

---

2 You might also have noticed that the above list of writers in the canon consists entirely of poets. The long tradition of privileging poetry over other forms of writing is also potentially a feminist issue. In the Romantic period (1789–1832), women writers of fiction were among the most admired and widely read writers of the day; but we continue to hear primarily of the six major male Romantic poets: Blake, Wordsworth, Coleridge, Keats, P.B. Shelley, and Byron.

Compact Oxford English Dictionary definition "Literature". By permission of Oxford University Press.
**Compact Oxford English Dictionary* definition "Literary". By permission of Oxford University Press.

attention to its use of language. First, the spelling of "luve," which is meant to approximate what is known as Scots language, draws our attention to (without telling us explicitly) who is speaking the line—most likely a rural Scotsman. Second, we notice that Burns has employed the use of a **simile**, which is to say, a direct comparison of two things using the words "like" or "as." From a logical point of view, it is difficult to imagine exactly how a person's love could be likened to a rose, especially since the one thing is an emotion and the other is a physical object. But literary language is not always logical, and in this case, allows us to contemplate two seemingly unrelated ideas simultaneously so that we might understand them in a more intuitive or impressionistic manner. Finally, Burns's line is perhaps most famous for the **rhythm**, repetition, and **alliteration** contained in the phrase "red, red rose," which together offer a luxurious sense of excess that a simpler, more direct reference to a rose might not otherwise have.

The popularity of Burns's rhythmical comparison between "luve" and a "red, red rose" suggests that there is pleasure to be had in certain uses of literary language. But literary language can hardly be considered unique in this way, since pleasurable uses of language are common in other kinds of writing— commercial advertising, for instance. The Nike slogan "Just do it" draws attention to and reproduces the pleasure people take in the goal-driven intensity of athletic discourse. Nike's slogan is, after all, little more than a copyrighted variation of the popular workout mantra "no pain, no gain"—which has a certain poetic rhythm to it, as well, albeit not a very subtle one. Furthermore, not all literary language is pleasurable. Many who admire James Joyce's literary accomplishments in *Finnegans Wake* (1938) could not honestly say they experienced pleasure in reading this very difficult novel.

Arguably, the best we can say about literary language is that by drawing attention to itself it works to further our understanding of how language works and what it makes possible. In the example of a "red, red rose," we do not just take pleasure in the rhythmical repetition of words and sounds. We are also made aware that literary language allows us to express ourselves and understand the world in ways that other kinds of language—or other artistic mediums such as music or painting—cannot. That is not to say that literature is superior to other art forms. Rather, literature is unique in what it teaches us about verbal language, which is perhaps why some of the most influential theoretical movements in literary studies have had a distinctly linguistic focus. We will consider some of these theories in Chapter 3. Suffice it to say for now that for some literary theorists, such as Paul de Man and Jean-Luc Nancy, literary theory is made possible by virtue of the fact that literary language is always already theoretical about itself. Literary language, in other words, allows literature to be self-reflexive—to think about itself in ways that inspire us to think with it. Its theory, you might say, is built in.

2. Literature is historical.

A discussion on literary language in no way exhausts a satisfactory definition of literature. Consider the following scenario taken from a children's television program: a computer-generated guinea pig rearranges the sentence "Once there was a girl who ate an ice-cream cone" so that it reads "Once there was an ice-cream cone who ate a girl." This example undoubtedly draws attention to language, and it would certainly teach a child (and even remind an adult) about the imaginative possibilities contained in inventive uses of language. Has our guinea pig therefore produced an example of literary language? If so, is it literature? One way for critics to hone their definition of literature has been to argue that, in addition to being literary, literature is also historical. This emphasis on history enables critics to define literature as a group of texts that demonstrate *historically significant* or *exceptional* examples of literary language. A person might argue, for instance, that the example of the girl eaten by an ice-cream cone is derivative of more noteworthy texts such as Lewis Carroll's *Alice's Adventures in Wonderland* and *Through the Looking-Glass*. Because the linguistic playfulness of Carroll's texts is determined to be historically unique and innovative, they are credited for making a significant contribution to a particular literary tradition—in this case, the tradition of nonsense literature.

This argument returns us yet again to the problem of literary excellence and who decides these things—the problem, that is, of who benefits from the supposed exceptionality of a text. Regardless of whatever biases we may locate in the selective tradition, however, the fact remains that literary traditions exist and have existed *in history* for quite some time. Certain texts and certain authors, for whatever reasons, have been and continue to be recognized for their significance. We cannot change the historical fact, for instance, that T.S. Eliot's recognition of the value of John Donne's poetry had a remarkable impact on Donne's reputation throughout much of the twentieth century. Likewise, literary critics and historians of the future will be unable to change the fact that the reputations of many of today's "best" writers are being decided with the conferral of Governor General's Awards and Pulitzer and Nobel Prizes.

That is not to say that people such as T.S. Eliot or the judges of contemporary literary prizes *should* be determining the shape of the canon. Rather, in addition to identifying the selectiveness, and therefore the partiality, of tradition, we need also to acknowledge the fact that those texts that get selected often acquire enormous historical and cultural significance. It would be possible to argue that sixteenth-century rivals Christopher Marlowe and William Shakespeare were equally skilled as playwrights, but you could not reasonably claim that Marlowe—or any other English writer—has had a more significant impact on English culture than Shakespeare. Shakespeare may or may not deserve such recognition, but his influence is indisputable. He is a major writer of the

English canon because he was *made* one—reiteratively identified as a major writer for over four centuries. Feminists, Marxists, and critical race theorists have understood this power of historical significance for a long time, which explains why they have been so interested in the canon and, more specifically, in changing our perception of the canon. They understand that exposing the biases of the canon is sometimes not enough. Rather, the more effective strategy may well be to harness and/or exploit the power of tradition and history, either by reconstructing the repressed lineage of competing traditions (e.g., working-class or women's literary traditions) or by actively forging new traditions. If the tradition is selective, then its selections are subject to revision and change.

There are many ways to discuss the historicity of literature, but we can conclude by stressing the fact that every work of literature is necessarily a product of its time. This thesis represents a basic assumption shared by New Historicist critics, who believe that literary works are best understood in light of their cultural-historical context. A work of literature will invariably make implicit and explicit references to ideas, values, texts, institutions, and other cultural activities that are specific to its time period. It makes sense, then, to assume that some of the text's meanings will be lost on readers from different historical periods who may be unfamiliar with or confused about such references. Conversely, New Historicists caution us about our own cultural frames of reference, which may include associations and biases that a text from the past might not share. Reading texts through their historical contexts essentially reminds us that interpretation is often a two-way street—or better yet, an intersection where the approach and passage of references and associations require a certain amount of traffic control.

3. Literature is political.

This chapter has already spent a good deal of time discussing the politics of literature. Like any other cultural category, literature continues to be an object of controversy and contentious debate. While literature departments across North America are increasingly associated with left-leaning political attitudes that value social justice and equality over traditions of privilege and entitlement, there are powerful and established voices that continue to resist change and speak out against it. Nevertheless, the politics of literature are not merely a matter of debating the racism or sexism of certain privileged texts or the canonical exclusion of others. Literature is also political insofar as literary works can, and often do, present their own devastating critiques of society. Whereas satirical social commentaries such as Jonathan Swift's "A Modest Proposal" or George Orwell's *Animal Farm* work to expose the follies and contradictions of a given nation or culture, other texts such as Ann Yearsley's "A Poem on the Inhumanity of the Slave Trade" or Alan Ginsberg's "America" are openly revolutionary in their desire to inspire political change. For many people, literature is not simply about commenting on society and its foibles but is interventionist in its aims. It seeks to make a political difference. One need only look at the latest list of persecuted authors across the world to see just how dangerous the business of writing literature can be and how frightened certain governments are by the political influence literary writings can have.[3]

4. Literature is powerfully affective.

If literature has political power, then it can likewise influence or *affect* its readers on a personal level. Drawing on the power of sentiment, literature often seeks to sway and/or manipulate its readers' passions and emotional responses. A **tragedy** such as Shakespeare's *Hamlet*, for instance, builds dramatic tension by deliberately frustrating its audience's desire for the swift execution of justice until relieving this tension in a final moment of **catharsis**, or purging of emotion (see Chapter 6). A **comedy** such as Shakespeare's *A Midsummer Night's Dream*, on the other hand, works to delight its audiences through light-hearted story lines and by encouraging laughter. When people say that a work is beautiful or sublime, they are really referring to the way that work makes them *feel*, since beauty and sublimity are, by definition, subjective states of mind that a person experiences when engaged in the act of reading—or in the case of drama, viewing a play. "Pathos" is another common affect of literary works; it occurs when readers are deeply moved or saddened by the suffering of otherwise sympathetic characters. Because readers subjectively respond in different ways, a definition of literature as affective will lack conviction without reference to one or more of the definitions above, just as those definitions will lack conviction without reference to literature's affect. There are, after all, plenty of highly affective texts (e.g., spy fiction, greeting-card poetry, etc.) that you would not typically find in the literature section of your average bookstore. By the same token, however, it would be difficult to imagine a work with literary, historical, and/or political significance that did not also *affect* its readers in powerful and compelling ways.

5. Literature is arguably so much more.

Without question, there will be readers who take issue with the characterization of literature that has been presented here so far, just as there will be readers who will have wanted more radical interpretation or definition. Among other

---

3 Every year the Human Rights Watch (HRW) organization awards a number of Hellman-Hammett Grants to writers "who have been victims of political persecution and are in financial need" (par. 1). In 2007, they awarded 45 grants to writers from 22 nations who had been harassed, censored, or imprisoned for what they had written. The grants are named after playwright Lillian Hellman and novelist Dashiell Hammett, who were persecuted in the United States under Senator Joseph McCarthy's anti-communist hearings in the 1950s.

things, it could be said that literature is *geographical*, inasmuch as literary traditions often contribute to the formation of national or (in the case of some Aboriginal literatures) more local identities. Geographical concerns, however, might well be subsumed under the category of politics. As the Greek origins of the word "politics" suggest, politics is as much about geography (*polis* means city) as it is about people (*politēs* means citizen). In any event, you have to begin somewhere, and the above list provides the starting points from which this guide will proceed.

Summary

WHAT IS LITERATURE?

1. Literature is literary.

    • literature often draws attention to its creative use of language

    • it exemplifies the power that language has to shape and/or change the way we view and understand the world around us

2. Literature is historical.

    • the word "literature" can refer to literary traditions (i.e., lists of major works and authors) that exist in history, but which are also subject to revision and change

    • literary works are necessarily products of their time and therefore make references that readers from other historical periods may not fully understand

3. Literature is political.

    • as expressions of social values, literary traditions can be biased in terms of race, class, gender, sexuality, and so on

    • individual literary works can present their own devastating critiques of society and may be interventionist, even revolutionary, in their aims

4. Literature is powerfully affective.

    • literature frequently draws on the power of sentiment to sway and manipulate its readers' passions and emotional responses

    • it aspires to *move* its readers in meaningful ways

5. Literature is arguably so much more.

WRITING ABOUT LITERATURE (AN OVERVIEW)

As is the case with writing about most things, writing about literature involves building an argument and proving that argument through examples. In the previous section, for instance, we set out to identify a subject (literature) and introduced a problem about that subject in the form of a question (what is literature?). We then constructed an argument to answer that question (literature is literary, historical, political, affective, etc.) and used various examples throughout to prove our claims. In this sense, writing about literature is not unlike the work of a court lawyer. In order to make a claim about a text, you need to collect your evidence (citations, references to secondary material, etc.) and build an argument around that evidence. The more convincing your evidence and argument are, the tighter your case will be.

In the next chapter, we will discuss different kinds of writing assignments that you can expect to encounter in both introductory and upper-year English courses. Since even short writing assignments require students to present some kind of argument, the chapter begins by considering different strategies for choosing a topic and building a thesis. The chapter then introduces three basic types of assignments: response papers, non-research essays, and research papers.

In addition to offering strategies for different kinds of writing assignments, this guide consistently underscores the importance of critical (or theoretical) approaches to thinking and writing about literature. At each stage in the process, you will be encouraged to consider not only the literary structures of a given text, but also the ways that texts are shaped ideologically by the cultures in which they are produced and consumed. Accordingly, Chapter 3 provides brief summaries of (and lists of suggested readings for) a number of critical methodologies, including New Criticism, deconstruction, reader-response criticism, psychoanalysis, Marxism, feminism, queer theory, New Historicism, and postcolonial criticism.

Drawing on examples of student writing, the chapters that make up Part 2 of this guide discuss the process of writing essays on works belonging to the major genres of English literature, including poetry, drama, and fiction. In addition to highlighting literary terms specific to each genre, each chapter in Part 2 offers a number of step-by-step demonstrations of interpretation, including some that utilize the insights of specific critical approaches to reading literature. Since courses that focus either partly or exclusively on the critical study of film are increasingly becoming a regular part of the curriculum in literature departments, Part 2 offers an additional chapter that prepares students to write about film.

Part 3 urges students to consider writing as a craft that requires discipline and a willingness to scrutinize and revise their own work. This section therefore guides students through the entire writing process, from the preliminary steps of building an outline to the writing, editing, and proofreading of multiple drafts of their assignments. Sample outlines and drafts provide concrete examples of how an essay can evolve from an initial rough draft to become a polished paper that is fit to print.

Beginning with a brief discussion on the seriousness of plagiarism and how to avoid it, Part 4 acts as a quick reference guide to documenting both primary and secondary sources in an essay. The chapter covers proper techniques and provides examples for citing from a wide range of electronic and printed texts within the body of an essay and offers guidelines for cross-referencing quotations in a bibliography or list of works cited.

WORKS CITED

Arnold, Matthew. *Culture and Anarchy*. 1869. Ed. J. Dover Wilson. Cambridge: Cambridge UP, 1932. Print.

Burns, Robert. "A Red, Red Rose." *The Age of Romanticism*. Ed. Joseph Black et al. Peterborough, ON: Broadview, 2006. 126. Print. Vol. 4 of *The Broadview Anthology of British Literature*.

Eagleton, Terry. "The Rise of English." *Literary Theory: An Introduction*. 3rd ed. Minneapolis: U of Minnesota P, 2008. 15–46. Print.

Human Rights Watch. "Human Rights Watch / Hellman-Hammett Grants." Human Rights Watch. Web. 22 May 2008.

Leavis, F.R. *Mass Civilization and Minority Culture*. Cambridge: Minority, 1933. Print.

"Literature." *The Compact Edition of the Oxford English Dictionary*. 2 vols. 1971. Print.

"Literary." *The Compact Edition of the Oxford English Dictionary*. 2 vols. 1971. Print.

Pound, Ezra. "In a Station at the Metro." *The Norton Introduction to Literature*. Shorter 9th ed. Ed. Alison Booth, J. Paul Hunter, and Kelly J. Mays. New York: Norton, 2006. 1003. Print.

Rich, Adrienne. "When We Dead Awaken: Writing as Re-Vision." *Criticism: Major Statements*. 3rd ed. Ed. Charles Kaplan and William Anderson. New York: St. Martin's, 1991. 535–50. Print.

Different Ways of Writing about Literature

WHAT A WRITING ASSIGNMENT IS ASKING YOU TO DO

Most writing assignments in the English classroom will ask you to perform the two fundamental activities of literary criticism: interpretation and analysis. Some people would argue that in literary studies interpretation and analysis refer to the same process, which is understandable since every good interpretation implies good analysis and vice versa. For pedagogical (i.e., teaching) reasons, however, it is useful to treat interpretation and analysis as two interdependent but nevertheless distinct aspects of the larger process of writing about literature. They are interdependent insofar as an interpretation of a text will remain speculative and tenuous if unaccompanied by supporting analysis; likewise, an analysis of a text will appear muddled and confused unless it is organized and driven by an intelligible interpretation of the text.

Just about anyone can, and likely will, have an interpretation of a book, a movie, or a poem, but not everyone will have reached that interpretation, or tested it, by way of analysis. After reading W.D. Snodgrass's poem "Leaving the Motel," for instance, a person's initial interpretation may be based primarily on an emotional or even a moral response to the poem. That person may insist that the poem's emphasis on a couple's attempt to conceal every trace of what appears to be an illicit sexual encounter is meant to highlight and condemn the deceptiveness of such affairs. Upon closer examination—which is to say, upon closer *analysis*—of the poem's literary devices, however, that interpretation may very well change. Let us read the whole poem and think about how we might come to a different interpretation:

Leaving the Motel
W.D. Snodgrass*

Outside, the last kids holler
Near the pool: they'll stay the night.
Pick up the towels; fold your collar
Out of sight.

Check: is the second bed
Unrumpled, as agreed?
Landlords have to think ahead
In case of need,

Too. Keep things straight: don't take
The matches, the wrong keyrings—
We've nowhere we could keep a keepsake—
Ashtrays, combs, things

That sooner or later others
Would accidentally find.
Check: take nothing of one another's
And leave behind

Your license number only,
Which they won't care to trace;
We've paid. Still, should such things get lonely,
Leave in their vase

An aspirin to preserve
Our lilacs, the wayside flowers
We've gathered and must leave to serve
A few more hours;

That's all. We can't tell when
We'll come back, can't press claims,
We would no doubt have other rooms then,
Or other names. (1–28)

This poem's various uses of language and other literary devices are too complex to consider here in their entirety, but we can narrow our focus on the metaphorical

---

significance of two objects in the poem—the checklist and the vase of lilacs. Twice the poem's speaker uses the word "Check" as though he or she were reciting a checklist to his or her partner while they clean their motel room. We could read this checklist literally inasmuch as we can imagine the speaker holding in hand, or in mind, an actual list of things to do before leaving the motel—a list that appears to have been prepared in advance and that may have been used in similar situations in the past. As a **metaphor**, however, the checklist implies a deeper meaning: namely, that the couple's rendezvous have become so routinized and predictable that their lovemaking culminates not with intensity or even intimacy, but with feelings more commonly associated with mundane tasks such as filling out a survey or doing the groceries. The speaker's preoccupation with the checklist, in other words, produces a **tone** of detachment that suggests the couple's passion for one another is being stifled by the rituals they must perform to keep their affair secret. From this brief bit of analysis, we can begin to extrapolate a new interpretation in which we understand the poem lamenting the consequences of—rather than straightforwardly condemning—the deception of extramarital affairs.

This interpretation of the poem is strengthened by analyzing the vase of lilacs, the one piece of evidence that the couple purposely leave behind in the room. Like the checklist, the vase of lilacs can be read literally insofar as it is an object into which the speaker intends to place some aspirin for the purpose of prolonging the life of the flowers inside. Also like the checklist, however, the lilacs in the vase have an underlying metaphorical function, which we can glean from the fact that the speaker says they "must" be left "to serve / A few more hours" (23–4). The poem prompts us at this point to stop and consider its use of language: Why must the flowers be left behind? Whom or what exactly do they serve? Although the speaker's meaning remains ambiguous, we could argue that the lilacs "serve" insofar as they *stand* for something—which is to say, they are *symbolic*. They stand as a **symbol** of the couple's passion, which strives to live on and bloom, as it were, despite being cut short from one secretive encounter to the next. (We assume the encounter is brief because, unlike the kids who "holler / Near the pool," the couple will not "stay the night" [1–2]). The aspirin used to preserve the lilacs a while longer also "serves" a metaphorical purpose by representing the speaker's desire to nourish the couple's passion, even as that passion continues to be stifled by their constant need for discretion.

We could continue to analyze the poem and build on our interpretation of it, but the key point here is that analysis has the power to change the way we read and understand a work of literature. Ultimately, literary analysis is about slowing down the reading process in order to discover why (and *how*) we come to a certain interpretation of a text and gain insight into how that text might be interpreted in different and possibly more compelling ways. A good way to approach an English writing assignment, then, is to think of the assignment as asking you to read *slowly*—to look carefully and closely at elements in a text that contribute to the production of the text's overall meaning and significance. This means analyzing not only recognizable literary devices in the text (such as symbols, metaphors, similes, and so on), but also extra-linguistic or non-literary elements such as the text's (and your own) historical, political, and cultural circumstances, all of which we will discuss in the chapters that follow.

The best place to begin reading slowly is the writing assignment itself. The next few sections offer overviews of, and advice on, different kinds of writing assignments; however, because these assignments vary in what they are specifically asking you to do, it is always wise to pay close attention to an assignment handout. Whether I assign specific writing topics or not, my own writing assignment handouts often provide rather detailed instructions, which I review when distributing the handout in class. These instructions can include the due date and expected length of the assignment; whether or not research is unnecessary, recommended, or required; what qualifies as a scholarly (i.e., peer-reviewed) secondary source; and where to find information on proper methods for documenting citations and formatting the paper. Regardless of my attempts to publicize these instructions, however, some students will inevitably submit papers that betray the fact that their reading of my instructions was neither careful nor accurate. I mention all this not to scold before the fact, but to warn you that a failure to follow instructions on an assignment can potentially irritate an instructor, which, if you want your paper to receive a fair assessment, you will obviously want to avoid.

WHAT TO DO WHEN YOU ARE GIVEN A WRITING TOPIC

In a first-year English class, you will typically receive a list of one or more writing topics with your writing assignments, especially in the early stages of the course. While students generally prefer having writing topics, there are a few pitfalls to avoid when beginning such an assignment. The first thing to consider is the fact that a writing topic is not a **thesis**. Writing topics can range from the very precise to the very broad, but they will invariably invite you to produce your own thesis. Finding room to explore your own interests in a list of topics can be difficult, especially when the topics are narrow and appear to steer you in directions you may not want to go. Sometimes talking to your instructor can help, and may even result in permission to pursue an idea that falls outside the list of topics. At other times your choice will be limited to three or four very specific topics. Here is a list of writing topics that affords students only limited freedom to pursue their own interests:

1. Compare and contrast representations of Caliban in Shakespeare's *The Tempest* and Aimé Césaire's *A Tempest*. How is Caliban different in these texts? How is he the same? What do these texts reveal about the category of "the monster"?

2. Compare and contrast representations of monstrosity in Shakespeare's *The Tempest* and Fred M. Wilcox's *The Forbidden Planet*. What does monstrosity symbolize in these works? How is it different in each text? How is it the same?

3. Consider Shakespeare's treatment of Caliban in *The Tempest*. Is the text's representation of Caliban ironic? In other words, is the text's depiction of Caliban a *symptom* or a *critique* of European assumptions about monstrosity and the colonized/native individual? Or is Caliban a mixture of both these possibilities?

One of these topics might appeal directly to a student's interest and that student would then be in a position to proceed to the next step of working toward building a thesis. For a student whose interests are not promptly piqued by these topics, the best strategy might be to re-read the topics and reflect on the general parameters of the assignment. You may want to make a list of questions about these parameters. What texts or works are you being asked to consider? The answer in this case is, of course, Shakespeare's *The Tempest*, Césaire's *A Tempest*, and Wilcox's *The Forbidden Planet*. What are your options with respect to these texts? The assignment above gives you some choice: you can write on either Césaire's *A Tempest* or Wilcox's *The Forbidden Planet*, or you can ignore both; but you have no choice but to write on Shakespeare's *The Tempest*. From this more or less obvious information, you can move to a more significant question: What kind of paper do you want to write—a comparative paper or a non-comparative paper? This is an important question, because (as discussed more fully below) comparative and non-comparative papers each present their own challenges and require different strategies and approaches.

You may need to ask yourself another broad question: What are the similarities and differences between the thematic focus of each topic? As it happens, all three topics above are concerned with literary and/or filmic depictions of monstrosity. Two of the topics (the first and the third) narrow this thematic focus by linking it specifically to the character of Caliban, who appears (albeit quite differently) in both Shakespeare's *The Tempest* and Césaire's *A Tempest*. Caliban is implicitly referred to in the second topic as well, since it would be difficult to imagine a comparison of monstrosity in *The Tempest* and *The Forbidden Planet* that did not consider Caliban. You might nevertheless prefer this topic if you were less intrigued by Caliban than you were by, say, the psychological insights of these works or by issues of modern adaptation. (*The Forbidden Planet* is a science fiction movie loosely based on Shakespeare's *The Tempest*.) Alternatively, if you were interested in representations of race and wanted to try your hand at postcolonial criticism (about which we will have more to say in Chapter 3), then you might be left with a decision to write a comparative paper for the first topic or a non-comparative analysis for the third topic.

There are still more questions to consider: Which topic will enable you to address problems you encountered or questions you had when you read the text? Which topic are you most prepared to address, whether it is because you are more familiar with certain texts or because you think the topic might inspire and challenge you through every stage of the writing process? The point is to read the topics carefully (and slowly) and ask questions such as these so you can find your passion and make the topic your own.

Checklist

WHAT TO DO WHEN YOU ARE GIVEN A WRITING TOPIC

- keep in mind that a writing topic is not a thesis

- find room to explore your own interests (talk to your instructor, if necessary)

- make a list of questions about the general parameters of the assignment (e.g., What texts am I being asked to consider? What are my options regarding these texts? What kind of paper do I want to write—comparative or non-comparative?)

- consider which topic will inspire or challenge you most

WHAT TO DO WHEN YOU ARE *NOT* GIVEN A WRITING TOPIC

When you receive an assignment without writing topics, it does not necessarily mean your instructor is being lazy. Assembling a list of writing topics does take time, but withholding topics can be pedagogically useful. After all, the ultimate goal of an English Department is to teach its students to convert their own unique interests in a work of literature into original literary criticism. Pursuing your own interests in the absence of specific writing topics is often difficult for first- and upper-year students alike. After distributing an assignment without topics, instructors can expect to receive office visits from students expressing their anxieties over not knowing what to write about. In many cases, these students already know generally what they want to write about; they just have trouble translating their interests into a topic narrow enough to manage in the space of five or six pages.

Consider the following scenario in which a first-year student seeks help for her term paper. When asked what she wants to write about, she claims not to know, but when pressed further admits to having thought about writing on Mary Shelley's *Frankenstein*. When asked why she might be compelled to write a paper on *Frankenstein*, she refers to a class discussion in which she was surprised to learn that Shelley was so young when she wrote the novel: "I find it fascinating," she remarks, "that an eighteen-year-old girl could write such a complex book, and one that would be so famous for so long." From this information, the student and her instructor draw two useful conclusions: (1) she is interested in the identity or "subject position" of the author (i.e., a young woman of the early nineteenth century); and (2) she understands *Frankenstein* to be a book of some complexity, one that has made a substantial impression on English culture. These conclusions are useful because they can become the building blocks of the student's own self-crafted writing topic. She could decide to investigate the historical and cultural circumstances of the text's publication and authorship. After learning that *Frankenstein* was published anonymously, for instance, she might write out her own topic in the form of a question (always a good idea): "What is it about *Frankenstein* and the culture in which it was first published that would compel its author to conceal her female identity?"

Alternatively, this student's research might lead her to conclude that despite Shelley's young age she had already endured many difficult life experiences, especially in regard to issues of maternity: Shelley's mother died eleven days after giving birth to her, her own first child (a daughter who remained nameless) died less than two weeks after being born, and her second child (a son named William) was born only a few months before Shelley began writing her novel. Although this second child died approximately eighteen months after *Frankenstein* was published, Shelley seems to have been anxiously clairvoyant about his death insofar as the boy's namesake in the novel (Victor Frankenstein's younger brother William) becomes the monster's first fatal victim. Concluding that *Frankenstein* is a complex book written by a woman of such tragic experience, the student might decide to write an essay on images of the maternal in *Frankenstein*, which is an especially interesting writing topic for a book that frightfully imagines the end of motherhood: in addition to eliminating the need for women in the act of producing new life, Victor Frankenstein fails to nurture and love his creation with the compassion of a mother, which is often said to be the primary cause of the monster's destructive behaviour.

In the end, this particular student decided not to pursue either of these topics, but opted instead to write a paper that considered *Frankenstein* as a feminist critique of science. Yet even this topic found its origins in the student's initial fascination with Shelley's identity as a young nineteenth-century woman and the complexity of her first novel. What is more, the student came to this topic after following her instructor's advice about re-reading the novel with a pen in hand, highlighting and annotating passages that related to her overall interest in the text's complexity and female authorship. As is often the case with this process, a more specific idea emerged as the student discovered commonalities between different passages and noticed connections that she had not recognized in her first reading of the text.

Checklist

WHAT TO DO WHEN YOU ARE *NOT* GIVEN A WRITING TOPIC

- identify your interests: are you drawn to any text(s) in particular; if so, how and why?
- use these interests as the building blocks for your own writing topic
- write out your topic in the form of a question
- re-read the text(s) with a pen in hand, highlighting and annotating passages that relate to your interests

---

Student Writing

Besides the difficulty of identifying and refining your interests, you will have to contend with the fact that even assignments without specific writing topics will ask you to develop your interests in particular ways. Here is an assignment that neither provides a list of specific texts nor gives suggestions for thematic focus, but it does insist on certain structural requirements.

> Compare and contrast any two texts from the anthology on whatever grounds you see fit. Be sure that you consider the significance of your comparison. For instance, if you insist that two poems approach a similar theme/subject in different ways, then be sure to articulate why that difference is important. What might that difference suggest about Romantic poetry, language, consciousness, etc.?

The assignment belongs to an upper-year course on Romanticism, which explains why it is broader in focus than topics you might find in a first-year English assignment. Below is the introduction to a paper that responded to the assignment. Although it is an example of advanced undergraduate writing, the introduction effectively illustrates how you can effectively turn a broad writing suggestion into a topic that is distinctly your own. Notice how it takes its cues from key words in the assignment question above:

> Romantic poetry has often been accused of being an escapist turning away from the political realm and a turning towards an apolitical exaltation of nature, yet the philosophical problems with which such poetry engages often have profound political consequences. The contrast between Samuel

Taylor Coleridge's "Frost at Midnight" and "Fears in Solitude," two poems published together in a pamphlet in 1798, offers a tangible connection between the philosophical and the political aspects of Coleridge's thought in that both poems participate in a coherent project to negotiate the relationship between self and other, the familial and the social. Both poems, I contend, attempt to understand otherness by translating it into a familial relationship, but while "Frost at Midnight" undertakes this act of translation on the individual level, "Fears in Solitude" extends it to the sphere of social and political relations. Moreover, I believe that the failure of the universalizing gesture in "Fears" reveals the inherent political difficulties of Coleridge's concept of organic unity.*

The student who wrote this introduction is clearly interested in what she calls the "political consequences" of Coleridge's poetry. In addition to being clear, her interests are uniquely her own insofar as they are not specifically derived from the writing assignment. Rather, she found a way to explore her own interests within the parameters of an assignment that asks her to compare two texts and to identify the significance of her comparison. In four complex sentences, the student's introduction accomplishes everything the assignment implicitly asks her to do. The first sentence introduces a *problem* that provides the grounds on which the paper's comparison will proceed: in contrast to conventional preconceptions about Romanticism, Coleridge's poetry appears to be profoundly political. The second sentence not only identifies what texts will be compared and contrasted but also suggests how the comparison will shed new light on, and perhaps even resolve, the problem. This second sentence thus prepares the reader for the paper's thesis, which is articulated with conviction in the third sentence: "Both poems, I contend, attempt to understand otherness by translating it into a familial relationship, but while 'Frost at Midnight' undertakes this act of translation on the individual level, 'Fears in Solitude' extends it to the sphere of social and political relations." This thesis statement is especially effective in that it says something original and structures itself in a way that directly corresponds to the task outlined in the assignment: it *compares* the similarities and *contrasts* the differences in Coleridge's two poems. The fourth and final sentence of the introduction does what few undergraduate papers do well: it attempts to extend the paper's thesis by drawing attention to the larger *significance* or possible *consequences* of the paper's argument. Granted, the sentence could have been more effective were it more forcefully written (i.e., if it said "I argue" rather than "I believe"), and the student might have been more precise about her use of the phrase

---

*From "Only Connect: Family Ties and Otherness in Coleridge's 'Fears in Solitude' and 'Frost at Midnight'" by R. Jayne Hildebrand. Reprinted by permission of the author.

"universalizing gesture." The sentence nevertheless suggests that the thesis is not just making a claim, but that there is something at stake in making the claim, namely, the integrity of "Coleridge's concept of organic unity." The student's reader is thus compelled to read on.

BUILDING A THESIS

Selecting a writing topic is, as they say, only half the battle. As mentioned earlier, a writing topic is not a thesis. This applies even to topics that you invent yourself. We have already seen two examples of this. In the case of the student who wrote a paper on *Frankenstein*, the student moved from a general topic of gender identity in *Frankenstein* to the more specific topic of considering *Frankenstein* as a feminist critique of science. Although this more specific topic sounds like a thesis insofar as it potentially makes a claim about Shelley's novel, the claim it makes is still too broad. The student would need to develop this claim in order to produce a thesis focused enough to support a compelling argument. As it happens, the student did sharpen her focus. She argued that, by imagining the destructive consequences of technological progress uncompromisingly fuelled by masculine ambition, *Frankenstein* represents a feminist-inspired cautionary tale of science fiction. Likewise, the sample introduction above does an excellent job of moving from a writing topic that focuses on the political implications of Coleridge's poetry to a thesis statement that makes specific claims about two poems, each of which engages political issues in a particular way.

A thesis or thesis statement, then, is a statement that makes a specific claim. It is not a statement of fact, but a statement that requires further proof and that could be argued *against*. This is not to say that facts have no place in an essay. Rather, an essay *uses* facts—it organizes and interprets them in order to prove an overall argument. This use of facts is what distinguishes an essay from a report. A report on blood imagery in Shakespeare's *Macbeth* (to use an old writing topic standard) would merely state the fact that the play contains blood imagery and then proceed to cite specific instances in the play where blood is either mentioned or alluded to. An essay on the same topic, on the other hand, would still use citations (which are facts in the sense that they represent actual lines from the play) but would also attempt to interpret the particular meaning of each citation while showing how the citation contributes to the essay's main argument. Typically, people argue that blood imagery in *Macbeth* is related in some way to Lady Macbeth's abiding sense of guilt—more specifically, that her famous line "Out, damned spot! out, I say" (5.1.35) represents her desire to be absolved or cleansed of her sins. Her hands are in fact clean, but her guilty conscience sees them as tainted by the murder of her husband's rival. This interpretation sounds obvious because it is conventional, when in fact it is not self-evident at all; meaning in literature is rarely, if ever, self-evident. The interpretation is, however, both reasonable and convincing, which is the goal of every good argument.

In addition to being reasonable and convincing, your argument needs to be perceptible to your reader, which is why your thesis statement is so important. Most effectively located in your paper's opening paragraph, a thesis statement introduces your argument by articulating its most essential elements. It gathers together the strength and flavour of your argument in concentrated form, and it should leave a lasting impression on your reader, since your reader will need to keep the thesis in mind, or be able to recall it without difficulty, throughout your entire paper. Let us look at some examples of weak and strong theses, many of which are based on actual student writing.

Thesis Category 1: The Non-thesis

The only thesis worse than a weak thesis is a thesis that is *not* a thesis. The non-thesis generally comes in two varieties. We have already alluded to the first variety above—namely, the thesis that is a statement of fact. Here is an example:

> Ann Radcliffe's use of the sublime in *The Italian* allows the reader to experience shock and terror within the confines of his/her own safety.

We might have used a more basic example here (such as the non-thesis about *Macbeth* containing blood imagery), but this Radcliffe example is interesting because the sentence *sounds* like a thesis that requires a supporting argument. If we look closely at the statement, however, we see that it does not in fact require such an argument. First, we are given an implied fact that is either true or false: Ann Radcliffe uses the sublime in *The Italian*, which happens to be true in the same way that we can truthfully say that *Macbeth* contains blood imagery. Second, we are told that this use of the sublime allows the reader to experience shock and terror from a position of safety. The problem with this claim is that it is less an argument about Radcliffe's novel in particular than it is a broad definition of the experience of the sublime itself. It is not a thesis any more than "A comedian's use of humour allows his audience to experience laughter" is a thesis. The statement would be equally true were we to substitute Radcliffe's novel with any other work that uses the sublime, such as Horace Walpole's *The Castle of Otranto*, Mary Shelley's *Frankenstein*, or even a painting such as Caspar David Friedrich's *Wanderer above the Sea of Fog*. All of these works allow us to "experience shock and terror" from a position of safety.

The second variety of non-theses includes statements of methodology masquerading as thesis statements. Confusing these two kinds of statements is a common mistake in first-year writing, especially when it comes to comparative essays. The following student introduction consists of two sentences, neither of which is a thesis:

> This paper will compare representations of Grendel in *Beowulf* and John Gardener's *Grendel* as well as the different relationships he has throughout each text. The paper will also consider what these two texts reveal about monstrosity.

This introduction tells us that the student has found a writing topic but has not moved to the next step of building a thesis. We know what the essay will be about (i.e., different representations of monstrosity in *Grendel* and *Beowulf*), but we do not know what it will argue. Instead of vague allusions to forthcoming comparisons and explanations, the student needs to identify precisely what it is that he or she thinks *Beowulf* and *Grendel* reveal about monstrosity.

Thesis Category 2: The Weak Thesis

The weak thesis generally lacks specificity. It makes a claim, but the claim is too broad to offer unique insight into the significance and meaning of a text. Here is an example:

> This essay will focus on the differences and similarities between the two texts, proving that both works warn us that progress can sometimes be very bad.

This student's essay mentions earlier which texts will be considered, so the absence of the names of these texts is not what makes this thesis too general. Rather, the references to differences and similarities are too vague. Generally speaking, any two texts (whether they are written by the same author or by different authors) will share similarities and differences. Without pointing to specific similarities and differences, your thesis will not tell your reader very much. The second half of this thesis is likewise too vague to be helpful. The reference to "progress" needs to be qualified further so that we know what kind of progress is being cited in this instance (social progress, technological progress, intellectual progress, etc.). The final phrase "can sometimes be very bad" is also problematic insofar as it is both informal and imprecise. What does the student mean by "bad"? Is progress bad for the environment, for society, or for humanity in general? Is it bad in terms of being destructive or in terms of being immoral?

This second example of a weak thesis begins with some strength but finishes with a bit of a whimper:

> While his poetry appears to strive consistently for the truth, Keats's stamp is noticeable throughout.

Since the pursuit of truth is a widely recognized feature of Keats's poetry, this thesis could be more specific about the kind of truth to which it alludes. Is it truth about suffering, about life, about poetry, or about oneself? More troubling than this, however, is the student's reference to Keats's "stamp." The essay topic for this assignment asked students to consider what makes Keats's poetry unique. Saying that Keats's "stamp" is noticeable throughout his poetry merely restates the essay topic in different words. If, on the other hand, the student had argued that Keats's poetry is marked by a consistent pursuit of one or more *particular* truths (identifying those truths by name) and that Keats's "stamp" is shown through the use of a specific form, then he or she would be closer to producing a strong thesis.

Thesis Category 3: The Strong Thesis

We have already witnessed one example of a strong thesis in the sample introduction cited above. That thesis reads as follows: "Both poems, I contend, attempt to understand otherness by translating it into a familial relationship, but while 'Frost at Midnight' undertakes this act of translation on the individual level, 'Fears in Solitude' extends it to the sphere of social and political relations." We noted that this thesis statement is strong not only because it says something original but also because it identifies specific differences and similarities. It is also worth noting that the thesis is provocative in that it makes a claim (or a series of claims) that the paper will need to prove. It prompts the reader to question whether or not such an argument can be made, which in turn entices that reader to continue reading.

More generally, a strong thesis makes connections between elements and ideas in a text. A strong thesis about W.D. Snodgrass's "Leaving the Motel" would not only point out that the poem emphasizes a cheating couple's deceptiveness instead of their passion for one another. Rather, it would also pinpoint a reason for this emphasis:

> W.D. Snodgrass's "Leaving the Motel" focuses on a couple's deceitful actions not to condemn their illicit affair but to lament a need to deceive that threatens to overwhelm and even destroy the couple's passion for one another.

Since even a strong thesis cannot stand on its own, this thesis would need to be surrounded by supporting sentences that alluded, for instance, to how the poem's complex use of figurative language (its checklist metaphor, the symbolism of the vase of lilacs, and so on) corroborates the paper's thesis. Likewise, the thesis would be further strengthened by a follow-up sentence that spoke to the significance of the paper's argument—a brief but provocative statement, perhaps, on the conflict between a society's moral strictures and the fulfillment of sexual desire.

Summary

BUILDING A THESIS

- a writing topic is not a thesis

- a thesis statement is not a statement of fact, but a statement that requires further proof and that could be argued *against*

- a thesis is most effectively located in your opening paragraph

- a strong thesis makes connections between elements and ideas in a text and speaks to the significance of your overall argument

- be specific: if you claim that two texts share similarities and differences, then identify those similarities and differences and explain why they are important to consider

JOURNAL ENTRIES AND RESPONSE PAPERS

It is always a good idea to build a strong thesis even for smaller writing assignments such as journal entries and response papers. To be sure, instructors often assign these kinds of shorter writing exercises to allow students to explore ideas that can be developed later in more formal and lengthier essay assignments. Journal entries are perhaps less straightforward than response papers and tend to cause more anxiety in students. The two most common concerns that students have about journal entries are (1) how to write them and (2) how they will be graded. Responding to the first concern is difficult, since journals are typically meant to be informal. They are usually more subjective or personal (i.e., "I" statements are not always discouraged) and are useful places to experiment with your own observations, speculations, and impressions. Occasionally, you will be given a choice to write either a *critical* entry, which involves some level of textual analysis and interpretation, or a *creative* entry that explores texts and/or ideas in a more artistic fashion (i.e., through writing poetry or fiction or producing graphic art). In either case, having a thesis will help focus your efforts, whether it be in terms of organizing your analysis in a critical entry or in terms of communicating the underlying idea behind your creative entry. How journal entries are marked is always left to the discretion of the instructor, but apart from following the explicit instructions of the assignment, a good rule of thumb is to make sure your entries demonstrate evidence of effort, deep thought, and the kind of slow reading and critical analysis discussed above.

Response papers (also called reflection papers) similarly require effort and deep thought. They, too, are personal insofar as they involve the writer's own particular responses to and reflections on a text, but they generally adhere to a more formal structure than journal entries. "I" statements are not entirely inappropriate, but since a response paper is more like a short essay, these statements should be used more sparingly than in journal entries.[1] While avoiding too much plot summary or paraphrase, a good response paper will often involve, and even combine, *commentary* (i.e., an overall understanding of the ideas and happenings in a text) or *explication* (i.e., a close reading that reveals a text's meaning as it unfolds one line or episode at a time). You would typically begin a response paper (as you would a strong essay) with an introductory paragraph that quickly introduces the topic or focus of the paper and offers a thesis statement (or thesis-driven question) provoked by your own particular interests in the text(s). The body of the response paper (which is to say, the paragraphs that fall between the introduction and conclusion) does more or less what the body of an essay does, but in a more economical fashion: it seeks to prove the validity of the thesis statement or, in the case of a thesis-driven question, seeks to prepare the reader for the paper's conclusions.

NON-RESEARCH ESSAYS (COMPARATIVE AND NON-COMPARATIVE)

Chapter 8 discusses the various steps involved in writing an essay, from building an outline to producing a final draft. Nevertheless, in keeping with this chapter's focus on the different kinds of writing assignments, the next two sections highlight, albeit in a general way, some of the principal components of non-research and research essays. A non-research paper is comparable to a response paper insofar as your primary aim will be to construct an argument that supports your own interpretation of a text, but that argument will consist of a longer, more detailed analysis. Whereas a response paper might focus on the recurrence of a single literary element throughout a text, such as an **image** or a **symbol**, an essay might either delve further into the nature and significance of that recurrence or widen the paper's analysis to include a more comprehensive discussion of several of the text's elements in relation to one another. A strong essay would also demonstrate how the analysis of such elements supports or proves a larger statement or thesis about the text as a whole. To return to the example of *Frankenstein*, a response paper might pinpoint and analyze a few **scenes** or **episodes** in which Victor Frankenstein's failure to offer compassion for his creature motivates that creature to unleash violence against Victor's friends and family. An essay that proceeds along the same lines, on the other

---

1 Basically, avoid "I" statements that express unsubstantiated opinions (e.g., "I feel" or "I like" or "I think"). On the other hand, "I" statements that are evidence-based or that refer in some way to your argument are perfectly acceptable (e.g., "I argue" or "I contend").

hand, might go further by considering these scenes within the larger context of Victor's ambition (which isolates him from his family and friends even before the creature awakens) as well as his desire to circumvent the need for women in the act of creation itself. Broadening the analysis in this way (and therefore connecting these different aspects of the text) would allow an essay to offer a more substantial thesis, like the one mentioned earlier in this chapter: "By imagining the destructive consequences of technological progress uncompromisingly fuelled by masculine ambition, *Frankenstein* represents a feminist-inspired cautionary tale of science fiction."

Although this thesis could be further supported through reference to historical or biographical research, such references would not be entirely necessary within the parameters of a non-research essay assignment. Remember that the point of a non-research writing assignment is to encourage you to become familiar with applying a form of analysis to a text based on your own perspective and experience with that text. Such an analysis need not be limited to a single text. As we have seen in earlier examples, a writing assignment (regardless of whether it has a research component or not) may ask you to write a comparative essay that analyzes two or more texts. The thing to remember here is that the word "comparative" refers both to comparing similarities and contrasting differences. As we discussed in the first example of "The Weak Thesis," a comparative paper must nevertheless do more than identify the fact that two or more texts share similarities and differences, since any two texts (regardless of their authorship, place in culture, or time in history) will invariably share similarities and differences. A comparative essay must demonstrate the larger significance or possible consequences of its comparison. The sample introduction earlier in this chapter (pp. 20–1) does an excellent job of this: after introducing a problem that provides the grounds for the paper's comparison, the essay not only highlights how Coleridge's "Frost at Midnight" and "Fears in Solitude" are similar and different, but also indicates how its analysis of those similarities and differences sheds new light on and perhaps even resolves the problem.

The student essay at the end of Chapter 5 also exemplifies a comparative essay's need to move beyond the mere identification of similarities and differences. It likewise offers a fruitful model for organizing a comparative analysis. Granted, there are no hard and fast rules to organizing a comparative paper, since it ultimately depends on personal preference or on the particular nature of the comparison. Some students prefer to conduct their comparisons by discussing one text at a time at length (or in alternating paragraphs); others prefer discussing texts together in the same paragraph, with each paragraph focusing on a major similarity or difference between the texts. You will want to stimulate and nurture your reader's interest, so it may be constructive on occasion to use a mixture of these approaches rather than remain devoted to just one. This kind of variation might allow your paper to feel more organic than mechanical.

RESEARCH ESSAYS

Training students to write convincing research essays is one of the primary goals of any English Department. The major difference between writing research and non-research essays is obviously the use of research. Incorporating research into your essay, however, is no obvious or simple matter. It requires more than reading background material that will help you become familiar with your topic or the text(s) on which you choose to write. It means making clear and documented references to your research texts (also called "secondary sources"). This can be done directly, by quoting the actual text of your secondary material, or indirectly, by referencing the original source of an idea that you paraphrase in your own words. If you were writing an essay on Jane Austen's *Pride and Prejudice*, for instance, and you wanted to reference what Elizabeth Fay says about Austen's reputation as a novelist, you could include Fay's words in a direct quote:

> According to Elizabeth Fay, Austen "has until recently been interpreted as a domestic novelist of limited range whose works shed no light on more important issues such as politics or war" (32).

Alternatively, you could paraphrase Fay's comments:

> Recent criticism challenges the idea that, by focusing on the domestic affairs of high society, Austen's novels ignore national and international politics (Fay 32).

Chapter 9 discusses proper ways to cite different kinds of texts (and explains why the parenthetical page references that follow the two citations above appear differently). Chapter 9 also considers some strategies for finding, evaluating, and using secondary sources. For the moment, we can identify some of the different kinds of secondary sources and briefly consider why you would want to refer to them in a research paper. Generally speaking, there are four kinds of references you can make to secondary sources. First, there are "biographical" references: these include references to texts and/or documents that provide information about an author, such as autobiographies, biographies, memoirs, diaries, and so on. References to such material are useful for supporting claims you wish to make about an author's intention or life experiences in relation to his or her work. Second, there are "historical" references: these include references to primary historical texts such as newspapers, periodicals, and legal documents; and secondary historical texts such as history books, historical surveys, and history-based literary criticism. These kinds of texts are useful for supporting claims you want to make about the historical or sociocultural contexts of an author's work. Third, there are "methodological" references: these include references to any particular theoretical approach to literature that you intend to pursue in your essay (e.g., formalism, structuralism, Marxism, feminism, etc.).[2] Lastly (and arguably the most common kind of reference to secondary sources in literary studies), there are "critical" references, which involve quoting or paraphrasing other literary critics who have written about the texts on which your paper focuses, or texts that are related in some way to those.

Citing critical references is a necessity for advanced students of literature, and it is an important aspect of essay writing for first-year students to get to know and to practice. If writing an argument about a work of literature (or anything else for that matter) involves making thesis statements that require further exposition and proof, then it makes sense to assume that others may or may not agree with what you have to say. Critical references allow you to confront the "debatable" aspect of your argument and at the same time demonstrate your willingness to entertain alternate perspectives. Before we look at the sample research essay below, it is important to reflect briefly on a couple of cautions regarding the citation of critical sources. First, when quoting a person whose argument reinforces a point or claim you wish to make, make sure that person's ideas merely *support* rather than *determine* or *overshadow* your own original argument. In other words, make sure that your most important ideas are your own, and avoid citing too often or more than you need to. Second, be respectful when citing someone whose argument you wish to challenge or question. Demonstrating a lack of respect for another perspective may tarnish your own credibility in the eyes of your reader.

SAMPLE RESEARCH PAPER

The following essay is an example of a strong research paper. The particular assignment to which this paper responded encouraged the student to engage a minimum of two scholarly texts that dealt with the literary work in question, in this case August Wilson's *The Piano Lesson*. The student went productively beyond this minimum insofar as her paper makes multiple references to a total of four scholarly works, all of which are listed on the paper's "Works Cited" page. In each instance, the student does a remarkable job of citing a critic's interpretation of the text in order to support aspects of her argument, without allowing the critic's ideas to overshadow her own. This strategy has the benefit of grounding the paper's argument by aligning it with existing criticism while also foregrounding the originality of the student's own possible contribution to such criticism. The essay also illustrates some elegant and effective ways of incorporating the words of a critic's text into the grammar and sentence structure of your own paragraphs.

---

2 For descriptions of these and other methodological approaches, as well as possible reasons and ways to use them in your essay, see Chapter 3.

Keely McFadden*
ENGL-1003(3)-001
Dr. Peter Melville
April 5, 2010

The Effects of Slavery in August Wilson's
The Piano Lesson

The era of slavery in the United States was a time wrought with pain and injustice. Yet even as slavery's stronghold on society began to weaken, the pangs of racial inequality continued to reverberate across the nation. Through the use of various dramatic elements, *The Piano Lesson* by August Wilson attempts to familiarize his audience with the after-effects of slavery on African Americans in the early twentieth century. Fuelled by racial injustices experienced in his own life, Wilson breaks from traditional dramatic structure and transports his audience into the midst of the Charles family's personal conflict with their past, which is best expressed through the symbolism surrounding the family's piano. The struggle between Berniece and Boy Willie as to what they should do with this family heirloom parallels their resistance to accepting their family's history and moving forward with their lives. Wilson employs Sutter's ghost to further develop the character conflict as a representation of the ongoing haunting of the past through many generations. Music is also used to emphasize the tone of the play.

August Wilson grew up feeling the effects of racism firsthand. During the early 1960s, he was the only Black student in his school and subsequently endured pervasive racism (Gantt 3), which drove him toward his goal of writing ten plays depicting Black-American experiences in each decade of the twentieth century. Wilson succeeded in writing "around, through, and against recorded history in order to give voice to the nameless masses of Africans in America" (Shannon 27), and to inform the world that Black culture exists (Gantt 2). In *The Piano Lesson*, Wilson focuses specifically on the struggles experienced by post-Emancipation Blacks in their efforts to gain inclusion in a society that has historically suppressed them (Singleton 41). By telling the story through the eyes of the subjugated, however, Wilson effectively distances his audience from the characters in the play, for at the time of the release of *The Piano Lesson*, the majority of the audience would have been Caucasian.

This distancing effect allows Wilson's audience to experience the alienation felt by so many Black people in the late 1930s when *The Piano Lesson* is set. The audience is thrust into the initial scene with barely any knowledge of what to expect, and are in many ways only bystanders, silent witnesses to the conflicts within the Charles family home. The time and place of the play are withheld well into the first act, and offhand references are made to details which only the characters are aware of, such as the Ghosts of Yellow Dog. The language is also difficult to understand at times; for example, when Boy Willie mentions Berniece's deceased husband, Crawley, he refers to his age as "three time seven" instead of twenty-one (1.1). These structural components are effectively used to create a nearly tangible fourth wall between the audience and the action on stage. Wilson intentionally wanted viewers to miss the significance of certain content and experience the uncomfortable feelings of exclusion felt by many African Americans at this time.

Wilson also strove, however, for his audience to notice the distinction between Black and White cultures early on so as to understand why the piano holds so much significance for Berniece and Boy Willie. Despite the fact that the piano was stolen from Sutter, the man who had enslaved their ancestors, both Berniece and Boy Willie feel that the piano is rightfully theirs, even if the law says otherwise. Boy Willie speaks of how he "don't go by what the law say. The law's liable to say anything. I go by if it's right or not" (1.1); and since the piano has their family history (including their ancestors faces) engraved on the side, the Charles' believe they have a valid right of ownership. For Berniece and Boy Willie, the piano is a symbol of the trials and tribulations that their ancestors experienced while enslaved, and it personifies their attempts to deal with the pain in their past. Jermaine Singleton reiterates this fact by claiming that the piano is "a symbol of the family's bondage and struggle for wholeness" (45), while Alexandre broadens its significance to embody all of "the black lives purchased, sold, and lost for White recreation and compensation" (Alexandre 82). This history contained within the piano sparks the main conflict in the play between the characters.

These characters contribute greatly to the overall theme, for as the tangible presence of the piano radiates throughout the Charles household, so do the effects of their family's past continue to repress them. While Boy Willie believes the piano should be sold and the profits used to buy Sutter's land, Berniece insists on keeping it for sentimental value, despite her refusal to play it. In this way, Wilson draws attention to the characters' resistance to accepting the antagonistic forces of their past. Boy Willie would rather rid himself of his family's baggage and be equal with the white men by legally owning the land that once enslaved his ancestors; to Wining Boy, however, selling the piano is the same as selling slaves (Alexandre 79). Boy Willie would essentially be profiting off of his family's hardships which Wining Boy sees as disrespectful to the dead. Berniece, on the other hand, struggles more with the psychological effects of the piano. Though she wants to keep it in her home, she is afraid to play it "cause I don't want to wake them spirits" (*Piano Lesson* 2.2). Though the wooden carvings on the piano are the only record of the Charles family's ancestors (Gantt 13), Berniece is afraid to acknowledge their presence for she would in turn be acknowledging the White oppressive force in their past.

The struggles faced by the protagonists are further complicated by the presence of Sutter's ghost, a fantastical character that represents the physical haunting of the past. Sutter's presence is mentioned in stage directions periodically throughout the play, though not all of the characters hear or feel him at the same time. Their recognition of the ghost, or lack thereof, is akin to their internal conflicts of recognizing their history of repression and exploitation (Singleton 45). As Berniece sees Sutter's ghost most often and is afraid of awakening more ghosts by playing the piano, the audience is made aware of her subconscious apprehension that White oppression may once again take away her family's freedom. Boy Willie, on the other hand, spends the majority of the play in denial of Sutter's ghost, saying that it "ain't nothing but in Berniece's head" (*Piano Lesson* 1.1). At the end of the play, however, Boy Willie has a physical fight with the ghost, representing his decision finally to face the facts of his family's history. These "divergent trajectories of transgenerational haunting" are further developed by the experiences Berniece's daughter Maretha has with Sutter's ghost (Singleton 48-9). While Berniece is determined that she "ain't gonna burden [Maretha] with that piano" and the history contained within (*Piano Lesson* 2.2), Sutter's ghost haunting her daughter is a symbol of the negative effects the unacknowledged past can have on succeeding generations.

Throughout *The Piano Lesson*, the resistance the characters feel toward their family's past and the antagonism it sparks between them is temporarily suspended through music, and it is music that provides the eventual resolution to their conflicts. When Boy Willie starts ranting about selling the piano and living "my life the way I want to live it" (1.2), Wining Boy sits down at the piano and the conflict is momentarily forgotten. Music is used as a subtle reminder of the characters' similarities and the common past they all share. Wilson

McFadden 4

employs this dramatic element to emphasize the tone of the play. Despite the characters' troubles, music leaves them with a sense of hope and optimism toward the future. At the play's climax, during the fight between Boy Willie and Sutter's ghost, music resolves what neither Boy Willie's punches nor Avery's divine blessing can achieve. It is a symbol of Berniece's final acceptance of her family's history when she at last plays the piano and rids her home of Sutter; the "song reaffirms the stories of the past, transforming the ugly and the awful, along with the beautiful and tender, into a joyous melody of hope" (Gantt 14). Music enables the characters to recognize their history. They realize that they "can neither ignore the past, nor let it lie dormant, nor sell it, nor give it away" (Gantt 14); the songs within the piano must be played, for it is a part of who the characters are.

It was August Wilson's goal for the world to become more aware of African-American history, and *The Piano Lesson* was his attempt to educate his audience of the strong after-effects slavery has had on many African-American families. At the start of the play, Wilson aims to familiarize his audience with the unfamiliar feelings of alienation felt by many African Americans at the time the play is set through various structural components. It was his hope that the audience would therefore understand the unique influence the piano had on the lives of the Charles family as a symbol of the struggles their enslaved ancestors faced; the tension between Berniece and Boy Willie about whether or not to sell the piano is a parallel to their internal conflicts of accepting their family's past. This is further exemplified by Wilson through Sutter's ghost—a literal haunting of their history. Yet it is music which eventually resolves the conflict and brings the characters together, encouraging them to accept their past of White oppression and subjugation and to move forward with their lives, finally free to look toward the future.

WORKS CITED AND CONSULTED

Alexandre, Sandy. "'[The] Things What Happened with Our Family': Property and Inheritance in August Wilson's *The Piano Lesson*." *Modern Drama* 52.1 (Spring 2009): 73–98. Print.

Gantt, Patricia M. "Putting Black Culture on Stage: August Wilson's Pittsburgh Cycle." *College Literature* 36.2 (Spring 2009): 1–25. Print.

Shannon, Sandra G. "Framing African American Cultural Identity: The Bookend Plays in August Wilson's 10-Play Cycle." *College Literature* 36.2 (Spring 2009): 26–39. Print.

McFadden 5

Singleton, Jermaine. "Some Losses Remain With Us: Impossible Mourning and the Presence of Ritual in August Wilson's *The Piano Lesson*." *College Literature* 36.2 (Spring 2009): 40–57. Print.

Wilson, August. "*The Piano Lesson*." *The Norton Introduction to Literature*. Shorter 9th ed. Ed. Alison Booth, J. Paul Hunter, and Kelly J. Mays. New York: Norton, 2006. 1205–62. Print.

WORKS CITED

Fay, Elizabeth. *A Feminist Introduction to Romanticism*. Oxford: Blackwell, 1998. Print.

Shakespeare, William. *The Tragedy of Macbeth. The Riverside Shakespeare*. 2nd ed. Ed. G. Blakemore Evans. New York: Houghton Mifflin, 1997. 1355–90. Print.

3

Different Critical Approaches

Many students are surprised to learn that (a) there are different schools of literary criticism and (b) these schools are often based on highly sophisticated theories of language and culture. Many of these critical schools are concerned primarily with how meaning is produced in a text. Is it just a matter of language? Or is it also a matter of psychology, history, culture, and politics? These critical schools also encourage us to consider our own position as readers. More specifically, they ask us to become reflective of and critical about the assumptions we make (either consciously or unconsciously) when we read a text. These assumptions may have to do with taking the complexity of linguistic communication for granted. They may have to do with our level of familiarity with literary form or literary history. Or they may have to do with our socially constructed identities as persons of a certain gender, race, class, or culture. Whatever the case, learning more about how a text produces meaning and how we participate (again, consciously or unconsciously) in that process promises to make us more alert readers not only of literature but also of the wide variety of cultural texts that surround us and with which we engage on a daily basis.

The following summaries do not presume to cover every critical approach to literary studies, nor do they presume to capture the full character of the critical approaches they do describe. Rather, they offer a brief glimpse into some influential developments in literary and critical theory that continue to shape the way literary studies are practised today. The summaries are followed by a list of works cited and consulted for the summaries and by brief lists for further reading on each of the approaches listed below.

FORMALISM/NEW CRITICISM

Depending on the context, the term "formalism" can refer, rather confusingly, to an array of different approaches to literature. Broadly understood, formalism denotes a reading methodology that looks at literature in terms of its various *forms*. It can be traced as far back as Aristotle, whose *Poetics* represents one of the first works of literary criticism in Western culture. *Poetics* is most famous for its discussion on the dramatic structure of **tragedy**, which Aristotle believed was not only fundamentally different than but also superior to other literary forms such as comedy and epic poetry. The basic assumption that underlies an Aristotelian view of literature, and indeed the majority of literary criticism since Aristotle, is the idea that literature has formal elements (such as dialogue, plot, rhyme, etc.) that allow us to classify literary works according to genre, subgenre, or type. Even criticism that challenges the very institution of formalized differences (see "Deconstruction," below, for instance) continues to rely on our ability to distinguish one literary form or genre from the other. In this sense, most criticism is formalist at some level.

More specifically, however, formalism calls to mind two very specific movements in literary criticism that emerged independent of one another in the early twentieth century: Russian Formalism and New Criticism. Both of these movements developed, at least in part, as reactions to prevailing criticism of the nineteenth century that privileged either an author's biography or a text's historical circumstances as the primary source of literary meaning. Russian Formalism and New Criticism each attempted in their own way to relocate the source of literary significance in the language and style of a text itself rather than something *outside* that text. Their proponents believed that literary criticism could be a discipline unto itself with its own particular aims and objects of analysis, and that it need not borrow so heavily from other disciplines such as psychology and history. To that end, the Russian Formalists, the best-known of whom was the linguist Roman Jakobson, sought to identify the various functions of literary language and form. Our discussion on literary language in Chapter 1, for instance, is indebted to Jakobson's definition of the "poetic function" of a verbal message, which "promotes" what he called "the palpability of signs" (69–70). This is Jakobson's typically dense way of saying that the poetic function measures the extent to which a text's language draws attention to itself *as language*, as letters and words that can be combined to form conspicuous and surprising visual arrangements and patterns of sound. Poetry in particular, but also literary language in general, is said to foreground the poetic function over language's other functions, including its referential, emotive, and conative functions. Since we often take language for granted in other forms of communication, a literary work's emphasis on language's poetic function is, according to the Russian Formalists, one way that literature distinguishes itself from other kinds of writing: it takes the familiar (i.e., language) and de-familiarizes it, making it seem new and strange.

Whereas the Russian Formalists focused, more often than not, on a rigorous linguistic analysis of literary language, the New Critics preferred to study the relationships in a given work between more traditional literary figures such as irony, ambiguity, imagery, and symbol—the significance of which they believed transcended biographical, historical, and social contexts.[1] The New Critics, many of whom taught in universities in the American South, saw their break from historical and biographical criticism as revolutionary. Influenced by the writings of Matthew Arnold, I.A. Richards, and T.S. Eliot, the best-known New Critics included Cleanth Brooks, William K. Wimsatt, Robert Penn Warren, John Crowe Ransom, and William Empson. According to Ransom, whose book *The New Criticism* (1941) gave the movement its name, literary criticism needed to become more systematic and objective insofar as it should "cite the nature of the object"—which for Ransom meant acknowledging "the *autonomy* of the work itself as existing for its own sake" and *not* for the sake of its author nor for the sake of its social and/or historical conditions (342, emphasis added 343). The word "autonomy" is emphasized because, more than anything, the New Critics viewed literary works as self-contained objects, each with its own intrinsic meaning. This meaning was thought to reside in the interplay of the text's formal elements—which is to say, in its use of rhetorical tropes such as figural (i.e., non-literal) language, symbolism, and paradox, all of which the New Critics believed were brought into harmony by the text's overall organic unity. For the New Critic, the point of literary criticism was to discover and expound upon this unity through a scrupulous and subtle "close reading" of the text. (For a demonstration of close reading, see the discussion of Walter de la Mare's "Slim Cunning Hands" in the following chapter.) Although the New Critical movement has been criticized over the years for undervaluing the importance of history, politics, and culture, the sophistication and subtlety of its reading strategies have had an enormous influence on other, more recent critical approaches to literature, the most obvious being deconstructionist criticism, which similarly involves close attention to textual detail.

STRUCTURALIST CRITICISM

With its intense linguistic focus, Russian Formalism is often considered a close relative of another linguistic movement of the mid-twentieth century called "Structuralism." In fact, some Russian Formalists, such as Roman Jakobson and Vladimir Propp, are often listed alongside the most prominent advocates of structuralism, including anthropologist Claude Lévi-Strauss, Marxist critic Louis Althusser, and literary theorist Roland Barthes. As these last three names indicate, however, structuralism was predominantly a French intellectual movement that was more interdisciplinary than Russian Formalism. It was

---

1 Terms like "irony," "symbol," and "imagery" are discussed more fully in subsequent chapters, and their definitions can be found in the glossary located in the Appendix.

also more exclusive in its indebtedness to the writings of an early-twentieth-century Swiss linguist by the name of Ferdinand de Saussure. Saussure also influenced some Russian Formalists to varying degrees, but what aligned structuralists from different academic disciplines was their shared effort to extend the insights of Saussure's posthumously published *Course in General Linguistics* (1916). For literary structuralists, this meant developing Saussure's differential theory of semantics—namely, that linguistic communication or "signification" as he called it (i.e., reading/writing, listening/speaking, etc.) does not simply refer to corresponding objects and ideas that exist outside language. Rather, as a "signifier," a word represents a mental concept, or what Saussure called the "signified," by virtue of its difference from other signifiers. Language, in other words, is not referential so much as it produces meaning through differences. The word "tree" does not simply refer to an actual tree, of which there are countless varieties with different shapes, sizes, and foliage. Rather, the word gains a certain meaning only when it is set in contrast to other related signifiers, like "shrub," "fern," and "vine." The differential relations between these signifiers enable the word "tree" to signify a particular classification of plant life (the signified). If we were to change the context by setting the signifier "tree" in relation to signifiers such as "skyscraper," "traffic," and "smog," then the signified will likewise change to something more symbolic like "nature" or (as in an advertisement for environmentalism) "going green." For a structuralist, this example highlights the arbitrary relationship between the signifier and the signified—a relationship that is always provisional and depends entirely on the presence of other signifiers. The example also demonstrates how language shapes and changes the way we perceive things in the world from one context to the other.

Structuralist literary critics viewed works of literature as complex arrangements of signifiers that work to produce a central signified meaning. But since this meaning is arbitrary and provisional, structuralists preferred to focus their critical attention on the relational structure of the text's signifiers. To put it plainly, they were less concerned about *what* a text meant than *how* its meaning was produced. The "structuralist activity," as Roland Barthes called it, often involved the study of oppositions in a text—hero/villain, self/other, inside/outside, nature/culture, light/darkness, male/female, young/old, and so on. The idea was that by analyzing not only the opposed terms within each opposition but also the interdependence of multiple sets of oppositions, the critic could discover the rules and conditions of the text's significance. As a case in point, an epic hero, whose function is to embody a set of ideal social values, is often defined "negatively," as Saussure would say, by the villains he encounters. If these villains are associated with darkness, otherness, death, and the outside (that is, as threats to society), then the hero might contrarily be linked to light imagery, selfhood, life, and the inside. A structuralist's job would be to illustrate how all these related oppositions work together throughout the text to produce and sustain the signifier–signified relation that exists between the hero and the social values he represents.

DECONSTRUCTION (POSTSTRUCTURALIST CRITICISM)

Insofar as "deconstruction" historically follows structuralism, it is said to be *post*-structuralist; however, it is also post-*structuralist* in the sense that it does not reject structuralism so much as it revises some of structuralism's basic assumptions about the signifier and the signified. First developed in the 1960s by the French theorist Jacques Derrida, deconstruction essentially radicalizes (i.e., extends through rigorous critique) the structuralist notion of the provisionality of signified meaning. Whereas structuralism saw the relation between the signifier and the signified as arbitrary and temporarily maintained by a complex but nevertheless predictable set of differential relations between signifiers, deconstruction argues that both types of relations are equally provisional. Replacing the structuralist's mechanical understanding of structure with a more fluid model of signification, Derrida insists that a signifier's dependency on other signifiers causes its meaning to be perpetually postponed, since those other signifiers will in turn depend on still more signifiers to maintain their own signified meanings, and so on. Because there is no place in the signifying chain where this dependency can finally stop— no one signifier that can bear the burden of confirming what all the other signifiers mean—meaning is never fully present, never stable. To account for this process of deferred dependency, Derrida invented the word *différance*, a French pun that denotes both difference and deferral. For Derrida, "meaning depends on structural difference but also on temporal relations of before and after" (Storey 98).

To illustrate the instability of *différance* in the chain of signifiers, we can return to our example of the signifier "tree" from the previous section. A deconstructionist would uphold the conclusion that the signifier "tree" will denote a particular classification of plant life in the presence of signifiers such as "shrub," "fern," and "vine," and that a context of signifiers like "skyscraper," "traffic," and "smog" might well transform the signifier "tree" into a symbol or metonym for "nature." The deconstructionist would additionally insist, however, that neither of these signifying contexts is closed unto itself, but that each context bears what Derrida calls "the trace" of the other, and not *just* the trace of the other, but the trace of countless other contexts in which the signifier "tree" functions in relation to different sets of signifiers. Because our culture so often associates trees with an idealized concept of nature (typically defined in opposition to culture itself), it is difficult for us to conceptualize a tree, whatever the linguistic context, without making this association. The signifier "tree" can never simply refer to a particular classification of plant life. It will always betray traces of its relation to a concept of nature that will in turn conjure up its own associations with human culture, urban environments, and pollution. Always already inside one another, these seemingly disparate signifying contexts cause the signifier to become undecidably self-different—referring as it does to multiple signified meanings. Contrary to what Freud may have said about cigars, a tree is never *just* a tree.

Literary deconstructionists, such as J. Hillis Miller, Paul de Man, and Barbara Johnson, insist that there exists no "transcendental signified" to a literary work, no one true meaning that rises above the play of *différance* in the text. Accordingly, a frequent reading strategy for deconstructionist criticism is to subvert—or decentre—what is called the "preferred reading" of a text. A preferred reading represents the most historically convincing (which is to say, most conventional) understanding of how and what a text means. This reading is "centred" not only in the sense that it is forcibly *made* central to the text's history of reception by certain authorities (i.e., prominent critics, popular opinion, etc.), but also in the sense that it is usually predicated on the assumption that the text achieves a cohesive or centralized unity. With special attention paid to the unstable play of oppositions in the text, deconstructionist readings aim to show that this assumption is an illusion and that a preferred reading only acquires its preferred status by actively repressing the self-divided and indeterminate nature of the text's language.

Deconstruction is not by any means exclusively devoted to subverting the centrality of preferred readings. It is also useful in exposing how texts, as socially constructed products of particular places and moments in history, disseminate discourses of power like sexism, racism, and classism. Consider the infamous and complicated example of Joseph Conrad's *Heart of Darkness* (1902). On the one hand, the novella itself participates in a kind of deconstruction of nineteenth-century racist assumptions about Africa. It does this primarily by subverting traditional associations between binaries such as white/black, good/bad, and life/death. Images of whiteness become linked in the novel to "darker" things like evil, death, and corruption, while images of blackness take on more positive, "lighter" associations. On the other hand, the novella's attempt to produce an anti-racist counter-discourse has been criticized for its failure to escape precisely the kind of racist stereotypes it aims to debunk. In particular, Chinua Achebe argues that Conrad's "fixation on blackness" continues to objectify the image of the African native as a mere supplement (or obverse mirror) to a European sense of "whiteness" (10). Unable to escape the precarious play of binary opposition, Conrad's novel confirms a basic premise of deconstruction: all writing, even deconstruction itself, is subject to further deconstruction.

READER-RESPONSE CRITICISM

Contrary to deconstruction, reader-response criticism argues that a text only appears self-divided and indeterminate because it requires a reader to fill in the "gaps," as it were. According to Wolfgang Iser, these gaps allow the reader to become an active participant in the production of literary meaning. This validation of the reader's participation does not mean the reader is free to interpret texts willy-nilly. Rather, as a form of critical *analysis* (and not personal reflection), reader-response criticism tends to emphasize the enormous responsibility readers assume as participants in the production of meaning. Reader-response considers both the interpretive demands of a text and the ability of the text's readers to recognize, respond to, or even resist such demands. In short, reader-response criticism is concerned with the reader's response-*ability*, which is largely determined by an individual reader's "idiosyncratic beliefs, knowledge bases, and ethnic, gender, and class backgrounds, among other things" (Hall 45). In this regard, reader-response analysis is "not simply an interpretation of a text, it is always an interpretation of the act of interpretation.... It is an analytical response to the reader's response" (Hall 45–46).

While reader-response criticism is more or less unified in its aim to account for how different readers read differently, it varies widely in methodology and application and depends entirely on how the individual critic views the author-text-reader dynamic. At one end of the spectrum is Wayne Booth, whose book *The Rhetoric of Fiction* (1961) is often cited as one of the earliest contributions to reader-response theory. Booth's view of literature was closer to New Criticism than it was to the views of later reader-response critics in that he located the primary source of literary meaning in the text itself, particularly in the text's rhetoric. Arguing that all literature is rhetorical and therefore designed to have specific and purposeful effects on its readers, Booth believed that readers are meant to detect the presence of what he called a text's "implied author," which is not an actual person so much as an authorial force that orchestrates the text's rhetorical manipulation of the reader. If literature is implicitly motivated in this way, then its intended meanings should be discernible through the study of its readers' responses.

While Booth privileged readers who possess enough training to recognize a text's rhetorical manoeuvres, Wolfgang Iser widened the scope of reader-response criticism to include detailed analyses of responses that an author (real or implied) might never have anticipated. Like Booth, Iser believed that a work of literature contains evidence of an implied author whose intentions shape the reader's responses to some degree. To this formula, however, Iser added a crucial distinction between the "implied reader," who represents a composite of the text's desired responses, and "actual readers," who struggle to fill in indeterminate elements or gaps in the text that make the text interpretable. Because the text's meaning is undetermined or incomplete without actual readers, and since each reader's interpretive sensibilities and frame of reference are conditioned by his or her own personal and social experiences, a multiplicity of interpretations is made possible. Actual readers who are wildly out of synch with the text's implied reader can still be accused of misreading, but Iser's interest in misreading was more anthropological than censorious. Rather than scold such readers, he sought to understand the reasons behind the choices that led them to misread the text.

Reader-response critic Stanley Fish goes even further than Iser in his validation of the reading practices of actual readers and is therefore at the other end of the spectrum from Booth. He does not dispense with the idea of an implied reader so much as he dislodges it, almost entirely, from its position of privilege. For Fish, the implied reader, as a composite of the text's desired responses, is not intrinsic to the text itself but is projected onto the text by the interpretive community to which the reader belongs, whether it is a group of friends in a book club, students in a classroom, or members of a specific school of literary criticism. The text's range of possible meanings will be different from one interpretive community to the next because each interpretive community will implicitly establish its own rules and conditions for reading. Although this means there are no universally correct ways of reading, it does not remove the possibility of misreading. Certain readings can still be considered inappropriate or mistaken, but only within the context of a particular reading community. An interpretation of a biblical text like the book of Judges, for instance, might be celebrated as provocative and insightful within a community of literary critics but criticized as erroneous and misguided within a community of biblical scholars. For Fish, the context of reading is all-important.

PSYCHOANALYTIC CRITICISM

The term "psychoanalytic criticism" covers a broad range of methodologies, but the most influential of these are all indebted in some way to the writings of Sigmund Freud, who not only applied psychoanalytic criticism himself to the literary works of Shakespeare, Dostoyevsky, and E.T.A. Hoffmann but also admitted that these and other literary works had already revealed many of the truths Freud would claim as his own. Sophocles' *Oedipus Rex*, for example, provided Freud with the prototype of one of his most famous psychological models, the "Oedipus complex," which describes the normal process through which a male child represses his desires to murder his father and have sexual intercourse with his mother. For Freud, literary texts such as *Oedipus Rex* allow us to fantasize about the fulfillment of a repressed desire at a safe distance and at the same time take pleasure in repression itself: we are simultaneously fascinated and horrified by Oedipus's story. In this sense, a literary work is, according to Freud, analogous to a dream or a daydream and can therefore be psychoanalyzed as such. Not surprisingly, a good deal of early psychoanalytic literary criticism resulted either in psychobiography (which treats an author's works as a series of complex wish-fulfillment fantasies) or in the psychoanalysis of fictional characters. In regard to the latter, for instance, a character's central conflicts in a narrative might be read in terms of an internal psychological struggle between the superego (Freud's term for a person's moral conscience), the ego (a person's conscious mind), and the id (the unconscious, instinctual part of the human psyche).

Even as Freud's influence over the methods and doctrines of twentieth-century psychology continued to wane, interest in his ideas experienced new life in literary studies, primarily with the help of psychiatrist Jacques Lacan but also through the influence of feminists Luce Irigaray and Julia Kristeva and cultural theorist Slavoj Žižek. (The feminist film critic Laura Mulvey, whose work is discussed in Chapter 7, has also been instrumental in establishing the importance of psychoanalysis in both film and literary studies.) Lacan revived Freudian psychoanalysis most famously by combining Freud's account of the unconscious (which is said to contain hidden impulses and desires that motivate our actions) with the insights of structuralism. According to Lacan, "the unconscious is structured like a language" (203). The use of the word "structured" is crucial in this instance, for the unconscious does not simply appear like a language. Rather, it is inscribed with structure, actively organized by the imposition (in early childhood) of what Lacan calls the "symbolic order," which comprises a given culture's "structures of language, rules of social organization, and interpersonal limits on behavior and desire" (Hall 105). Like signifiers, unconscious drives and desires are divided and forced into differential relations with one another, which means that, instead of expressing itself directly in reference to an object of desire, a desire can only find expression through related signifiers in the symbolic order. Resulting in a psychological subject who is "barred" or cut off from fully realizing his or her desires, this structuring of the unconscious prompts the individual to take pleasure in the pursuit of an endless parade of signifiers that continually postpone the fulfillment he or she seeks. For Lacan, this explains why reading in particular is so pleasurable, why it promises *jouissance*, or an excess of pleasure. It also explains why Lacan, like Freud before him, frequently turned to literary texts such as *Hamlet* and Edgar Allan Poe's "The Purloined Letter" to illustrate his theories of language and the unconscious. This turn toward the literary is extended by Irigaray, who revised Lacan's theories for the development of a new feminist form of writing called *écriture féminine*, and Kristeva, who located within Lacan's "symbolic order" a disruptive "semiotic" force that is most prevalent in what she calls the "revolution" of poetic language.[2] Žižek, who is well known for blending

---

[2] For more on Irigaray, Kristeva, and *écriture féminine*, see Grosz.

Lacanian psychoanalysis with Marxism, goes one step further by applying many of Lacan's most difficult theories to global politics and to examples of popular culture, his favourite being the films of Alfred Hitchcock.

MARXIST CRITICISM

Marxist literary criticism has undergone a number of developments and changes since it first gained prominence in the 1930s, but at its core lies a consistent belief in Karl Marx's theories about the relationship between economics and culture. Generally speaking, Marxists understand human history in terms of class struggle and class conflict. Even though Marx argued that the social relations between individuals in any historical period are determined by the material conditions and modes of economic production of that period, Marxists tend to focus almost exclusively on the advent, development, and spread of Western capitalism. As a mode of production, capitalism organizes social relations according to an individual's relation to the production of capital, which refers to the monetary surplus generated when commodities are exchanged or when they are purchased to create newer, more valuable commodities. Of particular interest to Marx were the proletariat (i.e., the working classes), who do not possess capital but rely instead on the exchange value of their labour to survive, and the bourgeoisie (i.e., upwardly mobile middle classes), who not only have capital but also consistently exploit the labour of the proletariat to accumulate more. Marxists recognize that capitalist social relations have become more complicated than this in our own historical period, but the point is that the capitalist mode of economic production forms what Marx calls the "base" upon which our society's "superstructure" (its social, cultural, and political organization) is determined. The relation between the base and superstructure is said to be supported by the "ideology" or worldview of the members of the dominant class (i.e., the bourgeoisie), who benefit from society's economic structure. This ideology provides a distorted view of the socioeconomic order by presenting it as "natural," which in turn alienates the subordinate class (i.e., the proletariat) and hinders its collective ability to articulate the injustice of its oppression.

One of the first influential Marxist critics in literary studies was the Hungarian-born Georg Lukács, who turned to Marxism shortly after the Russian Revolution of 1917. Lukács is perhaps best known for praising nineteenth-century "realism," which refers to literary attempts to represent the complexity of everyday life (usually in novels), over the experimental literature of early twentieth-century modernist movements such as expressionism and surrealism. Lukács believed that the depictions of contemporary society in the realist fiction of writers such as Honoré de Balzac and Leo Tolstoy would often purposely or inadvertently reveal the "objective reality" of the dehumanizing conditions of capitalist society. Contrary to Lukács, other early Marxist critics like Theodor Adorno, Max Horkheimer, Bertolt Brecht, and Walter Benjamin argued the opposite, suggesting that the experimentalism of modernist literature and art was in fact far more effective than realism in counteracting, rupturing, and exposing the ideological "distortions" of bourgeois culture. For these Marxists, the point of such literature was to rouse people from their complacency and to shatter their illusions about the socioeconomic order.

More recently, three Marxist literary critics in particular have had an enormous influence on the way literary criticism is practised today. The first is Raymond Williams, who developed a Marxist-inflected reading strategy called "cultural materialism" that has been embraced by advocates and practitioners of New Historicism (see "New Historicism," below, for more detail). Influenced by Antonio Gramsci's concept of "hegemony," which refers to the (often insidious) ways in which the dominant class gains "consent" for the cultural power it exerts over subordinate classes, Williams identified the literary canon—or "selective tradition," as he called it—as one instrument by which such consent is acquired. For Williams, texts selected for the tradition tend to validate and support the values of the bourgeoisie. The Marxist criticism of Williams's former student Terry Eagleton has likewise been influential in current literary studies. Turning from Williams to the writings of Louis Althusser, who re-framed Marx's ideas in structuralist terms to produce a theory of ideology as a material practice,[3] Eagleton is famous for viewing the practice of literary theory itself through a Marxist lens and arguing that university literature departments are, at least in part, complicit with "the ideological apparatus of the modern capitalist state" (174). Fredric Jameson extends this critique of literary critical practice by insisting that the study of literature (or any artistic object, for that matter) is incomplete without a rigorous historical analysis of the socioeconomic conditions of a text's production and consumption. For Jameson, this kind of Marxist historicism forms the "ultimate horizon" of literary studies (76).

FEMINIST CRITICISM

The preceding six summaries mention a total of forty critics and theorists of literature and culture. Of these, only four are women. The inequity betrayed by this fact only confirms Lana F. Rakow's thesis that "the exclusion of women from theoretical discourse . . . is typical of received academic histories" (200). Attempts to include women thinkers in anthologies (or summaries) of critical theory can also be problematic, especially when the category of feminism

---

3 For Althusser's definition of ideology as a "material practice," see his "Ideology and Ideological State Apparatuses."

functions as a kind of container into which these writers and their concerns are segregated, so to speak, from the rest of the theoretical canon. While it is important to recognize feminism as a general theoretical orientation and/or practice with its own unique aims (i.e., the critique and dissolution of male-dominated, or "patriarchal," social structures that inhibit female power and feminine knowledge), it is equally important to recognize feminist criticism and theory as being populated by a multiplicity of feminisms that often align themselves with other theoretical perspectives. These include deconstructionist feminism (Barbara Johnson, Hélène Cixous), psychoanalytic feminism (Luce Irigaray, Julia Kristeva), Marxist or socialist feminism (Gayle Rubin, Clara Fraser), postcolonial feminism (Gayatri Chakravorty Spivak, Uma Narayan), queer theory feminism (Eve Kosofsky Sedgwick, Judith Butler), and so on. What unites these different expressions of feminism is a common interest in correlations between differences in sex (or gender) and differences in political, economic, and social power.

Histories of feminism commonly isolate three movements or "waves" of feminist theory and practice. First-wave feminism is said to be concerned primarily with political inequality and includes the general fight for women's suffrage (i.e., voting rights) throughout the nineteenth and early twentieth centuries in Britain and North America. Second-wave feminism broadens the political scope of the first wave by bringing to light (with the aim of rectifying) economic and social inequalities between the sexes. Largely associated with the American "Women's Liberation Movement" of the 1960s and 1970s, and fuelled by the 1963 publication of Betty Friedan's *The Feminine Mystique*, this second wave continues to hold sway over contemporary feminist thinking, and many women writers still identify as second-wave feminists. For this reason, third-wave feminism is not regarded as the logical conclusion, or even an evolution, of second-wave feminism so much as it represents a competing alternative to it. Critical of the second wave's more or less universal or "essentialist" understanding of femininity, third-wave feminism generally views sexual identity as a social construct, the product of a complex network of socioeconomic and cultural relations. This post-structuralist perspective enables third-wave feminists to analyze gender not only in terms of sexism, but also in terms of racism and classism.

Feminist literary criticism arguably emerged out of second-wave feminism and continues to undergo profound development in light of third-wave feminism. There are, of course, pioneers of feminist literary criticism who predate second-wave feminism, including eighteenth-century political reformist Mary Wollstonecraft, modernist poet and novelist Virginia Woolf, and existentialist philosopher Simone de Beauvoir. But as an established and organized approach to literary studies, feminist criticism gained significant momentum in the early 1970s with the publication of works such as Kate Millett's *Sexual Politics* (1970) and Adrienne Rich's "When We Dead Awaken: Writing as Re-Vision" (1972). These and other early feminist literary critics argued that the English literary canon has been predominantly populated by male-authored texts with misogynistic views on sexual relations. Because these texts offer false representations of women that in turn confirm a patriarchal insistence on the superiority of men, writers such as Millett and Rich called for a revision or expansion of the canon that would unearth and celebrate women's writing suppressed by the selective memory of literary history. This challenge to the canon was extended later in the decade and throughout the 1980s by notable feminist critics such as Elaine Showalter, Sandra Gilbert, Susan Gubar, and many others. Advocating what Showalter called "gynocriticism" (i.e., women-centred criticism), these critics sought to reconstruct a specifically feminine tradition that included women authors such as Mary Wollstonecraft, Jane Austen, Mary Shelley, the Brontë sisters, Mary Ann Evans (a.k.a. George Eliot), and Virginia Woolf. Around the same time, French feminists Luce Irigaray and Julia Kristeva (see "Psychoanalytic Criticism," above) undertook *écriture féminine*, a similar project focused on women's writing. More recently, however, third-wave feminism has resulted in criticism that challenges the idea of an inherently feminine form of writing because that idea essentializes ideological (i.e., white, middle-class) assumptions about femininity. These third-wave feminists, who often prefer the term "gender criticism" to feminist criticism, argue that gender traits such as "feminine" and "masculine" are not inherent in either sex but are *performed* by individuals within particular cultural contexts.

GENDER CRITICISM AND QUEER THEORY

Occasionally combined under the rubric "Gender and Sexuality Studies," gender criticism and queer theory incorporate the lessons of feminism, but instead of focusing primarily on representations of women and/or femininity, they open their analyses to a plurality of sexual identities, including male, female, transgendered, two-spirited, heterosexual, gay/lesbian/queer, and bisexual identities. Though methodologically diverse, gender criticism and queer theory are centrally concerned with how and why certain sexual identities and relations (male, heterosexual) maintain social power and privilege, while others (female, transgendered, two-spirited, gay/lesbian/queer) continue to be marginalized and even criminalized. There is hardly space in this summary to account for the variety of approaches to gender criticism and queer theory, so we will narrow our focus to include critics and theorists who develop and refine one of the more dominant ideas in these two fields—namely, that gender and sexuality are less biologically determined than they are socially constructed and regulated according to cultural relations of power.

While gender criticism and queer theory are indebted to various forms of post-Freudian psychoanalysis, their greatest debt arguably belongs to the

French cultural historian Michel Foucault. Foucault's work on the history of sexuality in Western culture argues that our very idea of sexuality as a category of identification based on sexual preferences and practices was invented in the nineteenth century by the overlapping interests of what he calls "discourses of power" such as psychiatry, medicine, politics, religion, and literature. Foucault contended that, instead of merely describing natural inclinations, sexuality was and continues to be used as a regulatory ideal that normalizes or makes legitimate certain sexual activities and demonizes others as threats to society. The psycho-medical and moral "health" of the bourgeois family, for instance, was a key component of the bourgeoisie's hegemonic control over nineteenth-century European culture. Because this particular representation of the family depended, quite explicitly, on sanctifying heterosexual relations for its preservation, other configurations of sexual relations such as homosexuality were forcibly denounced for potentially undermining "normal" middle-class life. This condemnation of homosexuality was consolidated through the cooperation of multiple power discourses: psychiatric and medical discourses treated homosexuals as pathological or deviant; religious discourses considered them immoral; political discourses deemed them criminal; and literary discourses relegated them to the shadows of intelligibility.

Despite being labelled a cultural determinist (that is, a person who believes that identity is ultimately determined by cultural forces), Foucault conceptualized a "body" whose materiality pre-exists the regulatory ideals of culture but is nevertheless inscribed (i.e., shaped, organized, and/or transformed) by these ideals. Judith Butler, on the other hand, radicalized Foucault's emphasis on regulatory ideals in her famous theory of performativity, where she argues that the body does not reside outside of culture so much as it is materialized *through* (i.e., always already mediated by) culture, which makes any reference to biological or natural sexualities problematic. Such references are always already contaminated by cultural constructions of the body. Our concepts of gender and sexuality are therefore self-referential at best and unstable at worst. According to Butler, dominant (i.e., heterosexual) representations of sexuality and gender can only maintain cultural authority by obliging individual subjects to constantly rehearse or *perform* their gender and sexuality with constant reference to cultural norms. Butler's book *Gender Trouble: Feminism and the Subversion of Identity* (1990) is a landmark study in gender studies and queer theory insofar as it exposes heteronormative culture as performative and not natural, and offers strategies for validating the performance of alternative sexualities.

Eve Kosofsky Sedgwick, another prominent queer theorist, was likewise influenced by Foucault's thoughts on sexuality. Sedgwick is best known for her groundbreaking literary study *Between Men: English Literature and Male Homosocial Desire* (1985). *Between Men* uses nineteenth-century literary representations of love triangles between two men and a woman to produce a queer theory of homosociality (i.e., same-sex social relations). According to her theory, there is only a fine line separating sexual and social relations, and same-sex desire—particularly male-male desire—is historically mediated or prohibitively restructured through more acceptable homosocial relations. In literary love triangles, for instance, men express same-sex desire for one another through competition over the same woman. For Sedgwick, this "structuration" (15) of homosocial desire between men is not only homophobic and oppressive to women, it also indicates the extent to which same-sex desire, and the sublimation of such desire, is an essential component of heteronormative society. Queerness, in other words, lies at the heart of culture. As a result of Sedgwick's theories, identifying the underlying "queerness" of mainstream works of literature and film has become a common critical practice of queer theorists such as David Halperin, Lee Edelman, and Alexander Doty.

NEW HISTORICISM

Foucault's unique historical methodology has also been useful in the development of New Historicism. This methodology is not a matter of collecting historical facts that are then used objectively to reconstruct the historical context of a literary work. Rather, New Historicism treats the so-called historical fact as the ideological product of the vast network of power discourses, which includes literature itself. Literature is not simply informed by historical context; rather, it actively participates in the cultural struggle (between classes, sexes, etc.) for ideological control over the production of the dominant worldview of any given historical period. This worldview subsequently inscribes itself as the authoritative historical context of the period. New Historicist criticism aims to uncover the politics behind this process and tends to focus on marginalized or subcultural resistances to the dominant worldview as they are expressed not only through literature but also in other equally discursive cultural practices such as fashion (or self-stylization), shopping, burlesque theatre, and international trade. Obviously, New Historicism is not a simple return to history; it is a return to history with a difference—that is, with lessons learned from post-structural developments in psychoanalysis, deconstruction, Marxism, feminism, gender criticism, and so on.

The methodology of New Historicism is often described as a brand of "cultural materialism" that combines the class-based socioeconomic focus of Marxist analysis with a much broader interest in the cultural activities of politically disenfranchised groups, including (but not limited to) women, children, racial minorities, and the uneducated classes. Considered by many as the founder of the New Historicist method, Stephen Greenblatt studies these cultural activities as they are implicitly or explicitly represented in the literary works of early modern dramatists such as William Shakespeare, Edmund Spenser, and

Christopher Marlowe. According to Greenblatt, these works often betray what he calls "verbal traces" that may appear insignificant to present-day readers but when historically contextualized reveal a great deal about the cultural practices and frames of reference of early modern audiences and readerships. Failing to make certain contextual associations, present-day readers will likewise fail to recognize the early modern political struggles and cultural conflicts that the text engages (be it in terms of reinforcing or contesting dominant ideologies). Performing a kind of archaeology of a text's layers of cultural significance, Greenblatt's New Historicist method essentially aims to restore to the reading experience at least a partial sense of the "structure of feeling" (Williams 36) of the text's moment in history—a sense, for instance, of what was at stake for early seventeenth-century audiences attending performances of Shakespeare's *Richard II* or *Hamlet* (two plays about the legitimacy of royal succession) in the context of political uncertainty over who would succeed the aging Queen Elizabeth I. New Historicism is not exclusive to early modern literary studies. Among others in different fields, Jerome McGann applies New Historicist criticism to Romantic-period writers, and Catherine Gallagher has developed it for studies in Victorian literature.

POSTCOLONIAL CRITICISM AND CRITICAL RACE THEORY

Although they are related in significant ways and are often combined in application, postcolonial criticism and critical race theory are technically separate fields. For this reason, although they are included under the same heading, they will be discussed in sequence. Not unlike the term "post-structuralism," postcolonialism does not refer exclusively to literatures and cultures that have emerged *after* the age of European colonialism. Rather, due to the fact that nations and cultures previously subjected to colonial conquest and/or influence continue to experience the residual effects of their having been oppressed and restructured (demographically, economically, socially) by colonial forces, postcolonial criticism must necessarily concern itself with colonial history. Canada provides a useful example of this. To this day, many university English classes on Canadian literature will cover primarily Anglophone writers of European descent (with some Asian-, African-, and Caribbean-Canadian authors thrown into the mix), while Francophone and Aboriginal literatures are either relegated to specialized topics courses or outsourced, so to speak, to other academic departments. One need not look too hard to see the effects of Canada's colonial past (its complex history of Anglo-Franco-Aboriginal relations) structuring the way literature is organized and studied in Canada. In India, the case is similar; its history as a nation previously under British rule has rendered even its post-independence literature irrevocably influenced by British literary and cultural ideals, which partly explains why so many Indian novels are written in English. An obvious yet crucial difference between Canada and India is that the latter is predominantly populated by non-European-descended peoples. For this reason, India represents a prime example of a postcolonial critic's object of study: a nation whose post-independence literary and cultural identities are compromised by the impossibility of returning to the *cultural* independence of its precolonial past. Postcolonial cultures are hybrid cultures, the complex and conflicted product of precolonial history, colonization, and decolonization.

Postcolonial criticism owes many of its theoretical perspectives to literary critics such as Edward Said, Gayatri Chakravorty Spivak, and Homi K. Bhabha. Said is most famous for his definition of Orientalism, which he characterized as a vast network of European assumptions and prejudices about the so-called exoticism and/or savagery of "Eastern" cultures, prejudices that have been disseminated through travel narratives and other forms of literary discourse and used to justify Europe's abusive colonial activities in Asia and the Middle East. Spivak's most important contribution to postcolonial discourse has been her calling attention to the repressed presence of the "subaltern," by which she means radically marginalized groups (e.g., women, Aboriginal peoples, lower-caste people) whose experiences and perspectives are not always registered in literary and critical representations of postcolonialism. In a similar vein, Bhabha argues that the postcolonial condition differs from nation to nation and from culture to culture, and that the individual identities of postcolonial nations are unstable because the unresolved antagonisms of the colonial period tend to linger. According to Bhabha, postcolonial nations are often self-divided into different ethnic, cultural, and socioeconomic groups, all of whom compete to "narrate" (though literature and other media) the nation's official identity.

Postcolonial criticism, especially in the writings of Spivak, often addresses issues of race, but critical race theory as a discipline is most often associated with the history of race relations in the United States, a nation with its own unique colonial and postcolonial histories. Two of the most prominent literary critics in critical race theory are Henry Louis Gates Jr. and bell hooks. The critical writings of celebrated author Toni Morrison have also been influential in this field, especially her book *Playing in the Dark: Whiteness and the Literary Imagination* (1992), where she claims that literary criticism in America consistently overlooks what she calls a significant "Africanist presence" (6) in American literary history. Gates similarly points to the Eurocentric or white bias of the English literary canon, arguing that different literary traditions, including an African-American tradition, operate with respect to different aesthetic principles and should therefore not be subject to the so-called "universal" values of a single (i.e., European, white) culture. His ironically titled book *The Signifying Monkey: A Theory of Afro-American Literary Criticism* (1988) attempts to remedy this problem by linking the African-American literary tradition to African-American folklore. bell hooks extends Morrison's and Gates's criticisms of canonical biases in the literary tradition by linking issues of race with issues of sexism. Her work tends to highlight the otherwise neglected experiences of African-American women, which she claims even feminist criticism tends to ignore.

WORKS CITED AND CONSULTED

Abrams, M.H., and Geoffrey Harpham. *A Glossary of Literary Terms.* 9th ed. Boston: Thomson Wadsworth, 2009. Print.

Achebe, Chinua. "An Image of Africa." *Research in African Literatures* 9.1 (Spring 1978): 1–15. Print.

Althusser, Louis. "Ideology and Ideological State Apparatuses." *Mapping Ideologies.* Ed. Slavoj Žižek. London: Verso, 1994. 100–139. Print.

Baldick, Chris. *The Concise Oxford Dictionary of Literary Terms.* 2nd ed. Oxford: Oxford UP, 2001. Print.

Eagleton, Terry. *Literary Theory: An Introduction.* 3rd ed. Minneapolis: U of Minnesota P, 2008. Print.

Grosz, Elizabeth. *Sexual Subversions: Three French Feminists.* Crows Nest, Austral.: Allen & Unwin, 1989. Print.

Hall, Donald E. *Literary and Cultural Theory: From Basic Principles to Advanced Applications.* Boston: Houghton, 2001. Print.

Jakobson, Roman. "Linguistics and Poetics." *Language in Literature.* Ed. K. Pomorska and S. Rudy. Cambridge, MA: Harvard UP, 1987. Print.

Jameson, Fredric. *The Political Unconscious.* Ithaca, NY: Cornell UP, 1981. Print.

Lacan, Jacques. *The Four Fundamental Concepts of Psycho-Analysis.* Ed. Jacques-Alain Miller. Trans. Alan Sheridan. New York: Norton, 1977. Print.

Morrison, Toni. *Playing in the Dark: Whiteness and the Literary Imagination.* New York: Vintage, 1992. Print.

Rakow, Lana F. "Feminist Approaches to Popular Culture: Giving Patriarchy Its Due." *Cultural Theory and Popular Culture: A Reader.* 3rd ed. Ed. John Storey. Essex, Eng.: Pearson, 2006. 199–214. Print.

Ransom, John Crowe. *The World's Body: Foundations for Literary Criticism.* New York: Scribner's, 1938. Print.

Rice, Philip, and Patricia Waugh, eds. *Modern Literary Theory: A Reader*. 4th ed. New York: Oxford UP, 2001. Print.

Sedgwick, Eve. *Epistemology of the Closet*. Berkeley: U of California P, 2008. Print.

Storey, John. *Cultural Theory and Popular Culture: An Introduction*. 4th ed. Toronto: Pearson, 2006. Print.

Williams, Raymond. "The Analysis of Culture. *Cultural Theory and Popular Culture: A Reader*. 3rd ed. Toronto: Pearson, 2006. Print.

SUGGESTED FURTHER READING

General Introductions to Literary and Critical Theory

Eagleton, Terry. *Literary Theory: An Introduction*. 3rd ed. Minneapolis: U of Minnesota P, 2008. Print.

Hall, Donald E. *Literary and Cultural Theory: From Basic Principles to Advanced Applications*. Boston: Houghton, 2001. Print.

Formalism/New Criticism

Davis, Garrick. *Praising It New: The Best of New Criticism*. Athens, OH: Swallow, 2008. Print.

Spurlin, William J., and Michael Fischer, eds. *The New Criticism and Contemporary Literary Theory: Connections and Continuities*. New York: Garland, 1995. Print.

Steiner, Peter. *Russian Formalism: A Metapoetics*. Ithaca, NY: Cornell UP, 1984. Print.

Thompson, Ewa M. *Russian Formalism and Anglo-American New Criticism: A Comparative Study*. The Hague, Neth.: Mouton, 1971. Print.

Structuralism

Culler, Jonathan. *Structuralist Poetics: Structuralism, Linguistics, and the Study of Literature*. 2nd ed. New York: Routledge, 2002. Print.

Hawkes, Terence. *Structuralism and Semiotics*. New York: Routledge, 2003. Print.

Deconstruction (Poststructuralist Criticism)

Culler, Jonathan. *On Deconstruction: Theory and Criticism after Structuralism*. 25th anniversary ed. Ithaca, NY: Cornell UP, 2007. Print.

Sarup, Madan. *An Introductory Guide to Post-Structuralism and Postmodernism*. 2nd ed. Athens: U of Georgia P, 1993. Print.

Reader-Response Criticism

Fish, Stanley. *Is There a Text in This Class? The Authority of Interpretive Communities*. Cambridge, MA: Harvard UP, 1982. Print.

Freund, Elizabeth. *The Return of the Reader: Reader-Response Criticism*. New York: Methuen, 1987. Print.

Iser, Wolfgang. *Prospecting: From Reader Response to Literary Anthropology*. Baltimore, MD: Johns Hopkins UP, 1993. Print.

Psychoanalytic Criticism

Wright, Elizabeth. *Psychoanalytic Criticism: A Reappraisal*. New York: Routledge, 1998. Print.

Žižek, Slavoj. *How to Read Lacan*. New York: Norton, 2007. Print.

Marxist Criticism

Eagleton, Terry. *Marxism and Literary Criticism*. New York: Routledge, 2002. Print.

Hawkes, David. *Ideology*. New York: Routledge, 1996. Print.

Feminist Criticism

Gilbert, Sandra M., and Susan Gubar, eds. *Feminist Literary Theory and Criticism: A Norton Reader*. New York: Norton, 2007. Print.

Grosz, Elizabeth. *Sexual Subversions: Three French Feminists*. Crows Nest, Austral.: Allen & Unwin, 1989. Print.

Showalter, Elaine, ed. *The New Feminist Criticism: Essays on Women, Literature and Theory*. New York: Pantheon, 1985. Print.

Gender Studies and Queer Theory

Butler, Judith. *Gender Trouble: Feminism and the Subversion of Identity*. New York: Routledge, 1990. Print.

Jagose, Annamarie. *Queer Theory: An Introduction*. New York: New York UP, 1996. Print.

Sedgwick, Eve. *Between Men: English Literature and Male Homosocial Desire*. New York: Columbia UP, 1985. Print.

New Historicism

Gallagher, Catherine, and Stephen Greenblatt. *Practicing New Historicism*. Chicago: U of Chicago P, 2001. Print.

Vesser, Harold, ed. *The New Historicism*. New York: Routledge, 1989. Print.

Postcolonialism and Critical Race Theory

Delgado, Richard, and Jean Stefancic. *Critical Race Theory: An Introduction.* New York: New York UP, 2001. Print.

Said, Edward. *Culture and Imperialism.* New York: Vintage, 1994. Print.

Young, Robert J.C. *Postcolonialism: A Very Short Introduction.* New York: Oxford UP, 2003. Print.

Part 2

WRITING ABOUT LITERARY GENRES AND FILM

4

Writing about Poetry

WHAT IS POETRY?

Of the various definitions of **poetry*** in the *Oxford English Dictionary*, one stands out as particularly useful: "Composition in verse or some comparable patterned arrangement of language in which the expression of feelings and ideas is given intensity by the use of distinctive style and rhythm; the art of such a composition" (2220). There will always be poems that challenge this or any other definition of poetry, but for our present purposes we can accept the *OED*'s definition without too much trouble. "Composition" in this instance consists of putting something together or, to speak more technically, of combining individual elements or groups of elements into a larger whole. Musical composition, for instance, involves combining and arranging musical notes into an overall piece of music. Poetic composition similarly involves the arrangement of sounds: poets often consider the acoustic value of the words they select, be it in terms of **metre**, **rhyme**, **alliteration**, **assonance**, repetition, and so on. More than just an arrangement of sounds, however, poetry also implies the combination of **metaphors**, **symbols**, **allusions**, and other forms of **imagery** and the arrangement of lines grouped into **stanzas** and separated by **line breaks**.[1] The *OED*'s reference to "verse or some comparable patterned arrangement of language" is meant both to distinguish poetry from **prose** (i.e., non-metrical composition closer to ordinary speech) and to be inclusive of form-breaking poetry such as "concrete poetry" in which letters and words are arranged typographically into shapes, images, and other visual patterns (pillars, flowers, swirls, etc.). The notion that poetry gives "intensity" to "the expression of feelings and ideas" is a commonplace perception of poetic composition, though

---

1 Terms in bold are explained later in this chapter. For concise definitions, see the glossary in the Appendix.

**Compact Oxford English Dictionary* definition "Poetry". By permission of Oxford University Press.

emphasis tends to fall (perhaps, more often than it should) on "feelings" rather than on "ideas." This conventional overemphasis on feeling is likely the reason why students are so often protective of their personal interpretations of poetry. It is always a good idea to take note of your emotional responses to poetry; but literary criticism requires you to develop an analytical response that examines not only what you think and feel about a poem, but also, more importantly, how you came to have such thoughts and feelings in the first place. As discussed in Chapter 2, writing about literature involves both your interpretation of a poem's meaning and a critical analysis of the conditions (textual, historical, political, etc.) that make such meaning possible. The following sections are intended to help you acquire and/or develop the skills and knowledge needed to perform such analysis.

The previous chapter outlined a number of critical approaches to writing about literature. For the most part, the present chapter focuses on the formal elements of poetry and is therefore formalist in its approach. The Reading Demonstration section near the end of this chapter extends this formalist focus by applying a New Critical "close" reading strategy to a very short poem by Walter de la Mare. While subsequent chapters likewise consider the formal elements of other genres of literature and film, their Reading Demonstration sections offer examples of more political critical approaches to literature, including feminist criticism, New Historicism, and psychoanalysis.

WHO IS SPEAKING IN A POEM—AND HOW?

Even though poetry is commonly associated with the expression of personal feelings, it is important to keep in mind that the **speaker** of a poem is not always the poet himself or herself. Poets often use a **persona** (the Latin word for "mask"), who is presumed to be the person uttering the words on the page. A persona establishes a poem's **point of view**, which is crucial to the poem's meaning. In Chapter 1, we mentioned that Robert Burns's use of Scots language in his poem "A Red, Red Rose" is meant to draw our attention to who is speaking the poem— namely, a rural Scotsman who addresses his "bonny lass" (5). Burns was born and raised in the rural setting of Alloway, Scotland, but when he wrote his poem in 1794 he had long since given up farming to work as a British government official. More to the point, composed as a traditional Scottish folksong, "A Red, Red Rose" is based not on Burns's own experiences and/or perspective so much as it is inspired by points of view and experiences typically depicted in such songs. The speaker of "A Red, Red Rose," in other words, is not Burns but an **archetype** (i.e., a recurring, almost universal characterization) of Scottish folklore.

Sometimes the speaker is an obvious persona or mask, like the speaker of Sylvia Plath's "Mirror,"* whose identity shifts from being a seemingly

---

*'Mirror' taken from *Collected Poems* by Sylvia Plath, © the Estate of Sylvia Plath, and reproduced by permission of Faber and Faber Ltd.

unsympathetic mirror ("I am silver and exact") in the first stanza to being a slightly less indifferent body of water ("Now I am a lake") in the second stanza (1, 10). At other times, the difference between the speaker and the poet is almost imperceptible, which is the case in John Keats's poem "Ode to a Nightingale" (1819), the first stanza of which reads:

> My Heart aches, and a drowsy numbness pains
>   My sense, as though of hemlock I had drunk,
> Or emptied some dull opiate to the drains
>   One minute past, and Lethe-wards had sunk:
> 'Tis not through envy of thy happy lot,
>   But being too happy in thine happiness—
>   That thou, light-winged Dryad of the trees,
>   In some melodious plot
> Of beechen green, and shadows numberless,
>   Singest of summer in full-throated ease.   (1–10)

The story goes that Keats wrote the first draft of this deeply expressive poem while sitting under a plum tree listening to the "full-throated" warble of a nightingale that had built its nest just above the home of one of Keats's friends. Given these circumstances and the highly subjective nature of the poem, it would seem reasonable to equate speaker with poet. However, no one, not even Keats himself, would ever talk the way the speaker of "Nightingale" talks. As a carefully crafted lyric **monologue** (an extended speech given by a single character), the poem is far too polished and refined to have been an instance of a spontaneously spoken sequence of thoughts. As Keats's fellow Romantic poet William Wordsworth famously wrote, "Poetry is the spontaneous overflow of powerful feelings . . . recollected in tranquility" (208). What this means is that the spontaneity of a speaker like the one in Keats's "Nightingale" is only a simulated spontaneity reconstructed after the fact. If the speaker represents Keats as he sits listening to a nightingale under a plum tree, then he is at best an idealized simulation (or self-fashioned mask) of Keats. Making a distinction between the poet and a speaker who is an idealized version of the poet may appear to some as a mere quibble, but in the case of someone like Keats—a poet who struggled throughout his writing career with his own self-fashioned identity as a poet—such distinctions often lead to insight into the meaning of his poetry.

In cases where the speaker is noticeably different than the poet, it is always a good idea to ask yourself why the poet has chosen to portray a persona as opposed to some version of himself or herself. You might conclude, for instance, that Plath chose to portray her speaker ironically in "Mirror" as the **personification** of a mirror/lake in order to show that a mirror's reflection is not an objective process but is, rather, mediated by the subjective experience of an individual who projects his or her own feelings (of inadequacy, regret, etc.) onto the mirror's reflective surface. Consider the equally ironic use of persona in Robert Browning's widely studied "Soliloquy of the Spanish Cloister" (1842). Beginning his rantlike speech with a growl ("Gr-r-r—there go, my heart's abhorrence!" [1]), Browning's speaker attempts to communicate his seething hatred for a fellow monk named Brother Lawrence, but the reasons he lists for disliking the man do not appear to warrant such strong emotions. Complaining of Lawrence's trivial mealtime chatter, the speaker scoffs:

> *Salve tibi!* I must hear
> Wise talk of the kind of weather,
>   Sort of season, time of year:
> *Not a plenteous cork-crop: scarcely*
>   *Dare we hope oak-galls, I doubt:*
> *What's the Latin name for "parsley"?*
>   What's the Greek name for Swine's Snout?   (10–16)

Even if we sympathize with Browning's speaker (having ourselves been occasionally subjected to irritating dinner companions), it is important to recognize that the speaker's reaction to Lawrence (e.g., insulting his piglike proboscis) is disproportionate to the offence. The speaker is just being vindictive and petty, which is precisely the point of the poem: by taking advantage of a speaker who is clearly not the poet, Browning highlights how people can betray more about themselves and their own irritable natures when speaking negatively about other people.

This kind of **characterization** (or portrayal) of a speaker is likewise crucial to understanding the significance of a **dialogue** poem such as Thomas Hardy's "The Ruined Maid," in which neither position of the two arguing speakers (a "ruined maid" and a "country girl") appears to be endorsed by the poet. The purpose of Hardy's poem is not to determine which speaker is morally superior so much as it is tov consider how each speaker attempts to perform her identity in her choice of **diction** (i.e., word choice) and her **tone** (i.e., detectible attitude). Whereas the "ruined" maid displays a sophisticated urban sensibility in her use of irony, subtlety, and wit, the "country girl" discloses a no-nonsense rustic attitude in her dialect and parochial use of language. Like Plath's and Browning's poems, "The Ruined Maid" reminds us that identifying a poem's speaker(s) is not a trifling matter, but often unlocks a poem's raison d'être, its reason for being.

Summary

WHO IS SPEAKING IN A POEM—AND HOW?

- the speaker of a poem is not always the poet himself or herself, but is often a persona (or "mask") who is presumed to be the person uttering the words on the page

(continued)

Summary

WHO IS SPEAKING IN A POEM—AND HOW? (continued)

- when the speaker is noticeably different than the poet, ask yourself why the poet has chosen to portray a persona rather than some version of himself or herself?

- aspects of a speaker's diction (word choice) and tone (detectible attitude) can reveal how a speaker is being characterized

WHAT IS HAPPENING? WHERE DOES IT HAPPEN? AND WHEN?

When struggling to understand difficult poetry, a good strategy is to put aside your need to know exactly what a poem means when you first read it and instead start with the basics. Try to figure out what is happening on the surface. This involves ascertaining the identity of the speaker, as we considered above, but it also requires mentally reconstructing the *situation* (i.e., the action and goings-on) as well as the **setting** (i.e., the location and time) of the poem. Once you have a handle on these details, you can then begin to look for the poem's deeper meanings.

Let us return to Keats's "Ode to a Nightingale" for an illustration of setting. (Since we will return to this poem more than once in the next few sections, it is reprinted in its entirety at the end of this chapter. You are encouraged to read it through before proceeding.) Your first couple of readings of the poem should reveal the situation of the speaker, who, as we noted previously, appears to be speaking in the voice of the poet: he hears a nightingale's "full-throated" song, is enthralled by it, and meditates on its significance. That is the poem's situation. The setting of the poem, on the other hand, is more implied than explicitly described, but there are indications in the poem as to where the speaker is:

> I cannot see what flowers are at my feet,
>   Nor what soft incense hangs upon the boughs,
> But, in embalmed darkness, guess each sweet
>   Wherewith the seasonable month endows
> The grass, the thicket, and the fruit-tree wild;
>   White hawthorn, and the pastoral eglantine;
>   Fast fading violets covered up in leaves;
>   And mid-May's eldest child,
> The coming musk-rose, full of dewy wine,
>   The murmurous haunt of flies on summer eves.   (41–50)

The speaker claims that he "cannot see" the setting he describes in this passage. This may be a clue to the time of day in which the poem's action takes place. Nightingales are known to sing throughout the hour that precedes dawn, so the above passage likely alludes to the fact that the speaker is out-of-doors just prior to sunrise and is therefore unable to see clearly the objects before and beneath him. Through his keen sense of smell, however, the speaker is able to imagine the lush natural setting that surrounds him: there are flowers, grass, a dense forest or thicket of fruit-bearing trees, and a "soft incense" hanging in the air (aroma is also a matter of setting). That these natural objects are in full bloom is evidenced not only by Keats's emphasis on fragrance but also by the speaker's mention of the time of year: late spring/early summer ("mid-May"/"summer eves"). Since the poem does not refer to historical time (that is, beyond the time of year and day), and since the poem is written in the present tense, it is reasonable to assume that the poem's situation is set in May of 1819, when the poem is thought to have been composed. All these facts about the poem's situation and setting offer us a firm foundation on which to stand before proceeding to look more closely at the poem's densely lyrical and highly metaphorical language, which we will do in the next section. For the moment, we can conclude our current emphasis on situation and setting by noting that the poem takes place in a **pastoral** (i.e., idyllic, natural) setting and that the spell of the speaker's trancelike meditation of the nightingale's song is suddenly broken in the last **stanza**: "Forlorn! the very word is like a bell / To toll me back from thee [the nightingale] to my sole self" (71–72). Answering questions as to why the spell is broken and what this event means requires us to move beyond a basic consideration of what happens, where it happens, and when.

Summary

WHAT IS HAPPENING? WHERE DOES IT HAPPEN? AND WHEN?

- when trying to understand difficult poetry, start with some basic questions about what is happening on the surface:
    - Who is the speaker, and what is his or her role in the poem?
    - What is the *situation* of the poem? What is happening?
    - What is the setting of the poem? When and where does the poem take place?

POETIC LANGUAGE

One way to move beyond a basic consideration of a poem into a deeper understanding of its meaning is to analyze the poem's language. Most often, it is a poem's use of **figurative language** that challenges our sense of what the poem means. Figurative language is defined as language that refers to a meaning that is *other than* the literal meaning. When I say, for instance, that my mouth is on fire after eating a chili pepper, I am not suggesting that my mouth has literally burst into flames; I am simply using a figure of speech to communicate the simulated sensation of heat caused by the chili's active ingredient, capsaicin. The two most common forms of figurative language in poetry are **metaphor** and **simile**, both of which allude to figurative (or non-literal) meanings through some kind of analogy (i.e., comparison).

Metaphor

Generally speaking, a metaphor makes a comparison between two things (objects, feelings, ideas, etc.) where one thing is equated with, or described in terms of, the other. Shakespeare's Romeo offers a prime example when he espies Juliet on her balcony: "But soft! What light through yonder window breaks? / It is the East, and Juliet is the sun!" (*Romeo and Juliet* II.ii.2–3). Romeo actually makes two metaphorical comparisons through which he equates Juliet's entrance to the sunrise: first, he compares the balcony window to the eastern horizon; second, he compares Juliet to the sun. In both cases, the first object of the comparison is not said to be *like* the second object; rather, they are said to be *the same thing*: the window *is* the East, and Juliet *is* the sun. The objects under comparison, in other words, are not similar so much as they are the *same*.

A metaphorical comparison can also occur when only one of the things being compared is mentioned. Keats's "Nightingale" provides a good example: "Away! away!" the speaker proclaims, "for I will fly to thee, / Not charioted by Bacchus and his pards, / But on the viewless wings of Poesy" (31–33). Like Romeo, Keats's speaker makes more than one metaphorical comparison here, but the latter's are subtler in nature. The overall metaphor compares the imagination (which is roughly what "Poesy" means in this instance) to an invisible or "viewless" bird on which the speaker might sit in his desire to "fly" alongside the nightingale. What is more, the speaker specifically refuses to make such a flight on the leopard-powered chariot of Bacchus (the Greek god of wine), which is itself a metaphor for the anesthetizing and hallucinogenic properties of laudanum, the recreational drug of choice for early nineteenth-century poets. No, Keats's speaker will not fly to the nightingale by getting high, as it were—or worse, by overdosing and dying. Rather, he will soar soberly on the "viewless wings" of poetic inspiration. Throughout the poem Keats's speaker likens himself and his imagination to the nightingale in particular, that "immortal Bird" whose song universally connects it to all the nightingales that have sung the "selfsame song" since "ancient days" (61, 65, 64). For Keats, this idea of connectedness through song made an attractive metaphor for poetry itself as the immortal voice of humanity heard in the tenor of each individual poetic voice.

Simile

While metaphors often make *implicit* comparisons—or, as in the example of "Juliet is the sun," do not make comparisons so much as they make *equations*—a simile is a figure of speech that draws an *explicit* comparison between two things using verbal signals such as "like" and "as." We might say that the simile makes a spectacle of its comparison: it asks us openly to think about the comparison, to mull it over in our heads for a moment. As mentioned in Chapter 1, Robert Burns's famous first line, "O, my luve's like a red, red rose," candidly invites us to contemplate two seemingly unrelated ideas simultaneously so that we might understand them in a more intuitive or impressionistic manner. The simile never makes an equation, but insists only on similarities between the two otherwise distinct terms of the comparison. In Canto 2 of Lord Byron's *Don Juan*, for instance, the narrating speaker compares the tenderness with which a young woman named Haidée cares for Juan to a mother nursing her child: "And she bent o'er him, and he lay beneath, / Hushed as the babe upon its mother's breast" (2.148). This example of an "as" simile ("Hushed as the babe") does not *equate* Juan to an infant (as a metaphor might do) but merely emphasizes similarities between two distinct situations. Juan is not a baby; he only sleeps like one in Haidée's arms.

For another example of simile, let us revisit the final stanza of Keats's "Nightingale": "Forlorn! the very word is like a bell / To toll me back from thee to my sole self" (71–72). Up to this point in the poem, Keats's speaker has been lulled into a sort of daydream by the sounds of the nightingale's warbling. The daydream is textured by his desire to escape "[t]he weariness, the fever, and the fret" of everyday reality, and by his wavering back and forth between thoughts of death ("Now more than ever seems it rich to die" [55]) and a restored faith in the compensatory nature of poetry. Before these tensions can be resolved, however, the speaker's melancholy gets the best of him. The casual use of "forlorn" in line 70 ("in faery lands forlorn") falls on his ears "like a bell" in line 71. This simile's comparison works on several complex levels. On the one hand, Keats draws our attention to the sound of the "very word" *forlorn* which, with its equally stressed repetition of the *or-* sound (for-lorn), resembles the resounding double strike of a swinging bell. On the other hand, the word *forlorn*'s associations with hopelessness and abandonment are bolstered by this acoustic resemblance to the sound of a bell, which in the context of the poem's reflections on mortality cannot help but connote the "toll" of a death bell that abruptly calls the speaker back from his imaginary flight with the nightingale to the mortal sufferings of actual life "where men sit and hear each other groan" (24).

Ambiguity

There are, of course, other uses of figurative language beyond metaphors and similes. **Ambiguity** is another kind of figurative language in which words express multiple (sometimes contradictory) meanings or a diverse range of emotions or attitudes. Given the emphasis that Keats places on the forlorn/bell simile, it would appear that "Nightingale" ends with the speaker having lost faith in the uplifting power of poetry: "the fancy cannot cheat so well / As she is famed to do, deceiving elf" (73–74). Like many of Keats's concluding lines, however, the final **couplet** of "Nightingale" ultimately remains *ambiguous* on this point: "Was it a vision, or a waking dream? / Fled is that music—do I wake or sleep?" (79–80). The speaker appears too disoriented to be conclusive about "fancy's" failure. His inability to tell whether he is awake or asleep suggests that his "vision" or "waking dream" has not left him entirely. His return to harsh reality seems to have changed his perspective—if not completely, then at least enough for him to picture the "meadows" and the "still stream" that he himself cannot see but that he can imagine through the eyes of the bird who disappears over the "hillside" without him. The speaker, in other words, remains ambiguously caught in a state of reaching for the ideal from a position of real life.

Personification, Allusion, and Symbol

Keats's "Nightingale" also uses figurative language such as **personification** and **allusion**. Although the nightingale is said not to have the capacity for human suffering (which it "hast never known" [22]), it is nevertheless personified as having a "voice" that "[s]ingest of summer" as though it were consciously composing an ode of its own (63, 10). The poem's allusions (i.e., its references to literature, myth, art, etc.) are perhaps easier to spot than to understand: in line 4, the phrase "Lethe-wards" refers to the Greek mythological river of Lethe, which is associated with forgetfulness; "Flora" in line 13 alludes to the Roman goddess of flowers and spring; and "Hippocrene" in line 16 refers to the fountain of inspiration held sacred by the Greek Muses. These are just a few of the poem's many classical allusions (see also "Dryad" [7], "Bacchus" [32], "Fays" [37], and "Ruth" [66]). For a **symbol** (i.e., a figure that represents itself but at the same time stands for something else), we can remember from Chapter 2 our example of the vase of lilacs in W.D. Snodgrass's "Leaving the Motel," or we can consider the sudden disconnect between Keats's speaker and the nightingale in "Nightingale" as *standing for* Keats's own struggle to pursue "truth" and "beauty" (as he refers to them in his poem "Ode on a Grecian Urn") in a world so full of melancholy and painful experiences.

Summary

POETIC LANGUAGE

- poems often use figurative language (e.g., metaphor, simile, ambiguity, etc.), which is language that refers to a meaning that is different than the literal meaning

- a metaphor makes an *implicit* comparison between two things (objects, feelings, ideas, etc.) where one thing is equated with, or described in terms of, the other

- a simile draws an *explicit* comparison between two things using verbal signals such as "like" and "as"

- ambiguity involves language that expresses multiple meanings or a diverse range of emotions or attitudes

- personification occurs when human qualities and characteristics are attributed to non-human entities

- allusion refers to a poem's indirect references to literary, mythological, or historical figures and/or events

- a symbol is a figure or object that represents itself but at the same time stands for something else

---

PROSODY: SCANNING FOR SOUND

As we see with Keats's acoustical interest in the word "forlorn," sounds in poetry can bear a great deal of significance. Consider the **alliteration** (i.e., the repetition of initial consonant sounds) in the following line from "Ode to a Nightingale": "With beaded bubbles winking at the brim" (17). This line extends the repetition of "b" sounds found in the word "bubble," which is itself a sort of **onomatopoeia** that approximates the sound of its referent—namely, spherical beads that "wink" at the "brim" of "a beaker full of the warm South" (i.e., wine) (15). This alliteration of "b" sounds adds an acoustic aspect to an otherwise visual image, and in the process expresses more fully the desire the speaker attaches to these bubbles that entice him to drink and "leave the world unseen" (19). **Consonance** (i.e., the repetition of final consonants in stressed syllables) and **assonance** (i.e., the repetition of vowel sounds in words with different endings) are also commonly used for emphasis. For a mixture of consonance and assonance, we can look to the sequence of "m," "r," and short "u" sounds in line 50 of Keats's "Nightingale": "The murmurous haunt of flies on summer eves." Not unlike the "beaded bubbles" of line 17, the sounds of this line are also onomatopoeic in suggesting the sound of humming flies.

As far as poetic sounds go, however, nothing is perhaps more noticeable and familiar than the **rhythm** and **rhyme** of poetry, which, along with the sounds we have just considered, make up the prosody of poetry (i.e., the principles of metrical composition). Rhyme would appear to be straightforward because, stereotypically, it has become the telltale sign of poetry. Sophisticated readers of poetry will know that rhyme is not a feature of all poetry; but even more sophisticated readers will know that rhyme is more complicated than simply determining which poems have it and which ones do not. Even poems without a consistent rhyme scheme may use **internal rhymes**, where one word rhymes with another word in the same line. (Rhymes that occur at the end of lines are called end rhymes.) Alternatively, poems with definite rhyme schemes will often employ **half rhymes,** in which the final consonant sounds of two words are identical but the preceding vowel sounds disagree (e.g., in her sonnet "In an Artist's Studio," Christina Rossetti rhymes "dim" and "dream"); or such poems may use **eye rhymes,** where words *look* like they rhyme but do not (e.g., Keats's sonnet "The Poetry of Earth Is Never Dead" places "dead" in a rhyme scheme with "mead" and "lead").

Rhythm is most often measured in terms of **metre**, which refers to the overall pattern of stressed and unstressed syllables in a line of poetry. Each sequence or group of stressed and unstressed syllables is called a **foot**. The number of feet in a line determines its metre. Let us look, for instance, at the most famous metrical pattern in English poetry, which occurs in the sonnet form as well as in the **heroic couplet** of some **epic** poetry. Here is an example from Shakespeare's "Sonnet 12": "When I do count the clock that tells the time" (1). This line consists of five syllabic sequences (or feet) in which an unstressed syllable is followed by a stressed syllable. We can express this typographically as follows: Whĕn Ī | dŏ coūnt | thĕ clōck | thăt tēlls | thĕ tīme. The feet in this example are separated by vertical bars, the ˘ characters represent unstressed or light syllables, and the ˉ characters represent stressed or hard syllables. When a foot consists of two syllables, the first unstressed and the second stressed (e.g., "Whĕn Ī"), it is called an iamb. Since this line contains five iambs, it is said to be written in **iambic pentameter** (*penta* is Greek for five, as in *penta*gram or *penta*gon). Iambic pentameter is said to resemble everyday English speech more than any other metre, but we should qualify this characterization by pointing out that it represents only an idealized form of everyday speech, since no one speaks in consistent iambic pentameter. Poetic metre is, after all, stylized language that conspicuously draws attention to itself.

Reading for metre (known as **scansion**) is most appropriate for poetry with **fixed form** (discussed in "Poetic Form and Structure," below), but all poems contain metre even when they do not produce consistent patterns. Depending on the number of feet present, lines of poetry are said to be written in monometer (one foot), dimeter (two feet), trimeter (three feet), tetrameter (four feet), pentameter (five feet), hexameter (six feet), heptameter (seven feet), octameter (eight feet), and so on. Here is a list of different kinds of feet:

Iamb (adjective: iambic): a light syllable followed by a stressed syllable (e.g., re-VOLT)

Trochee (trochaic): a stressed syllable followed by a light syllable (e.g., PE-ter)

Anapest (anapestic): two light syllables followed by a stressed syllable (e.g., in the RAIN)

Dactyl (dactylic): a stressed syllable followed by two light syllables (e.g., SYLL-able)

The above metrical feet are often sustained through an entire line and can be used to build any kind of metre: you can have iambic trimeter, trochaic tetrameter, anapestic pentameter, and so on. There are, however, a few "variant" feet that occur most often as exceptions within a line dominated by one of the above four metres. These include the following:

Spondee (spondaic): two syllables of approximately equal stress (e.g., RUM PUNCH)

Amphibrach (amphibrachic): a stressed syllable between two light syllables (e.g., ma-CHINE gun)

Amphimacer (amphimacic): a light syllable between two stressed syllables (e.g., READ-y MADE)

Summary

PROSODY: SCANNING FOR SOUND

- always keep in mind that sounds in poetry usually carry a good deal of significance

- alliteration refers to the repetition of initial consonant sounds (e.g., "beaded bubbles")

- onomatopoeia refers to words that sound like the actions or objects they denote (e.g., "thump")

- rhythm and rhyme are important aspects of a poem; they enable certain words to have emphasis and give readers a sense of what to expect

  - there are many different kinds of rhyme, each with its own effects; they include end rhymes, internal rhymes, half rhymes, and eye rhymes

  - rhythm is most often measured in terms of metre, which refers to the overall pattern of stressed and unstressed syllables in a line of poetry

(continued)

Summary

PROSODY: SCANNING FOR SOUND (continued)

- each sequence or group of stressed and unstressed syllables is called a foot
- reading for metre is called scansion; it consists of determining how many and what kind of feet occur in a single line, or sequence of lines, of poetry

POETIC FORM AND STRUCTURE

The term **fixed form** refers to poetry that adheres to historically established structural requirements. Examples include the haiku, which consists of an unrhymed **tercet** (i.e., a three-lined stanza) that contains a total of 17 syllables (five in the first line, seven in the second, and five in the third) and the ballad, which consists of an undetermined number of **quatrains** (i.e., four-lined stanzas) with a rhyme scheme of *abcb* (i.e., the second and fourth lines rhyme) and written in alternating tetrameters and trimeters. One of the best-known fixed form in English poetry is the **sonnet**. Although sonnets can vary to some degree in their rhyme schemes, all sonnets are composed of fourteen lines of iambic pentameter. The two dominant varieties of sonnets are the **Shakespearean** (or English) **sonnet**, consisting of three quatrains with an *abab/cdcd/efef* rhyming pattern and a concluding couplet that rhymes *gg*; and the **Petrarchan** (or Italian) **sonnet**, which is organized into an eight-line **octave** that rhymes *abbaabba* and a six-line **sestet** that usually rhymes *cdecde*. It is important to be familiar with the various rules of the sonnet, not least because many of the most distinguished sonneteers in literary history often bend or break such rules for emphasis or dramatic effect. Take William Wordsworth's "Nuns Fret Not" for example, a sonnet in which the speaker finds comfort in the rigid confines of the sonnet form:

Nuns fret not at their convent's narrow room;	a
And hermits are contented with their cells;	b
And students with their pensive citadels;	b
Maids at the wheel, the weaver at his loom,	a
Sit blithe and happy; bees that soar for bloom,	a
High as the highest Peak of Furness-fells,	b
Will murmur by the hour in foxglove bells:	b
In truth the prison, unto which we doom	a
Ourselves, no prison is: and hence for me,	c
In sundry moods, 'twas pastime to be bound	d
Within the Sonnet's scanty plot of ground;	d
Pleased if some Souls (for such there needs must be)	c
Who have felt the weight of too much liberty,	c
Should find brief solace there, as I have found.	d

We know this sonnet is Petrarchan (or Italian) in structure because the rhyme scheme, though somewhat inconsistent with Petrarchan rules, clearly separates an octave (*abbaabba*) from a sestet (*cddccd*). In addition to changing the usual rhyme scheme of a Petrarchan sestet, Wordsworth takes some liberty with a few other conventions, including the use of iambic feet: the poem's very first foot, to mention only the most obvious example, is more of a spondee than an iamb. Wordsworth even takes liberty with "liberty" itself, since his use of this word in line 13 leaves the line with one syllable too many (eleven instead of ten). This irregularity, like the others, is both intentional and ironic. As it turns out, the poem is not simply about finding comfort in the sonnet form (i.e., its "scanty plot of ground"). It is, more importantly, a tribute to the possibilities afforded by the strictures of a fixed form. Because the rules of the sonnet are well known (especially during Wordsworth's time), the occasional break from such rules plays on the reader's expectations and consequently provides opportunities for emphasis and meaning that a more **open form** of poetry might not otherwise allow.

Somewhere between fixed form and open form lies a kind of poetry called **blank verse**, which is not the same as the **free verse** that has become dominant in the twentieth and twenty-first centuries. Whereas blank verse retains a consistent metre (usually iambic pentameter) but avoids rhyme, free verse eschews both rhyme and metre altogether. Blank verse in iambic pentameter first became popular in Elizabethan (i.e., sixteenth-century) drama, but the English Romantic poets of the late eighteenth century made it a common practice in poetry. Here is a sample from Coleridge's "Frost at Midnight":

> Dear Babe, that sleepest cradled by my side,
> Whose gentle breathings, heard in this deep calm,
> Fill up the interspersèd vacancies
> And momentary pauses of the thought!   (45–48)

Even as this example of blank verse appears spontaneous and unstructured, it adheres to iambic pentameter. The following short example of free verse, entitled "Gentlemen Take Polaroids" by Gil Anderson,* is quite different:

> Imagine me
> hung out to dry
> crying honey
> don't leave me this way.   (1–4)

This poem does not appear to conform to the established structure of a fixed form or even to a specific metrical pattern the way Coleridge's poem does. But that does not mean the poem lacks structure. You might ask yourself: why does this poem, which comprises a single sentence broken into four lines, use **line**

---

*Excerpt from "Gentlemen Take Polaroids" by Gil Adamson in *Primitive* by Gil Adamson. Published by Coach House Press © 1991. Reprinted by permission of the author.

breaks this way? Why not just write the entire sentence across a single line and be done with it? **Enjambment** is the term used when the syntax and grammar of one line runs into another. There is never a single explanation as to why a poet uses line breaks and/or enjambment. In fact, the ability of enjambment to produce ambiguity and uncertainty is part of its attraction. It can likewise be used to emphasize certain words or ideas. In "Polaroids," Anderson may have wanted us to read her poem slowly, one grammatical step at a time, while pausing and reflecting at the end of each line so that we might flesh out the full scope of the poem's imaginative space. *Imagine me*—this imperative demands that we not only envisage the speaker but also linger over this initial image before filling in any details. Now imagine me *hung out to dry*—an addition pregnant with both literal and figurative significance. Now imagine me hung out to dry *crying honey*. The pause between line 3 and 4 is exemplary in capitalizing on the kind of ambiguity that enjambment allows. On the one hand, the poem's grammar suggests that "crying" refers to the speaker's desperate plea to an intimate addressee: "Honey, don't leave me this way." Standing on its own, however, the phrase "crying honey" offers an alternate image, not of a person calling out to another, but of a person crying tears as thick and sticky as honey. This strikingly vivid second impression further accentuates the distress of the final line: *don't leave me this way*. Apropos its title, the poem's structural use of line breaks allows its **imagery** to emerge gradually, like the contents of a Polaroid picture.

Summary

POETIC FORM AND STRUCTURE

- fixed form refers to poetry that adheres to historically established structural requirements, such as the haiku and the sonnet

- sonnets come in two main varieties:

  - Shakespearean (or English) sonnets consist of three quatrains with an *abab/cdcd/efef* rhyming pattern and a concluding couplet that rhymes *gg*

  - Petrarchan (or Italian) sonnets are organized into an eight-line octave that rhymes *abbaabba* and a six-line sestet that usually rhymes *cdecde*

- blank verse is a form of poetry that uses consistent metre (usually iambic pentameter) but avoids rhyme

- free verse is a form of poetry that does not follow a consistent metre or rhyme scheme

READING DEMONSTRATION: POETRY AND NEW CRITICISM

We have already performed a kind of formalist reading of Keats's "Ode to a Nightingale" by focusing on that poem's speaker and its use of figurative language and sound. But we will end this chapter with a brief demonstration of a New Critical "close" reading (also a kind of formalism) of Walter de la Mare's* "Slim Cunning Hands," a poem that consists of a single **quatrain** (i.e., four-line stanza).[2] As close readers, we should pay particular attention to the interplay of the poem's various rhetorical elements (especially its ambiguity) and how that interplay achieves unity in the poem's attempt to express a conflicted set of emotions.

> Slim cunning hands at rest, and cozening eyes—
> Under this stone one loved too wildly lies;
> How false she was, no granite could declare;
> Nor all the earth's flowers, how fair.   (1–4)

This poem is nothing if not ambiguous. Presenting itself as though it were an epitaph (i.e., words etched on a tombstone), the poem draws on the multiple meanings produced by its **diction** (word choice) and its grammar in order to portray the speaker's ambivalence toward the woman buried "[u]nder this stone." The speaker cannot help but begin with an implicitly negative, and typically chauvinistic, representation of the woman: she was manipulative ("cunning hands") and deceitful ("cozening eyes"). In addition to being negative, this depiction of the woman also implicitly reveals the speaker's interest in the woman's physical appearance, which he has reduced to a pair of body parts. The second line is more explicit in expressing the speaker's feelings towards the woman: he loved her "too wildly"—that is, with a passion that he could not control and that may have caused him pain. This second line, however, turns ambiguously on its own grammar and on the play of the word "lies." First, the speaker's passive omission of the personal pronoun ("I") in "one loved too wildly" suggests that he may not have been alone in loving her. In this light (and in light of his suspiciousness vis-à-vis her cunning hands and cozening eyes), the excess implied by "too wildly" points to a possessive jealousy that likely drove him senseless or crazy, so to speak, while she was alive. Second, the pun on "lies" (so close to the word "false" in the next line) suggests that her alleged deceptions continue to haunt him after her death: she "lies" both *in* and *from beyond* the grave.

We should be careful not to believe the speaker's representation of his former lover, since he writes his epitaph from the biased position of having felt spurned

---

2 For a summary of New Criticism, see Chapter 3.

*"Slim Cunning Hands" by Walter de la Mare from *The Complete Poems of Walter de la Mare* © 1975. Reprinted by permission of the Literary Trustees of Walter de la Mare and the Society of Authors as their representatives.

by her in some way. To be sure, the situation of this poem is rather misogynistic (i.e., sexist). Less a literal epitaph engraved on an actual tombstone (who would allow such a thing?), the poem more accurately represents the speaker's fantasy of having the final word on a woman whom he seems to have despised as much as, if not more than, he was attracted to her. But the speaker's words seem not to be enough, for as the poem's third line claims, "How false she was, no granite could declare." This is another way of saying that even a fantasized epitaph written on stone (i.e., the poem itself) could never fully capture or *clear up* (which is what the word "declare" means) the extent of the woman's dishonesty. This impossibility is paralleled by the poem's inability to register the vastness of the woman's beauty in the final line. While this line appears to end the poem on a positive note, two things trouble the close reader. First, returning to his misogynistic fixation on the woman's body, the speaker praises not the woman's identity but an aspect of her appearance: she is fairer than all the earth's flowers. Second, given the poem's emphasis on suspicion and deception as well as its previous pun on "lies," the speaker's actual last word—"fair"—could never limit its **connotation** (i.e., its range of reference) to a simple matter of beauty. De la Mare uses the word "fair" partly because he needs to complete the rhyme initiated by the previous line (". . . no granite could declare"). But it is difficult not to hear other associations in light of the poem's playful language. First we are told the woman is precisely the opposite of "fair" insofar as she is dishonest and manipulative, and now we are told that she is "fair" beyond words. Although these two meanings of "fair" operate on different levels, the word remains paradoxically charged with both negative and positive connotations. For this reason, it fittingly concludes (i.e., brings a kind of unity to) a poem that expresses, more than anything, the speaker's deeply ambivalent feelings about the woman beneath the stone.

STUDENT WRITING

The following writing sample by a first-year student focuses on the importance of tone and speaker in Audre Lorde's "Hanging Fire." The paper originally received a decent (albeit not exceptionally high) grade, and although it appears here in revised form, it remains imperfect. We will look more closely at both the virtues and the flaws of this essay in our discussion of the drafting and revision process in Chapter 8. Suffice it to say for now that some of the paper's limitations include its lack of attention to the importance of race in Lorde's poem, its tendency to dismiss the validity of the speaker's troubles, its occasional reliance on gender stereotypes, and its repetitiveness. Regardless of these imperfections (or perhaps because of them), the paper remains a good example of first-year writing. It is generally well written and demonstrates a good understanding of how specific literary elements, such as **hyperbole** (exaggeration) and diction, contribute meaningfully to a poem's overall message or theme.

The Crucial Role of a Mother: Loneliness and Insecurity in Audre Lorde's "Hanging Fire"*

The speaker of Audre Lorde's poem "Hanging Fire" is a lonely, young woman who experiences the confusing hormonal changes of puberty without a mother's guidance. The poem's emotional tone reveals the speaker's feelings of isolation, insecurity, and directionlessness—all of which stem from an unfulfilled desire to have a meaningful and close relationship with her otherwise absent mother. Unable to turn to her mother for support, the speaker is incapable of overcoming her own anxieties; as a result, the poem ends not with hope for the future, but on a note of despair. "Hanging Fire" thus makes a powerful statement on the importance of a nurturing maternal presence in the life of a young girl.

Although the speaker's identity remains vague throughout the poem, we know she is young ("I am fourteen" [1]) and we can infer that she, like Lorde herself, is African-American: she complains, for instance, that "my skin has betrayed me" (2). While the precise meaning of this complaint is unclear, the reference to "skin" and the pun on "betrayed" (i.e., her skin both exposes and undermines her) suggest that the speaker's troubles, for which she seeks maternal guidance, consist partly in being a visible minority. The speaker likewise reveals her adolescent immaturity indirectly in the way she expresses herself. Moving quickly and indiscriminately from one topic to the next, she discusses her displeasure at being excluded from the math team, wearing braces, having nothing to wear, facing an uncertain future, and her mother's unavailability, all in one short stanza (24–35). While some of the speaker's concerns are clearly significant (her mother's absence being perhaps the most important), other concerns appear overstated and unfounded (e.g., "what if I die / before morning [8–9]). The uninterrupted flow and juxtaposition of exaggerated and legitimate worries indicates an illogical thought pattern commonly associated with those going through puberty. In other words, she lacks the kind of perspective that a mother's guidance might afford.

This lack of perspective is heightened in each stanza by the speaker's expression of disjointed, unpunctuated, and incomplete thoughts that culminate in the repetition of the phrase, "and momma's in the bedroom / with the door closed" (10–11, 23–24, 34–35). The door here acts as a symbol for an invisible barrier set up between the mother and daughter, keeping them from communicating meaningfully. If each stanza lists of a series of scattered complaints about being lonely, isolated, or excluded, then the speaker seems

---

*Essay by Jasmine Dyck. Reprinted by permission of the author.

to see her mother's inaccessibility as the sum of all her problems; indeed each problem is amplified by the separation between mother and daughter. The speaker laments the closed door, wishing she had the support of her mother instead of the coldness of a door she cannot, or will not, open herself. By closing each stanza with an expression of her mother's unavailability, the speaker underscores its significance to her.

The alienation and loneliness caused by this unavailability is particularly evident in the speaker's brief commentary on the boy she cares for. While claiming that she "cannot live without" him, she also admits that he himself "still sucks his thumb / in secret" (3–5). This revelation suggests that even her boyfriend is incapable of supporting her. The repeated "S" sound in the phrase "still sucks his thumb / in secret" imitates the sound of the boy sucking his thumb, adding to the immature picture she paints of the object of her affection. He does not sound mature enough to help her navigate the early teen world. To be sure, his thumb sucking indicates that he is need of greater guidance and comfort himself. This leaves the speaker to deal with her problems on her own, as the two people that arguably mean the most to her (her mother and her boyfriend) retreat into their own private worlds--one hiding in a bedroom, the other sucking his thumb in secret. She is alone in the world, trying to survive high school, confounded by the problems that plague young teens, and wishing that "momma" would open the door and help her to make sense of all the trials of adolescence.

The speaker is clearly uncertain of her ability to navigate her way to adulthood on her own. This uncertainty leads her to hyperbole. "What if I die?" (8), she asks in the first stanza, repeating the sentiment in the second stanza with the speculation "suppose I die before graduation" (150) and again in the third stanza with the question "will I live long enough / to grow up" (32–33)? Although she rephrases this worry concerning death, the speaker's insecurity about life is always evident. The poem's silence regarding anything that could threaten her life suggests that her fears are unfounded and instead reflect a general fear for the future in her journey through adolescence. Her repetition of this exaggerated worry, in other words, betrays an unstable emotional state exacerbated by a lack of parental support.

Any direct commentary on the speaker's mother is limited to repeated reference to her unavailability. She is always portrayed as being behind a closed door. The daughter does not appear to know, or is unwilling to admit, what her mother is doing behind that door. The bedroom setting alludes to the possibility of an illicit sexual encounter. In any event, the speaker clearly portrays her mother as a bad role model, ineffective in offering guidance to a daughter who needs and wants it. No matter what the mother is doing, she is inaccessible and unhelpful to her daughter's maturation.

The speaker's insecurity and her mother's unavailability are the only ideas repeated clearly throughout the poem and they are inextricably linked to one another. It is because the daughter lacks the benefit of a mother's guidance and perspective that smaller troubles seem large to her. She has difficulty mounting the stepping-stones that lead to maturity because she is doing so alone, without the help of someone who knows and cares for her, and has already endured many of these difficulties alone.

The speaker unveils more information about herself through her ambiguous punctuation and word choice. An example of this occurs when she says:

> Suppose I die before graduation
> they will sing sad melodies
> but finally
> tell the truth about me
> There is nothing I want to do (15–19)

The last two lines in this passage have two levels of meaning. One possible interpretation is that the ideas presented (i.e., the "truth" about her and her sense of apathy) do not fit together, but the speaker has juxtaposed them in a distracted state of mind. The capitalization of the "T" in "There" infers the start of a new sentence, which supports the idea that these are unrelated subjects; but, the absence of a period at the end of line eighteen supports another idea, that the ambiguous relation between these two lines offers insight about the speaker. When considering the lines "tell the truth about me" and "There is nothing I want to do" together, it seems that she fears the truth that mourners will finally tell about her is that there was nothing she wanted to do with her life, that she was without ambition or personal direction to guide her life; her death, though sad, was less disappointing because she had no purpose to her existence.

All of this information aids in understanding who the speaker is: a lonely, insecure girl. Her identity is crucial to the message the poem presents. Her youth, for instance, is necessary for the reader to remain open-minded to the message that she presents. If someone already grown up spoke about the need for mothers to be involved in their children's lives, it might sound more like a lecture or sermon. Spoken from the perspective of someone experiencing the hardships of growing up alone, on the other hand, the poem is more likely to enlist the sympathy and understanding of its readers. The female identity of the speaker is arguably important as well because the expression of a female's feelings may well be more effective in arousing compassion than a young male voice expressing similar concerns. This is perhaps due to the dual standards for men and women regarding the social acceptability of verbalizing emotions. Women are often allowed, indeed expected, to verbalize their feelings, whereas men are discouraged from expressing themselves in this way. For these reasons it is more effective for the speaker of "Hanging Fire" to be a young female so that her message is taken seriously.

The speaker's loneliness and her insecurity about her ability to reach adulthood on her own suggest that she is not content with her mother's lack of involvement in her life. The lonely tone is necessary to clarify that the speaker does not enjoy the freedom and independence that she has from her mother. Her discontentedness at facing maturation alone shows that the speaker believes that the way her mother treats her is not how mothers should interact with their daughters. Her displeasure at being left alone by her mother indicates that she believes that a mother should be an active source of guidance for her child. Communication should flow freely, unhindered by closed doors separating the two.

Each aspect of the speaker's identity forms a part of the foundation that supports the meaning of the poem. They work together to produce the message that a girl benefits greatly from the meaningful involvement of a mother in order to mature. Her identity as a girl, lost in the confusion of puberty without a mother's influence is important in order to understand the meaning of her words. Her identity shapes the topic of a mother's role in her teen daughter's life into the message that a mother's influence is desired and needed for a girl to become a woman.

WORK CITED

Lorde, Audre. "Hanging Fire." *The Norton Introduction to Literature*. Shorter 9th ed. Ed. Alison Booth, J. Paul Hunter, and Kelly J. Mays. New York: Norton, 2006. 650. Print.

WORKS CITED

Browning, Robert. "Soliloquy of the Spanish Cloister." *The Norton Introduction to Literature*. Shorter 9th ed. Ed. Alison Booth, J. Paul Hunter, and Kelly J. Mays. New York: Norton, 2006. 644–45. Print.

Burns, Robert. "A Red, Red Rose." *The Age of Romanticism*. Ed. Joseph Black et al. Peterborough, ON: Broadview, 2006. 126. Print. Vol. 4 of *The Broadview Anthology of British Literature*.

Byron, George Gordon, Lord. "*Don Juan*, Canto 2." *The Age of Romanticism*.
    Ed. Joseph Black et al. Peterborough, ON: Broadview, 2006. 567–93. Print.
    Vol. 4 of *The Broadview Anthology of British Literature*.

Coleridge, Samuel Taylor. "Frost at Midnight." *The Age of Romanticism*. Ed.
    Joseph Black et al. Peterborough, ON: Broadview, 2006. 302–3. Print.
    Vol. 4 of *The Broadview Anthology of British Literature*.

de la Mare, Walter. "Slim Cunning Hands." *The Norton Introduction to
    Literature*. Shorter 9th ed. Ed. Alison Booth, J. Paul Hunter, and Kelly J.
    Mays. New York: Norton, 2006. 687. Print.

Keats, John. "Ode to a Nightingale." *The Age of Romanticism*. Ed. Joseph Black
    et al. Peterborough, ON: Broadview, 2006. 719–20. Print. Vol. 4 of *The
    Broadview Anthology of British Literature*.

Plath, Sylvia. "Mirror." *Sound and Sense: An Introduction to Poetry*. 11th ed. Ed.
    Thomas R. Arp and Greg Johnson. Boston: Thomson Wadsworth, 2005.
    35. Print.

"Poetry." The Compact Edition of the Oxford English Dictionary. 2 vols. 1971.
    Print.

Shakespeare, William. *Romeo and Juliet*. Ed. Brian Gibbons. London: Methuen,
    1980. Print.

Wordsworth, William. "From *Lyrical Ballads, 1800, 1802*." *The Age of
    Romanticism*. Ed. Joseph Black et al. Peterborough, ON: Broadview, 2006.
    202–19. Print. Vol. 4 of *The Broadview Anthology of British Literature*.

—. "Nuns Fret Not." *The Norton Introduction to Literature*. Shorter 9th ed. Ed.
    Alison Booth, J. Paul Hunter, and Kelly J. Mays. New York: Norton, 2006.
    781. Print.

APPENDIX: "ODE TO A NIGHTINGALE" BY JOHN KEATS

The following reproduction of Keats's "Ode to a Nightingale" has been
annotated (i.e., marked up) in order to highlight many of the poetic elements
discussed above. Annotating a poem in this way is a good reading strategy to
develop when writing about poetry—or any work of literature, for that matter.
Paying such close attention to the poem should bring to light some of what
it is trying to accomplish with its use of language. Making a few photocopies
of the poem might work best; that way you can mark the poem up more than
once.

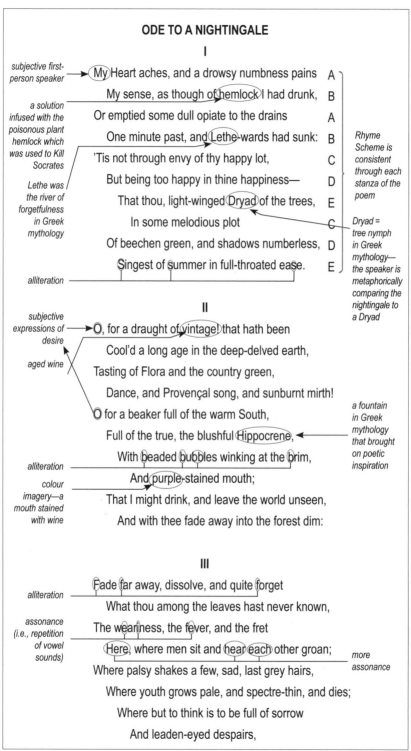

ODE TO A NIGHTINGALE

I

subjective first-person speaker

My Heart aches, and a drowsy numbness pains   A
My sense, as though of hemlock I had drunk,   B

a solution infused with the poisonous plant hemlock which was used to Kill Socrates

Or emptied some dull opiate to the drains   A
One minute past, and Lethe-wards had sunk: B

Rhyme Scheme is consistent through each stanza of the poem

'Tis not through envy of thy happy lot,   C
But being too happy in thine happiness—   D

Lethe was the river of forgetfulness in Greek mythology

That thou, light-winged Dryad of the trees,   E
In some melodious plot   C

Dryad = tree nymph in Greek mythology—the speaker is metaphorically comparing the nightingale to a Dryad

Of beechen green, and shadows numberless,   D
Singest of summer in full-throated ease.   E

alliteration

II

subjective expressions of desire

O, for a draught of vintage! that hath been
Cool'd a long age in the deep-delved earth,

aged wine

Tasting of Flora and the country green,
Dance, and Provençal song, and sunburnt mirth!
O for a beaker full of the warm South,
Full of the true, the blushful Hippocrene,

a fountain in Greek mythology that brought on poetic inspiration

With beaded bubbles winking at the brim,

alliteration

And purple-stained mouth;

colour imagery—a mouth stained with wine

That I might drink, and leave the world unseen,
And with thee fade away into the forest dim:

III

alliteration

Fade far away, dissolve, and quite forget
What thou among the leaves hast never known,

assonance (i.e., repetition of vowel sounds)

The weariness, the fever, and the fret
Here, where men sit and hear each other groan;

more assonance

Where palsy shakes a few, sad, last grey hairs,
Where youth grows pale, and spectre-thin, and dies;
Where but to think is to be full of sorrow
And leaden-eyed despairs,

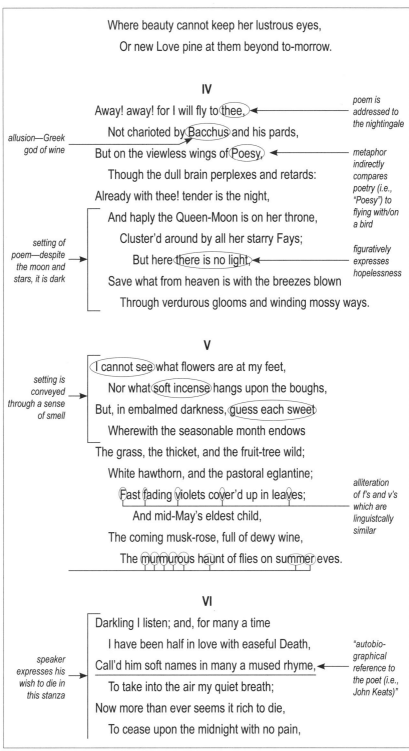

Where beauty cannot keep her lustrous eyes,

Or new Love pine at them beyond to-morrow.

IV

Away! away! for I will fly to thee,

Not charioted by Bacchus and his pards,

But on the viewless wings of Poesy,

Though the dull brain perplexes and retards:

Already with thee! tender is the night,

And haply the Queen-Moon is on her throne,

Cluster'd around by all her starry Fays;

But here there is no light,

Save what from heaven is with the breezes blown

Through verdurous glooms and winding mossy ways.

poem is addressed to the nightingale

allusion—Greek god of wine

metaphor indirectly compares poetry (i.e., "Poesy") to flying with/on a bird

setting of poem—despite the moon and stars, it is dark

figuratively expresses hopelessness

V

I cannot see what flowers are at my feet,

Nor what soft incense hangs upon the boughs,

But, in embalmed darkness, guess each sweet

Wherewith the seasonable month endows

The grass, the thicket, and the fruit-tree wild;

White hawthorn, and the pastoral eglantine;

Fast fading violets cover'd up in leaves;

And mid-May's eldest child,

The coming musk-rose, full of dewy wine,

The murmurous haunt of flies on summer eves.

setting is conveyed through a sense of smell

alliteration of f's and v's which are linguistcally similar

VI

Darkling I listen; and, for many a time

I have been half in love with easeful Death,

Call'd him soft names in many a mused rhyme,

To take into the air my quiet breath;

Now more than ever seems it rich to die,

To cease upon the midnight with no pain,

speaker expresses his wish to die in this stanza

"autobiographical reference to the poet (i.e., John Keats)"

While thou art pouring forth thy soul abroad

In such an ecstasy!

Still wouldst thou sing, and I have ears in vain—

To thy high requiem become a sod.

VII

Thou wast not born for death, immortal Bird!

No hungry generations tread thee down;

The voice I hear this passing night was heard

In ancient days by emperor and clown:

Perhaps the selfsame song that found a path

Through the sad heart of Ruth, when, sick for home,

She stood in tears amid the alien corn;

The same that oft-times hath

Charm'd magic casements, opening on the foam

Of perilous seas, in faery lands forlorn.

metaphor— the nightingale is indirectly compared to an immortal voice heard throughout time by emperors and clowns alike

Break between these final stanzas indicates a shift in tone and focus

VIII

Forlorn! the very word is like a bell

To toll me back from thee to my sole self!

Adieu! the fancy cannot cheat so well

As she is fam'd to do, deceiving elf.

Adieu! adieu! thy plaintive anthem fades

Past the near meadows, over the still stream,

Up the hill-side; and now 'tis buried deep

In the next valley-glades:

Was it a vision, or a waking dream?

Fled is that music—Do I wake or sleep?

repetition of the word "forlorn"—which is itself comprised of a repetition of "or-" sounds

the poetic imagination

simile—the word "forlorn" is directly compared to a bell

the poem ends with an inconclusive and/or ambiguous set of questions

5

Writing about Fiction

WHAT IS FICTION?

Fiction is often defined in opposition to fact. In a criminal investigation, a police detective examines evidence, talks to witnesses, and interrogates suspects in an attempt to separate "fact" from "fiction." In this context, fiction refers negatively to that which is *false*—false testimony, false alibis, false conclusions, and so on. In literary studies, fiction is similarly opposed to fact—or, more precisely, to writing that is based on fact. One need only look for confirmation of this in the lists of national bestsellers in a newspaper such as *The Globe and Mail*. Unlike the detective's view of the facts and fictions of a criminal case, however, *The Globe and Mail*'s maintenance of separate categories for fiction and non-fiction does not seek to disparage fiction. Books of fiction are not dishonest or mistaken in comparison to non-fiction; rather, fiction distinguishes itself only inasmuch as it invents tales about imaginary (as opposed to real) events and people. Even when these events and people are loosely (or even closely) based on real life, they are ultimately the products of creative invention.

As a literary genre, fiction sets itself apart from poetry and drama in its combined use of **prose** and **narration**.[1] Poetry occasionally uses narration to tell a story, but it will most often do so in **verse** (i.e., metrical composition; see Chapter 4) rather than prose; and while drama can be written in either prose or verse, it will generally rely on **dialogue** rather than narration to convey its plot. Only fiction makes consistent use of narrative prose in recounting imaginary stories. *Narration* implies the presence of someone—a **narrator**—who tells the story, and *prose* implies writing that resembles everyday speech and/or ordinary

---

1 Terms in bold are explained later in this chapter. For concise definitions, see the glossary in the Appendix.

processes of thought. Works of short fiction, also called **short stories**, can range from being very short (Jamaica Kincaid's "Girl" is little more than a single page in length) to very long (e.g., Franz Kafka's twenty-two-thousand-word "The Metamorphosis"). **Novella** is the term for a work of fiction that is longer, more developed, and more complex than a short story, but shorter than a novel. Famous examples of the novella include Henry James's *Turn of the Screw* and Joseph Conrad's *Heart of Darkness*. Longest and most complex of all are **novels**, which vary in length but generally seek to "give form" to what Georg Lukács called the "extensive totality of life" (46). The length of a novel can fall anywhere between 50,000 and 1.5 million words—the latter being the approximate length of the world's longest published novel, *In Search of Lost Time* (*À la recherche du temps perdu*) by Marcel Proust. Because short stories are easier to summarize than novels and novellas (and are thus better suited for our purposes), this chapter will focus mainly on examples of short fiction—though it does briefly discuss a novel by Steven Hayward, as well as a book of short stories by Alice Munro that resembles a novel.

PLOT

Plot is a defining feature of fiction; without it there is no story and thus no fiction. Although the words "story" and "plot" are used interchangeably in ordinary conversation, there is a subtle terminological difference between them. A story refers to what happens in a work of fiction, whereas plot refers to *how* the story is arranged and told. When a work of fiction *tells* a story, it will not always do so in a straightforward manner. Take John Cheever's short story, "The Country Husband," for example. "The Country Husband" does not simply describe what happens in the life of its main character, Francis Weed, so much as it focuses on a specific set of events in Francis's life and organizes those events in a particular order. After surviving a plane crash, Francis returns to his suburban New York home, where he becomes increasingly disillusioned with—even bored by—his comfortable middle-class life. He is rude to his neighbours, fights with his wife (who threatens to leave him), and has a sexual encounter with his teenaged babysitter. Recognizing the signs of a possible midlife crisis, Francis finally visits a psychiatrist, who advises him to seek distraction and refuge in a hobby, which Francis does by building a coffee table in the cellar of his home. That is Francis's story, in a nutshell.

The plot of "The Country Husband," however, transforms Francis's story into compelling fiction by arranging the story's **action** in a way that is less concerned with chronology than it is with the depth of Francis's psychological experience. For one thing, Cheever makes effective use of **flashback**—which is to say, he interrupts the main **narrative** to recall **episodes** (i.e., series of events) from the past. At a neighbourhood party, Francis flashes back after recognizing his neighbour's maid as a woman he once saw publicly flogged and humiliated while he was stationed in Normandy during the Second World War. This distant memory of wartime brutality starkly contrasts with the story's otherwise tranquil depiction of suburban life. The interruption of the main narrative offers us a greater perspective on the events of the story and anticipates (through **foreshadowing**) Francis's failure to reconcile his own complex psychology with the repressive social environment of the subdivision in which he lives, where people appear to be "united in their tacit claim that there had been no past, no war—that there was no danger or trouble in the world" (76). This emphasis on the disconnect between Francis's inner turmoil and the serene exterior of the suburb is not afforded by the story alone, but by the plot's *arrangement* of events—its juxtaposition of past and present actions. The subtlety here between story and plot amounts to a difference between the event as it happens and the retelling of that event *in relation to* other events in the story. Context determines significance.

Many (though certainly not all) works of fiction abide by a conventional plot pattern that was first identified by the nineteenth-century German novelist and playwright Gustav Freytag. According to Freytag, there are five phases through which the average plot passes. This movement is captured in the rise and fall of a diagram known as "Freytag's pyramid":

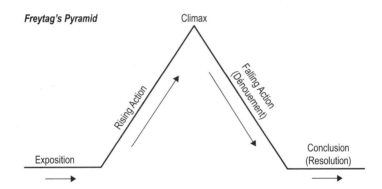

Many university and college students will remember some variation of this diagram from high school, but it is useful to reacquaint ourselves with it. The diagram allows us to take a step back and get a better sense of a story as a whole; at the same time, it conveniently compartmentalizes a story into manageable parts for closer analysis. Discovering how parts relate to a whole is one of the primary goals of literary study.

We can define the five plot-points of Freytag's pyramid with brief references to Cheever's "The Country Husband" (which you will not need to have read to follow along). The five points of the pyramid trace the development of a story's central **conflict** (i.e., a struggle or confrontation between characters or between one character and forces beyond his or her control). The central conflict is the engine that drives a story's plot from beginning to end. We are typically made aware of the central conflict during or just after a story's **exposition**, which consists of the reader's early introduction—or *exposure*—to the story's main characters, the situation of the story, and its **setting** (discussed later in this chapter). In the first few pages of "The Country Husband," we are introduced to Francis Weed as he survives a rather sensational plane crash; we are then introduced to Francis's family and the subdivision where he lives. We already begin to sense the emergence of the central conflict between Francis and his family: he has neither the right words nor even the opportunity to communicate to them his feelings about the plane crash. Throughout the **rising action** (which is represented on Freytag's pyramid as a steep incline and which refers to a series of events related either in terms of causality or significance), we witness the escalation of the central conflict. In the case of "The Country Husband," events such as Francis's flashback to Normandy, his initial sexual encounters with the babysitter, his progressively impolite interactions with neighbours, and the major fight he has with his wife (during which he actually strikes her "full in the face" [83]) all work steadily to heighten—or *raise*—the intensity of the story's action and its central **crisis**. It is no longer simply his family with whom Francis finds himself in conflict; rather, he finds himself at odds with the whole structure of middle-class, suburban life. The rise of this action leads to the story's **climax** (or "turning point"), where the conflict necessitates an irrevocable confrontation or decision. Reflecting back on recent events, Francis "wonder[s] how he could have avoided arriving at just where he was" (86). The "trouble" of his life converges on him: "he s[ees] clearly that he ha[s] to make a choice" (86).

The climax of "The Country Husband" is not a spectacular moment—as some turning points are—but a moment of realization. Francis realizes that his next few steps in life will have long-lasting repercussions and may lead either to stability or misery. As it happens, he chooses to rescue his marriage from disaster by visiting a psychiatrist, who tells him to seek therapy in a hobby. The remaining paragraphs of the text present the story's **falling action** or **dénouement** (French for "untying"), which refers to events that comprise the outcome and consequences of the climax. We find Francis building a coffee table in the cellar, while the innocuous sounds of suburbia (dogs, neighbours, etc.) resonate in the yard outside his house. While a story's falling action typically yields a sense of resolution to the story's conflict, the **conclusion** of "The Country Husband" is ultimately ambiguous and therefore calls for interpretation. Will therapeutic woodworking help Francis to endure the demands and limitations of suburban life? Or is the ending ironic, with his escape into the basement signalling an unhealthy withdrawal from the world around him? While the story remains unresolved, its finale nevertheless leaves us feeling that the plot has run its course.

Summary

PLOT

- in works of fiction, the terms "plot" and "story" do not refer to the same thing

  - *story* refers to what happens; *plot* refers to how the story is arranged and told

- stories are rarely conveyed in a straightforward way; plot devices like foreshadowing and flashback add depth and context

- works of fiction typically develop a central conflict (struggle or confrontation) through a five-part plot pattern that consists of exposition (introduction to characters, situation, and setting), rising action (events that intensify the central conflict), climax (turning point), falling action (events depicting the consequences of the climax), and conclusion (resolution)

NARRATION AND POINT OF VIEW

If plot refers not to the story of a work of fiction so much as to the specific arrangement of events that comprise the *telling* of that story, then it is equally important to consider the perspective around which the plot is organized. From whose **point of view** is the story being told? The question is not always as straightforward as it sounds, primarily because the character whose perspective is central to the story and the person who actually *tells* the story (i.e., the **narrator**) are not always the same person. "The Country Husband," for instance, is clearly told from the perspective of Francis Weed. We know this because we are privy to his innermost thoughts and desires; we also journey with him through his flashback to Normandy, even though he chooses "not to tell anyone" about it (76). Yet, even as his perspective dominates throughout, Francis does not tell his own story. If he did, we would be dealing with a **first-person narrative**, when in fact "The Country Husband" uses a **third-person narrative**; its narrator acts as a kind of disembodied consciousness with a point of view that penetrates Francis's mind and observes his thoughts. In technical terms, we say that the story is told from a third-person point of view but is *focalized* from (i.e., conveyed with particular insight into) Francis's perspective. Why would an author choose to use one kind of narrator over another? Would it not be simpler and more direct to have Francis narrate his own midlife crisis? Perhaps. But as we shall see in a moment, John Cheever has other purposes in mind precisely in *not* letting Francis tell the story in his own words.

A major difference between first- and third-person narrators concerns the extent of knowledge the narrator has about the events in a story. A first-person narrator has only *limited* (i.e., subjective) knowledge, which makes him or her more or less an **unreliable narrator**. A first-person narrator may also be unreliable in the sense that he or she may even try to cultivate, if only to manipulate, the reader's sympathies. A narrator's unreliability might also be the result of inexperience, as in the case of a child narrator or a narrator who is outside his or her own cultural setting. Third-person narrators, on the other hand, tend to be more objective and have greater knowledge of events in a story than first-person narrators do. There are degrees to this knowledge, however. Some third-person narrators, such as the one in Jane Austen's *Pride and Prejudice*, are **omniscient narrators**, meaning they have unlimited knowledge of everything and everyone in a story (including the inner thoughts of multiple characters). Other third-person narrators, such as the one in "The Country Husband," only know events as they are experienced by one character (or perhaps two), and are therefore considered to have "selective" or **limited omniscience**. While the point of view of a selective omniscient narrator is limited, it is not always as limited—or not limited in the same way—as a first-person narrator, since the former, unlike the latter, may choose to retract or distance himself or herself temporarily from the main character's perspective in order to widen or alter the story's point of view.

To illustrate this last point, we can return to our earlier question about why John Cheever would utilize a third-person, selectively omniscient point of view in "The Country Husband" instead of allowing Francis to narrate his own story. Arguably, the freedom of a third-person narrator to shift his or her perspective enables Cheever's story to end ambiguously, which is necessary for the social commentary the story tries to make. We can expand on this thesis by saying that this shift in perspective occurs on both temporal and spatial levels (i.e., on levels of time and space). Temporally speaking, the narrative changes abruptly in the final few paragraphs from the past tense to the present tense. The peculiar logic of this shift, whereby the story loses its original retrospective view from the future (which is always the implicit structure of the past tense), suggests that Francis himself has no future. At the end of his story, he remains perpetually frozen in the present, always "building a coffee table" in the cellar of his house (87), never knowing whether it will help him find peace or further frustrates his desires. We can interpret this shift from past to present tense to mean that the possible outcomes of Francis's current predicament (whether he will get better or worse) are less important or interesting than the predicament itself. Cheever wants the reader to linger over and ponder the significance of Francis's present condition as an individual struggling with the social circumstances of 1950s middle-class America.

This narrative focus is further complemented by the *spatial* shift in perspective that we experience in these final moments of the story. In addition to the change from the past to the present tense, we move from a position of selective omniscience with respect to Francis's internal thoughts to observing him from the point of view of a more **objective** (or "dramatic") **narrator**. That is to say, we lose our special view into Francis's mind, and he becomes just another figure blending into the background of the text's closing portrait of mid-twentieth-century suburbia. If his future is perpetually postponed by the shift in tense, then our loss of access into his consciousness hinders our ability to make even a reasonable guess as to which direction his future mental health may take. Again, it is the psychological crisis that Francis faces at the end of the story—and not any particular resolution of that crisis—that is the story's primary concern. While an essay on Cheever's innovative narrative technique would do well to continue developing this line of analysis, we can already see how important it is to consider narration and point of view when writing about fiction.

Summary

NARRATION AND POINT OF VIEW

- always ask yourself, "From whose point of view (perspective) is the story being told?"

- the character whose perspective is central to a story and the person who actually *tells* the story (the narrator) are not always the same person

- typically, narrators present either a first-person point of view, which uses personal pronouns such as "I" and "me," or a third-person point of view, which avoids using such pronouns

- narrators can range from having *limited* knowledge of a story's characters and events to having *unlimited* (or omniscient) knowledge over all aspects of a story

- identifying how a narrator's point of view and scope of knowledge mediate (and even shape) a reader's access to a story is crucial to understanding the story as a whole

FICTIONAL CHARACTERIZATION

You may be asked at some point to write an essay that executes a study of one or more characters in a work of fiction. The first thing to keep in mind when writing such an essay is the difference between **character** and **characterization**. The first of these terms hardly requires much elaboration: a "character" refers to a person—or in the case of a science fiction or fantasy novel, a being with human attributes—who takes part in a fictional story. Fictional "characterization," on the other hand, is a more complex term; it refers to the many ways character traits are revealed through narrative. Characterization can occur directly, as when a narrator describes a character's personality, or indirectly, as when we learn about characters through their actions (what they do, think, and say) as well as the actions of others (e.g., how others treat them; what others say to or about them). A character's appearance should not be confused with characterization. Take the example of Patrick Blatchford from Alice Munro's *Who Do You Think You Are?* At age twenty-four, Patrick is described as being "tall, thin, fair, and good-looking, though he had a long pale-red birthmark, dribbling like a tear down his temple and his cheek" (67). This passage describes Patrick's physical appearance, but it does not reveal any character traits. The first *direct* revelation of Patrick's character occurs only after his appearance is described:

> There was something edgy, jumpy, disconcerting, about him. His voice would break under stress—with her [Rose, the text's main character], it seemed he was always under stress—he knocked dishes and cups off tables, spilled drinks and bowls of peanuts, like a comedian. He was not a comedian; nothing could be further from his intentions. (67–68)

Notwithstanding the indeterminate "something" in the first sentence of this passage, we get the distinct impression that Patrick is a nervous individual, especially around Rose, his current love interest and future ex-wife. The narrator adds that despite being nervous, Patrick is "also full of cruel judgments [and] full of conceit" (68). These character traits are confirmed *indirectly* in his conversations with Rose. When Rose jokingly refers to him as a "timid scholar," Patrick is noticeably offended, but instead of openly contradicting her, he resorts to self-pity: "I suppose I don't seem very manly," he admits (77). It does not take long, however, before his vulnerability turns to aggressive condescension. After comparing their situation to an obscure nineteenth-century work of art, Patrick takes "scornful" pleasure in Rose's ignorance: "Don't you know that painting?" (78). We are encouraged at this point to concur with the narrator's (and Rose's) opinion that "[Patrick's] arrogance and humility were both oddly exaggerated" (78).

Despite our present focus on Patrick's character, Rose is easily identified as the main character of all of the stories collected in *Who Do You Think You Are?* That is to say, she is the text's central **protagonist**—a term that combines the Greek words *prōtos* (meaning "first") and *agōnistēs* (meaning "actor"), as in "an actor who plays the first part" (*OED* 2334). The protagonist is the **hero** (or in Rose's case, the **heroine**) of the story. In literary criticism, the term "hero" does not necessarily imply heroism or valour so much as it designates a general category for identifying the chief character of a story whose goals and interests are frustrated by the competing interests of an **antagonist** or villain. Of course, not all works of fiction have recognizable antagonist characters; they may rely instead on antagonistic *forces* that oppose the aspirations and well-being of a protagonist. While Rose, for instance, faces antagonist characters (such as Flo, her controlling stepmother) in some of the stories in *Who Do You Think You Are?*, other stories in the collection present only abstract forces such as societal expectation, sexism, and social inequality that frustrate her self-determination and personal growth.

As is often the case with protagonists, Rose is a *round* character, which means she demonstrates the complexity of a real person. She has multiple character traits and is generally *dynamic* insofar as her personality undergoes significant development and change throughout the text. While even minor characters in *Who Do You Think You Are?* (such as Patrick and Flo) are portrayed with some depth, they are *flat* in comparison with Rose. Traditionally, flat characters are closer to **stereotypes**, exhibiting as few as one or two character traits. More *static* (or unchanging) than dynamic, they tend not to develop as characters and usually serve a very limited, one-dimensional purpose in a story. The babysitter in "The Country Husband" is a perfect example: embodying the stereotype of an emotionally confused and sexually vulnerable teenaged girl, she functions solely to attract the absurd attentions of an equally confused middle-aged man.

Summary

FICTIONAL CHARACTERIZATION

- character refers to a person who takes part in a fictional story; characterization refers to the ways character traits are revealed and developed through narrative

- characterization can occur *directly* when a narrator describes a character's personality, or *indirectly* when we learn about characters through their own thoughts and actions as well as the thoughts and actions of other characters

- protagonist is the term for the chief character (or hero) of a story whose goals and interests are frustrated by the competing interests of an antagonist or villain

- *round* characters have multiple character traits and undergo significant development throughout a narrative; *flat* characters serve a more limited, one-dimensional purpose

SETTING

Setting refers to a story's evocation of place and time, which includes its geographical, cultural, and historical-temporal contexts. Knowing where and when a story takes place helps to make sense of the story's action, but setting should never be dismissed as a mere backdrop. In "The Country Husband," the reader's sense of time and place is crucial to understanding the text's purpose. The 1950s New York suburb does not just happen to be where Francis's midlife crisis takes place; its repressive social atmosphere is precisely the major force of antagonism in Francis's life. Likewise, the cultural contrast in setting between the small town of Hanratty, Ontario, and the city of Toronto in Munro's *Who Do You Think You Are?* does far more than contribute to Rose's development as a character; as a literary technique, this kind of contrast between small towns and big cities has helped define part of the Canadian literary identity.

While the plot of Cheever's "The Country Husband" is set in and around the time it was written and published, many fictional works, like Steven Hayward's *The Secret Mitzvah of Lucio Burke*, purposely situate their plots in the past. Hayward's playful mixture of historical realism and fantasy seeks to recreate the culturally assorted character of Toronto in the 1930s, and in doing so, presents another instance where setting gradually moves from the background into the **foreground**. Hayward's novel tells a compelling tale of romance and political activism on the surface, but as the novel unfolds a much broader story emerges about the depth and colour of urban life during the Great Depression. In reconstructing the mood of Depression-era Toronto, Hayward focuses on the array of social differences that structured 1930s city life in and around Toronto's Chinatown, particularly in terms of ethnicity (Jewish, Italian, and Chinese), class (the underemployed poor), and gender (women's exploitation in the workplace). This kind of socioeconomic emphasis in setting is essential for fiction that aims to draw attention to the life experiences of underrepresented social groups. Examples of such fiction include Gabrielle Roy's *The Tin Flute*, which sets its fiction during the Depression in order to characterize the cultural legacies of poverty in the city of Montreal; James Baldwin's "Sonny's Blues," which focuses on the African-American music scene in 1950s Harlem and reminds us of the importance of race in the setting of a story; and Margaret Atwood's *The Handmaid's Tale*, which reveals how the dystopian setting of a science-fictional future can contain within it an explicit critique of gender politics in the present.

The writing sample at the end of this chapter considers examples of the ways in which setting can likewise function as a metaphor for personal experience. In particular, the essay compares Andrea Barrett's figurative use of setting in "The Littoral Zone" with Amy Tan's similar use of setting in "A Pair of Tickets." You are encouraged to read the essay closely, since in addition to comparing these two short stories on the basis of setting, the paper is a fine example of effective first-year writing.

Summary

SETTING

- setting refers to a story's evocation of place and time, which includes its geographical, cultural, and historical contexts

- setting may constitute a central aspect of a story's social commentary—by foregrounding socioeconomic and/or cultural issues and concerns, for instance

- setting may even function as a metaphor for personal experience, as is the case in Andrea Barrett's "The Littoral Zone" and Amy Tan's "A Pair of Tickets"

SYMBOLISM AND THEME

Like poetry, fiction often draws on the figural power of **similes** (which compare similarities between two things using "like" or "as") and **metaphors** (which describe one thing in terms of another as if both things were one and the same). The narrator of *Who Do You Think You Are?* uses a simile when describing Patrick's "pale-red birthmark, dribbling *like* a tear down his temple and his cheek" (67, emphasis added). And Francis from "The Country Husband" uses metaphor when he complains of having "to come home every night to a battlefield" (73).[2] Even more than simile and metaphor, however, fiction thrives on the kind of figurative language known as **symbolism**. Symbolism offers a much wider range of reference than simile or metaphor, and occurs in a more general way when one thing refers indirectly to or suggests something else. A **symbol**, it is said, *stands* for something (an idea, perhaps, or a whole system of ideas) that is not mentioned but is merely inferred by the symbol's presence. For example, a flag that features a red maple leaf in the centre of a white background flanked by two vertical red bands *stands* for Canada, or a series of related ideas about Canada's national identity.

Unlike similes (and even metaphors), the association between a symbol and the idea it represents is not typically achieved through comparison—the Canadian flag is not *like* Canada in any way. Rather, the association is forged either by convention (Canada's national flag has represented Canada since

---

2 For an extended discussion of the differences between similes and metaphors, see the section on "Poetic Language" in Chapter 4.

1965) or by personal invention. In the latter instance, an author might invent a situation in which an object is invested with significance that exceeds its most immediate or obvious meaning. That object's symbolic associations may also be developed by its being reintroduced under different circumstances throughout the course of a narrative. Nathaniel Hawthorne provides a classic example of a personal symbol in "Young Goodman Brown." When Brown, the story's protagonist, bids farewell to his wife, Faith, before embarking on his journey through the woods, the narrator makes a kind of spectacle of "the pink ribbons of [Faith's] cap" (233). Perhaps the most conspicuous objects in the story, these colourful accoutrements draw our attention in a way that suggests a meaning deeper than we might ordinarily expect ribbons to have. Hawthorne encourages our further interest in their significance through repetition: the next time Faith speaks, she is referred to as "Faith, with the pink ribbons;" and when Brown finally turns to leave, his wife is said to carry "a melancholy air, in spite of her pink ribbons" (233). This repeated association between Faith and her pink ribbons gives to the ribbons the ability to symbolize what their "aptly named" owner represents, namely, a concept of pious devotion (233). Later in the story, when Brown is alone in the forest enduring a crisis of religious conviction, he witnesses the dramatic descent of a solitary "pink ribbon" that falls from the sky, "flutter[s] through the air," and gets "caught on the branch of a tree" (238). Like the proverbial thrown-in towel, the ribbon in this context now symbolizes for Brown the potential loss of the very idea for which his wife stands—faith.

It is widely accepted that the whole narrative of "Young Goodman Brown" is symbolic—that it presents an **allegory** for a particular kind of religious experience. The story, in other words, draws a parallel between Brown's experience in the woods and a more general early-American Christian struggle to maintain faith in a world full of hypocrisy and sin. This conflict (between the Christian individual and society) is also the story's main **theme**—its overall idea or message. The story's overall thematic statement, however, is not simply that a person should remain faithful in spite of the hypocrisy of others. The story seems to suggest instead that a resolute devotion to God is not enough, since the Christian faith also entails compassion for others, even if these others occasionally demonstrate moral depravity. Unable to accept the actions of his fellow townspeople who preach piety but practise sin, Brown alienates himself from society: "he shrank [even] from the bosom of Faith" (241). He lives a life of resentment and dread; when he dies "no hopeful verse [is carved] upon his tomb-stone; for his dying hour was gloom" (241). If "Young Goodman Brown" is an allegory for Christian faith, then it is also an allegory for a person's moral obligations to the Christian community as a whole.

Summary

SYMBOLISM AND THEME

- like poetry, fiction draws on the power of figurative language, especially symbolism (which occurs when one thing refers indirectly to or suggests something else)

    - stories often use individual symbols that stand for other things—e.g., the pink ribbons of Faith's cap that represent pious devotion in "Young Goodman Brown"

    - when a whole narrative functions as an extended metaphor or symbol wherein characters, places, and things signify abstract ideas, the story is called an allegory

- theme refers to a story's central idea or message

READING DEMONSTRATION: SHORT FICTION AND FEMINISM

The reading demonstration in the previous chapter illustrated the formalist approach to reading literature known as New Criticism. The preceding sections on the elements of fiction are also primarily formalist in their approach. There are, however, many different ways to read literature, some of which are concerned with politics in addition to form—or may even treat form itself as a matter of politics. Feminist criticism is a prime example. There are (as noted in Chapter 3) a plurality of feminisms, each with its own approach to the correlation between sex (or gender) and social power. Not surprisingly, the practice of feminist literary criticism is similarly diverse. While critics such as Kate Millett seek to identify and critique the chauvinism of male-dominated literary traditions, others, such as Elaine Showalter, aim to recover important women's writing that has been forgotten by history while also identifying more recent and emerging female literary traditions. Showalter invented the term "gynocriticism" (*gyno* is the Greek word for woman) to describe a women-centred literary criticism that analyzes women's writing not on the basis of patriarchal ideals but according to literary values and standards derived from female experience. The reading demonstration below attempts to briefly shed a gynocritical light on Katherine Govier's "Sociology"—a very short story, published in 1985, about a woman named Ellen and her experience with pregnancy, prenatal class, and childbirth.

That Govier's story has such a gynecological focus is itself something of a feminist gesture. A woman's medical and social preparation for childbirth is by no means a frequent topic of narrative fiction, and yet it falls squarely within the range of common (though by no means universal) female experience. Giving birth to a child is, of course, an experience that *only* a woman can have. This fact alone makes Govier's story the ideal object of gynocritical analysis. As if to stress the dramatic possibilities of her story's subject, Govier measures the apparent banality of anticipating childbirth against action that is more sensational and less common. When an armed man ambushes Ellen and her husband on the doorstep of their own home, demanding their wallets and jewellery, the mugging reaches its "greatest point of risk" when Ellen fails to remove her wedding ring: "My fingers are swollen," she explains, "because I'm pregnant" (398). Looking the armed man "in the eye as she said the word pregnant" (399), Ellen secretly challenges the man to become the object of one of her most peculiar prenatal anxieties: "She was testing. It had been her fantasy during these last months that she would run into one of those maniacs who shot pregnant women in the belly or cut them open with a knife" (399). While her fears of feticidal madmen are exaggerated, their resurfacing during an actual situation of danger suggests something extraordinary (as opposed to mundane) about the psychic life of Ellen's pregnancy.

As a thesis, we could argue that "Sociology" reveals the intensity and depth of this psychic life, which is something Ellen evidently shares with the other women in her prenatal class. The story suggests, moreover, that despite being a common condition, pregnancy confers on these women acute feelings of isolation and trepidation that the women never openly acknowledge but communicate to one another through implicit recognition and knowing glances. Although men are present throughout the story, they remain always on the periphery, their partner's experiences of pregnancy and childbirth being ultimately inaccessible to male understanding. During prenatal class, the men are referred to as mere "supporters," while the women—"making each other seem more grotesque than ever"—ready themselves "to go *alone* into the perilous future" (400, emphasis added). When it is revealed at a reunion for the class that June (the only class member absent from the gathering) gave birth to a stillborn baby, everyone (including the men) agrees that "[t]he worst part . . . must have been having to carry the dead baby for another week" (402). And yet, only the women of the group seem truly able to empathize with June. What is more, each woman implicitly understands what June's story means to the other women in the room. They address one another without speaking: "[their] eyes connected and their lips pressed down. . . . They could not help but feel relief, lucky to have been missed. But with luck came fear that luck would not last, and the long, hard oval of dread that had quickened in Ellen along with her offspring was born" (402). From a feminist point of view, this passage, with its powerful metaphor of emotional afterbirth, speaks directly to the kind of women's experience the story aims to uncover through fiction—namely, the repressed "sociology" of maternal dread. Govier's story, in other words, gives literary expression to a profoundly human set of conflicted emotions that some women may have with respect to pregnancy and childbirth but about which they may feel obligated to remain silent. Recognizing a story's power to thus reflect the complexity of female experience—as well as its contribution to a particular (in this case Canadian) tradition of women's writing—is a fundamental aspect of the gynocritical enterprise.

STUDENT WRITING

As mentioned earlier, the writing sample below compares Andrea Barrett's figurative use of setting in "The Littoral Zone" with Amy Tan's similar use of setting in "A Pair of Tickets." In addition to offering an effective example of a first-year comparative research paper, the essay also demonstrates how the setting of a story is not always a simple matter of when and where a story happens to takes place. As the paper's title suggest, setting can become a metaphor for character conflict and development.

Choy 1

Anna Choy*
ENG-1001/6-010
Dr. Peter Melville
April 6, 2009

Setting: A Figurative Representation of Character Struggle in Amy Tan's "A Pair of Tickets" and Andrea Barrett's "The Littoral Zone"

The significance of setting is easily overlooked, when in fact it can contribute to or create greater meaning within a work of fiction. According to Laura Van der Berg, "nature is not just a backdrop, but serves as a metaphor, catalyst, and an essential companion to the examination of the character's inner lives" (208). Amy Tan's short story, "A Pair of Tickets," and Andrea Barrett's short narrative, "The Littoral Zone," both illustrate this use of setting. In these stories, setting does not simply consist of the time and place of the action; it also serves a greater purpose by figuratively

*Essay by Anna Choy. Reprinted by permission of the author.

depicting the struggles of the characters. In "A Pair of Tickets," the protagonist, Jing-mei, has difficulty accepting her Chinese heritage when living in the United States, but by visiting China she learns what it means to be Chinese and eventually accepts who she is. In Barrett's short fiction, the secluded island enhances the loneliness experienced by the two protagonists, causing them to engage in an adulterous affair, which later in their lives instils them with further feelings of solitude. Ultimately, Barrett uses setting to catalyze the struggles of the characters, whereas Tan uses setting to resolve the inner struggles of the protagonist.

The setting in "A Pair of Tickets" reveals Jing-mei's difficulty in defining who she is. While visiting Hong Kong, Jing-mei, who is of Chinese decent, recounts her life in the United States, and explains how she never considered herself to be Chinese, for she had grown up in the setting of San Francisco: "I was fifteen and had vigorously denied that I had any Chinese whatsoever below my skin. I was a sophomore at Galileo High in San Francisco, and all my Caucasian friends agreed: I was about as Chinese as they were" (205). Living in the United States serves as a barricade, preventing the protagonist from understanding her Chinese roots. She is of Chinese decent, but because she lives so far from China, she is unfamiliar with her heritage, and detaches herself from her Asian background. Jing-mei's mother assures her that she will soon learn what it means to become Chinese; however, Jing-mei is unable to understand her mother, and instead views becoming Chinese as "transforming like a werewolf" (205). By comparing her heritage to a werewolf, an unreal and unnatural character, she reveals that her Chinese heritage is alien to her, and that she does not really consider it part of her identity.

Furthermore, Jing-mei describes the humiliation she felt as a teenager when her mother would act Chinese: "a cluster of Chinese behaviours, all those things my mother did to embarrass me--haggling with store owners, pecking her mouth with a toothpick, being blind to the fact that lemon yellow and pale pink are not good combinations for winter clothes" (205). Jing-mei's embarrassment over her mother's Chinese customs reveals her failure to relate to her mother's Chinese ways, for she considers herself to be purely American. Jing-mei's incapability to accept her mother's behaviour, as well as her lack of comprehension for what it means to be Chinese, prevents her from understanding and accepting who she really is: a Chinese descendent. The setting in Tan's story ultimately emphasizes the protagonist's inner struggle to accept her own identity.

Similar to "A Pair of Tickets," Barrett's short story uses setting as a metaphor for the emotional turmoil the protagonists experience. The trivial annoyances on the island reveal the solitude that Jonathon and Ruby feel in their lives. Boring lectures, poison ivy, lack of fresh water, uncomfortable sleeping quarters, and cold, damp weather are all aspects of the setting that enhance both the scientists' frustration and loneliness:

> They were so tired by then, twelve days into the course,
> and so dirty and overworked and strained by pretending to
> the students that these things didn't matter that neither of
> them could understand that they were also lonely.   (Barrett 198)

The seclusion and irritation the main character's experience on the island is symbolic of the isolation and discontent that the characters experience in their home lives, and foreshadows the feelings of solitude that the scientists experience further on. The characters, at the beginning of the story, admit "that the days before they became so aware of each other . . . blurred in their minds;" however, they are both able to remember the exact details of the island, further emphasising the importance of the setting in their lives, and the feelings of loneliness it enhanced: "They both remember the granite ledge where they sat, and the raucous quarrelling of the nesting gulls" (198). "The Littoral Zone" uses the setting of the secluded island to illustrate the emotional isolation of the two scientists.

In "A Pair of tickets," as Jing-mei travels from Hong Kong to Guangzhou, she gradually becomes more comfortable with her Chinese heritage. During her stay at Hong Kong, Jing-mei wore make-up; however, due to the hot weather, she decides to not wear anything on her face at the Guangzhou border: "I wear no makeup; in Hong Kong mascara had melted into dark circles and everything else had felt like layers of grease" (208). Cosmetics are associated with more Western practices; therefore, by not wearing make-up, Jing-mei is starting to lose her predominately American identity, and is slowly "becoming Chinese" (204). The protagonist's physical transformation is symbolic of the inner transformation she is experiencing. Jing-mei even starts to relate to some aspects of Guangzhou. Jing-mei notices crowds of "people wearing drab Western clothes," pushing in line to get through customs, which reminds her of home life in the United States: "I feel as if I were getting on a number 30 Stockton bus in San Francisco. I am in China, I remind myself" (207, 208). Jing-mei's familiarity with some behaviours and customs in China allows her to slowly realize that she is not completely alien to her Chinese heritage.

Nonetheless, Jing-mei's process of self-acceptance is slow, for she is hesitant to understand her Chinese identity at the beginning of her visit to Guangzhou. She still feels that "even without make-up, [she] could never pass for true Chinese" (208). Jing-mei continues to see differences between her and the rest of the Chinese citizens, noting how her "head pokes above the crowd so that [she is] eye level only with tourists" (208). The fact that Jing-mei so easily identifies the differences between people from China, further illustrates the struggles she has with accepting her Chinese roots. Jing-mei, instead of comparing herself to Chinese citizens, compares herself to tourists, in other words, people who are not from China, showcasing the fact that she believes herself to be more of an outsider than a member of the Chinese culture. Upon her arrival to Guangzhou, Jing-mei feels lost and turns to "a man who looks American" for directions (208). Jing-mei feels lost in China, because she does not feel Chinese, and turns to a man who appears to be American for comfort and guidance, because she is more comfortable and places more significance on her American identity. The setting of Guangzhou gradually aides the protagonist with her difficulty in comprehending her own background.

Eventually, after experiencing the city and people of Guangzhou, Jing-mei's accepts her hybrid identity. While visiting Guangzhou, Jing-mei notices the infusion of Western culture in China. She realizes that Guangzhou "looks like a major American city," where she even stays in westernized hotels and is able to eat American food: "We are going to dine tonight in our rooms, with our family, sharing hamburgers, french fries, and apple pie à la mode" (210, 211). The combination of western culture and Chinese culture causes Jing-mei to realize that she can have both an American and a Chinese identity. Jing-mei's acceptance of her true identity and her ability to understand what it means to be Chinese is revealed when she asks her father to speak in Chinese: "Tell me in Chinese . . . Really, I can understand" (213). By asking her father to speak Chinese, Jing-mei makes a decision to understand and be a part of her Chinese culture. Jing-mei further embraces her heritage, by confronting her Chinese half-sisters. By hugging her sisters, she is accepting the fact that part of her family is Chinese; thus, she is Chinese as well:

> I look at their faces again and I see no trace of my mother
> in them. Yet they still look familiar. And now I also see what part of me
> is Chinese. It is so obvious. It is my family. It is in our blood. After all
> these years, it can finally be let go.   (217)

Scholar Kiyoko Sueda concurs, asserting that by confronting her sisters, "Jing-mei Woo is in the stage where she starts to understand the Chinese culture inside her with a feeling of competence" (90).

Jing-mei's journey from the city of Hong Kong, where she recounts her youth and the embarrassment she had for her Chinese heritage, to Guangzhou, a city infused with both Western and traditional Chinese customs, serves as a metaphor for Jing-mei's self-transformation. During her time in Hong Kong, she is unable to embrace her Chinese heritage; yet by the end of her journey in Guangzhou, Jing-mei becomes Chinese. The setting of Tan's short story causes the main character to grow and resolve her incapability of accepting her true identity. Ben Xu, argues, however, that when Jing-mei becomes Chinese, she does not necessarily experience personal growth, for when she returns to the United States she will no longer be able to relate to her American identity; thus, she will be "going home as a stranger" (16). What Xu fails to realize, is that Jing-mei does not have to choose between her American culture and her Chinese culture, rather, she is a hybrid of both. When Jing-mei notices Western traditions practiced in Guangzhou China, she realizes that she can be both Chinese and American. Ultimately, her stay in Guangzhou helps instil this insight, causing her to experience personal growth.

     Although the setting of Guangzhou assists the protagonist in Tan's narrative, the environment in "The Littoral Zone" does exactly the opposite. The poor conditions on the secluded island catalyze the feelings of loneliness the main characters experience. The irritations of the island cause the scientists to search for a moment of relief from their suffering, by engaging in a passionate and adulterous love affair. The night of the scientists' infidelity, the wind is extremely cold and powerful; hence, the protagonists seek shelter and warmth under a fireplace. The strong wind gives the main characters the "pretext they needed to crouch side by side on the cracked tiles, brushing elbows as they opened the flue and crumpled paper and laid kindling in the form of a grid" (203). The blazing fire that protects them from the icy wind, serves as a symbol of the hot passion the scientist have for one other, which derives from their need for protection and relief from the isolation and frustrations they experience on the island. The setting of the island ultimately causes the scientists to consummate their relationship in hopes to eliminate their feelings of seclusion; however, the outcome is quite the opposite. The protagonists' struggle to end their seclusion results in infidelity, which ironically, further enhances the feelings of isolation they experience in their lives. After their consummation, the adulterers divorce their spouses and live together in order to preserve their passion. However, while living together, the fervour in their relationship gradually fades, and the main characters "struggle to conceal their disappointments" with one another (202). Instead of being together to end the discontent and solitude they experienced on the island and in their previous marriages, they are filled with regret and an even greater sense of loneliness: "All they have lost in order to be

Choy 6

together would seem bearable had they continued to feel the way they felt on the island" (202). Ultimately, Barrett uses the setting of the island to augment the protagonists' feelings of discontent and isolation.

Both Tan and Barrett use setting effectively and uniquely to figuratively portray the inner struggles of the characters. Tan reveals the power setting has on shaping one's own identity, whereas Barrett gives caution to the influence the natural environment has over human behaviour and motivations. Both authors creatively explore the remarkable relationship between human beings and their surrounding environments, and the astounding influence setting has on individuals. In the battle between man and nature, perhaps human beings are not as powerful as it is commonly believed.

WORKS CITED AND CONSULTED

Barrett, Andrea. "The Littoral Zone." *The Norton Introduction to Literature.* Shorter 9th ed. Ed. Alison Booth, J. Paul Hunter, and Kelly J. Mays. New York: Norton, 2006. 90–94. Print.

Sueda, Kiyoko. "An Analysis of *The Joy Luck Club* from the Perspective of the Intercultural Communication. *Hokusei Review* 30 (1993): 79–105. Print.

Tan, Amy. "A Pair of Tickets." *The Norton Introduction to Literature.* Shorter 9th ed. Ed. Alison Booth, J. Paul Hunter, and Kelly J. Mays. New York: Norton, 2006. 77–89. Print.

Van der Berg, Laura. "About Andrea Barrett." *Ploughshares* 33.2–3 (2007): 207–12.

Xu, Ben. "Memory and Ethnic Self: Reading Amy Tan's *The Joy Luck Club*." *MELUS* 19.1 (1994): 3–18. Print.

WORKS CITED

Cheever, John. "The Country Husband." *The Norton Introduction to Literature.* Shorter 9th ed. Ed. Alison Booth, J. Paul Hunter, and Kelly J. Mays. New York: Norton, 2006. 71–88. Print.

Govier, Katherine. "Sociology." *The Oxford Book of Canadian Short Stories in English.* Ed. Margaret Atwood and Robert Weaver. Toronto: Oxford UP, 1986. 389–403. Print.

Hawthorne, Nathaniel. "Young Goodman Brown." *The Norton Introduction to Literature*. Shorter 9th ed. Ed. Alison Booth, J. Paul Hunter, and Kelly J. Mays. New York: Norton, 2006. 232–41. Print.

Lukács, Georg. *The Theory of the Novel: A Historico-Philosophical Essay on the Forms of Great Epic Literature*. Trans. Anna Bostock. Cambridge, MA: MIT P, 1971. Print.

Munro, Alice. *Who Do You Think You Are?* Scarborough, ON: Macmillan-NAL, 1978. Print.

"Protagonist." *The Compact Edition of the Oxford English Dictionary*. 2 vols. 1971. Print.

Writing about Drama

WHAT IS DRAMA?

Drama is similar in many ways to fiction, particularly in it use of **character**, **plot**, and **setting**, but also in its utilization of **symbol** and **metaphor**.[1] It is also similar to fiction in that it typically employs all these elements to comment on or express an overall **theme**. Perhaps the most obvious difference between fiction and drama is the fact that, while fiction depends primarily on **narration** to tell a story, drama relies principally on **dialogue** (or speech) to achieve the same end. There are always exceptions to the rule: some works of fiction, such as Ernest Hemingway's "Hills Like White Elephants," offer more dialogue between characters than narration, and some dramatic works use prologues, epilogues, and/or detailed **stage directions** to introduce, summarize, or advance their plots. But when it comes to story and plot, fiction generally *tells* (through narration) and drama *shows* (through dialogue).

The demonstrative nature of drama calls to mind another major difference between fictional and dramatic works: traditionally, fiction is meant to be read (either privately or aloud to a group), whereas drama is meant to be performed before an audience. That does not mean that you cannot read and appreciate a dramatic work as words on a page, which is, after all, how you will most often approach drama in an English class (as opposed to, say, a theatre arts class). On the contrary, what makes reading drama an especially exciting prospect in the English classroom is the fact that, in addition to being analyzed as a written text, a work of drama encourages us to imagine the ways it *could be* played (or "brought to life") on stage or through film. To account for this double life of

---

1 Terms in bold are explained later in this chapter. For concise definitions, see the glossary in the Appendix.

drama, literary criticism makes a distinction between the "dramatic text" and the "play," whereby the former refers to the complete written text of the work (stage directions and all) and the latter refers to its (potential for) performance. What is more, every performance or "play" is said to be an interpretation of the dramatic text. Attending a performance of Shakespeare's *The Tempest* at the Manitoba Theatre Centre in Winnipeg, Manitoba, for instance, will be a far different experience than attending the same play at the Stratford Festival Theatre in Stratford, Ontario—and not simply because the Stratford venue will have access to more internationally known and experienced players and directors. Rather, what separates performances of the same play more than anything else is the **dramaturgy** of each production, which refers to directorial decisions regarding stage and costume design, lighting and sound effects, character movement and action on stage, acting style, and so on.[2] These dramaturgical aspects of performance are especially important to consider when you are asked to write about a particular performance or film adaptation of a dramatic work. But they are also important to keep in mind when writing about the text itself, since the dramatic text will invite you to envision a kind of mental dramaturgy of your own. Your understanding of what the text means, in other words, will depend largely on how you conceptualize a stage, a set, a group of players, their movements, their manner of speaking, and their props.

CHARACTER AND CHARACTERIZATION

A good place to begin visualizing the "play" within the text is in the text's dramatis personae—its cast of characters. Dramatic characters are not unlike characters in fiction insofar as they can be complex or simple, but dramatic **characterization** (i.e., drama's means of establishing personality traits for its characters) normally operates without the benefit of narrative description. Granted, some character traits can be conveyed through stage directions. In Tennessee Williams's *A Streetcar Named Desire*, Stanley (the leading male character) is first introduced with the following stage direction: "*[He is] about twenty eight, or thirty years old, roughly dressed in blue denim work clothes. [He] carries his bowling jacket and a red-stained package from a butcher's*" (1540). Although we learn some things about Stanley in this brief description, we do not learn very much, and what we do learn is rather vague. We are not sure of his exact age; we are encouraged to assume he is a working-class labourer (he wears "blue denim work clothes"); his "bowling jacket" suggests that he likes to socialize with other men, and the "red-stained" package he carries arguably foreshadows his brutish behaviour. In all honesty, much of what can

---

2 Performances will even vary from one night to the next: opening night jitters might cause a few missed cues; a prop might misfire the next night; and closing night might energize the players and the audience alike.

be extrapolated from the above passage is based on hindsight. It is really what Stanley says and does throughout the rest of the play that characterizes him in the eyes of his audience. His verbal and physical interactions with other characters (particularly his wife Stella and her sister Blanche) reveal him to be chauvinistic, crude, and short-tempered. In fact, Stanley's actions communicate enough about Stanley's character that even if his sexual assault of Blanche near the end of the play is upsetting or surprising, the text has partially prepared its audience for this outcome by showing that the assault is not entirely *out of character* for Stanley. Among other violent outbursts, the audience sees (or at least *hears*) Stanley beat his wife in Scene 3.

Even more dignified characters such as Shakespeare's Prince Hamlet are characterized by the things they say and do. Hamlet's famous **soliloquies**— solitary speeches addressed to himself and heard by the audience—reveal him to be profoundly reflective and philosophical ("To be or not to be, that is the question" [3.1.56]), while his constant hesitation and *in*action demonstrate his abiding self-doubt and deep insecurity. But Hamlet is also a prime example of how a character is partially characterized through the expressions and reactions of the characters around him. His fellow courtier Laertes, for instance, is increasingly appalled by what he calls Hamlet's "wicked deed[s]" (5.1.197). Although Laertes' criticisms of Hamlet cannot be taken at face value (largely because he does not know the full story behind Hamlet's actions), the audience can nevertheless infer from Laertes' perspective that Hamlet is rather shortsighted, even cavalier, about the impact his behaviour has on other people. On an ill-guided course toward vengeance, Hamlet inadvertently devastates Laertes' entire family, killing his father, Polonius, and driving his sister, Ophelia, to suicide. While Polonius's motives are not always honourable, Laertes and his sister are innocent with respect to Hamlet's aspiration "to set it [the world] right" (1.5.188). More to the point, they are typically well liked and admired by audiences: after all, who in *Hamlet* is more sympathetic than the heartbroken Ophelia, or more righteous than her devoted brother? That these two characters suffer the fallout of Hamlet's actions reflects poorly on Hamlet and forces the audience to question the integrity of his character.

Like characters in fiction, characters in drama fall into different categories. Despite his flaws, Hamlet is a **protagonist**—that is, a major character or hero, albeit in his case a tragic one (see **tragic hero**, below). He is also a "round" (i.e., dynamic and complex) character, perhaps the roundest Shakespeare ever invented. The primary **antagonist** or villain of *Hamlet* is Hamlet's uncle, Claudius, who kills Hamlet's father (the previous king of Denmark) and marries the queen (Gertrude, Hamlet's mother) to become the new king of Denmark. Claudius is also somewhat "round" in that he demonstrates inner reflection (and is even remorseful at times); however, he is by no means as complicated or as fully developed as Hamlet.

Dramas also have minor characters that are said to be "flat" (i.e., static and one-dimensional) and that are occasionally used as **foils** (i.e., characters who define rounder, more major characters by way of contrast). There are exceptions to such categories: Laertes, for example, although he is minor, cannot be said to be strictly flat, since he technically develops as a character after learning (very late in the play, mind you) that he has been misled and manipulated by Claudius. And yet, Laertes is also a foil, as Hamlet's famous pun on "foil" indicates: "I'll be your foil, Laertes" (5.2.219). Shakespeare is being ironic here, since it is Laertes who is Hamlet's foil, not the reverse. Laertes' resolve and strength of character are meant to remind the audience—through contrast—of Hamlet's own indecisiveness.

Apart from protagonists, antagonists, and foils, dramas are also populated by **stereotypes**, sometimes referred to as "stock characters." An example of a stereotype in *Hamlet* is the clever gravedigger who exchanges witticisms with Hamlet in Act V, Scene 1. That he is identified by no other name than "Clown" is the first indication that he functions as a stereotype. In Elizabethan (i.e., late sixteenth-century) tragedies, clowns provided momentary **comic relief** from the tragedy's mounting dramatic tension. In additional to being impish and comical, clowns stereotypically impart insight and wisdom to those who listen to them. Shakespeare uses this convention to great effect in *Hamlet*. The partly humorous, partly serious conversation between Hamlet and the grave-digging Clown of Act V does more than inspire Hamlet's final determination to kill Claudius; it also results in some of Shakespeare's most profound meditations on the nature of mortality and death.

Summary

CHARACTER AND CHARACTERIZATION

- dramatic characterization (i.e., drama's means of establishing personality traits for its characters) normally operates without the benefit of narrative description

- what a character *says* and *does* throughout the play characterizes him or her in the eyes of the audience

- dramatic characters fall into different categories: protagonists (major characters or heroes); antagonists (villains); foils (minor characters who define major characters by way of contrast); and stereotypes (stock characters)

- like fictional characters, characters in drama can be round (dynamic and complex) or flat (static and one-dimensional)

STRUCTURE AND PLOT

As in many dramatic works, the **plot** of *Hamlet* (i.e., the play's action and events) is driven by a central **conflict** whose resolution or outcome is not entirely certain. Although the audience has some idea of what *might* happen in the play, it does not know for sure what *will* happen. In the case of *Hamlet*, the audience is even given a strong sense as to what *ought* to happen. Shakespeare's Elizabethan audience would have been especially appalled by Claudius's murder of Hamlet's father because of its implications of regicidal treason and fratricide. (Hamlet's father was both the king of Denmark and Claudius's brother). Such an audience would not only have approved of Hamlet's revenge, it would also have been deeply desirous of its execution. As I tell my students, the Elizabethans would have been "out for Claudius's blood." The central conflict is thus between Hamlet and Claudius, but this conflict must necessarily be viewed in light of the audience's desire for blood, since this desire allows Shakespeare to produce a subtler, more ingenious conflict between what the audience wants (or thinks it wants) and what it gets. Again, what ought to happen (i.e., vengeance) does not happen, at least not immediately. Hamlet initially swears that he will exact "swift" (1.5.29) revenge on Claudius but constantly postpones doing so, which in turn "puts off" the audience's demand for retribution. As a plot device, the deferral of vengeance does more than structure the action in *Hamlet*; it also heightens the play's tension, which the audience is supposed to enjoy before being relieved by the resolution or **catharsis** (this term is discussed later in this chapter) of the final act. This structure of deferral is in fact so dominant in *Hamlet* that one could persuasively argue that the central conflict organizing the play's action is not between Hamlet and Claudius so much as it is between Hamlet and himself. Internally conflicted, Hamlet is constantly at odds with himself: he wants to be loyal to his father's memory, but needs proof of Claudius's guilt. He wants to "set [the world] right" (i.e., kill Claudius), but he hesitates when given the chance to do just that.

Although conflict is effective in organizing plot in drama (as it does also in fiction), it is not the only plot-structuring device at the dramatist's disposal. Consider the more recent example of August Wilson's *The Piano Lesson*. First performed in 1987, this Pulitzer Prize-winning play takes place in Pittsburgh in the 1930s and tells the story of an African-American woman named Berniece and her brother, Boy Willie, both of whom claim ownership of an old upright piano inherited from their deceased parents. How the piano first came into the family's possession is complicated. Suffice it to say, the instrument connects Berniece and Boy Willie to their family's long and troubled history with slavery in America. (For one thing, the piano's legs are engraved with the faces of their enslaved ancestors.) The central conflict of the drama exists between brother and sister: Boy Willie wants to sell the piano in order to purchase the land on which their family worked as slaves, but Berniece is determined to keep the piano in the parlour of her Pittsburgh home, despite the fact that she refuses to play it.[3] This conflict is certainly a factor in shaping the plot of *The Piano Lesson*, but the piano itself structures much of the play's action. First, as the subject of much dialogue, the piano functions as a plot device for recounting **subplots** of hardship endured in the family's past. Second, as a **symbol** of family history (ancestral faces and all), the piano epitomizes how the past influences the present; it "[d]ominat[es] the parlour" (1205) and acts as a reference point for everything that happens on stage. Lastly, the fate of the piano determines the play's outcome: will the dispute over its ownership tear the family apart or bring the family together? Affecting the plot in this way, the piano reminds the audience of the play's overall subtext: slavery may be a thing of the past, but its residual effects continue to complicate the lives of African-Americans in the twentieth century. In addition to teaching its audience about slavery, in other words, *The Piano Lesson* teaches a lesson on the relationship between dramatic objects and dramatic structure.

Another aspect of dramatic structure involves the division of a play into **acts** and **scenes**. Why is *Hamlet* written in five acts, whereas *The Piano Lesson* has only two acts? What about *A Streetcar Named Desire*, which consists of eleven scenes but no acts? Whether a traditional arrangement of acts and scenes or an innovative departure that better serves the demands of a particular story, the way any dramatic work is divided is primarily a means of organizing the plot; in that respect, a dramatic work is similar to a work of fiction. A five-act play, for instance, might reasonably deploy **exposition** (i.e., an introduction to characters, etc.) in its first act, where the audience learns about what has happened and to whom prior to the time and setting of the play. Subsequent acts might move from exposition into **rising action,** where significant events and exchanges between characters are dramatized on stage.[4] Where the **climax, falling action**, and **conclusion** (or "resolution") occur varies from one work to the next. In *Hamlet*, they occur in quick succession in the final scene of Act V, where Hamlet is mortally wounded and Horatio is left to tell Fortinbras how the play's final **catastrophe** (i.e., tragic outcome) came to pass. The climax, falling action, and resolution of *The Piano Lesson* also occur in the final scene, and *Streetcar* differs only insofar as its climax or "turning point" takes place just prior to the final scene.

---

3 The conflict between Boy Willie and Berniece is extremely complicated by the impact of slavery on their family history—so much so that it is difficult to identify one of them as the play's protagonist and the other its antagonist. Rather, they are both protagonists whose relation to one another has been *antagonized* by their own personal responses to the family's experiences with slavery.

4 For a fuller description of terms such as "exposition," "rising action," "climax," "falling action," and "resolution," see the discussion on Freytag's Pyramid in the "Plot" section of Chapter 5.

Summary

STRUCTURE AND PLOT

- dramatic plot (the organization of action and events) is often driven by a central conflict (a major struggle or confrontation) whose resolution is not certain

- dramatic texts can be divided into acts and scenes: *Hamlet* is divided into five acts, *The Piano Lesson* has only two acts, and *A Streetcar Named Desire* consists of eleven scenes but no acts

- dramatic structure often follows a five-part plot pattern that consists of exposition (introduction to the characters, situation, and setting), rising action (events that intensify the central conflict), climax (the turning point), falling action (events depicting the consequences of the climax), conclusion (resolution)

SETTING . . . THE STAGE

As mentioned at the beginning of this chapter, your interpretation of a dramatic text will depend partly on how you envision a stage on which the text might be performed. There are different kinds of stages, so you will want to ask yourself: what type would best suit the play? This question implicitly asks you to consider how the audience should engage the action. While you may not recognize its name, the arrangement of a *proscenium* stage is likely most familiar to you. Most dramatic performances (and most television sitcoms) use a proscenium arrangement, which more or less consists of three walls—at the back and on both sides of the stage—and a primarily front-on view for the audience, who is said to look through an imaginary "fourth wall" that separates them from the action on stage. Less conventional (or "off-Broadway") theatre companies will occasionally use a *thrust* stage arrangement (where the audience envelops three sides of the stage) or an *arena* stage arrangement (where the audience surrounds all sides of the action). Thrust and arena stages are said to increase an audience's sense of involvement in the play and offer more varied perspectives on the play's action.

After imagining a stage, the next step is to envision a "set" to be built into or on top of that stage for the purpose of portraying **setting** (i.e., where and when the action takes place). Again, without recourse to narrative description, a dramatic text relies mainly on stage directions to convey its setting. Shakespeare rarely provides much description of setting at all. He describes the entire "scene" of *Hamlet* as follows: "*The action takes place in or near the royal castle of Denmark at Elsinore*" (1325). As an actor and entrepreneur of the Elizabethan theatre,

Shakespeare would have known that travel and scarce resources made elaborate sets unfeasible. At the other end of the spectrum is Tennessee Williams, whose directions for setting in *Streetcar* move well beyond a straightforward account of situation, time, and place in their attempt to evoke ambience and mood: in Scene 1, the sky is said to be "*a peculiarly tender blue, almost a turquoise, which invests the scene with a kind of lyricism and gracefully attenuates the atmosphere of decay*" (1141). August Wilson likewise uses provocative, abstract language when describing the atmosphere of *The Piano Lesson*: "*there is something in the air that belongs to the night. A stillness that is a portent, a gathering, a coming together of something akin to a storm*" (1206). Practically speaking, how might one stage (mentally or otherwise) the "lyricism" of Williams's sky or the ominous ambiguity of Wilson's "stillness"? If these descriptions of setting challenge our understanding of what stage directions are meant to do, then they also remind us that the dramatic text must be interpreted before it becomes a "play."

Summary

SETTING . . . THE STAGE

- your interpretation of a dramatic text will depend partly on how you envision a stage on which the text's dialogue and action might be performed

- most dramatic performances (and most television sitcoms) use a proscenium stage arrangement, which consists of three walls (at the back and on both sides of the stage); the audience views the performance through an imaginary "fourth wall"

- in a thrust stage arrangement, the audience envelops three sides of the stage; in an arena stage arrangement, the audience surrounds all sides of the action

- dramatic texts rely mainly on stage directions to convey a sense of setting (i.e., where and when the action takes place) as well as a sense of how we might envision a "set"

LANGUAGE AND STYLE

Not unlike other kinds of literature, dramatic works make frequent use of stylized or "literary" language—which is to say, language that refers to levels of meaning beyond the literal and/or that draws conspicuous attention to itself *as* language. Drama uses symbols, as we saw in the case of the piano in *The Piano Lesson*. It uses metaphor, as we saw in Chapter 4's brief discussion of *Romeo and Juliet*, where Romeo compares Juliet and her balcony to the sun rising in the east. In Chapter 2, we discussed dramatic uses of **imagery** (specifically *blood* imagery) in Shakespeare's *Macbeth*. Dramatic works even use language more commonly associated with poetry, such as **allusion**, **alliteration**, **assonance**, and so on (see Chapter 4). To be sure, a good number of dramatic works written before the nineteenth century use what is called "dramatic **verse**," wherein dialogue is written in both **metre** (i.e., specific patterns of syllables) and **rhyme**. Some of Shakespeare's plays even alternate between dramatic verse and prose. For example, aristocratic characters in *A Midsummer Night's Dream* speak in elegant verse, whereas more lowly characters of the same play (like Bottom and his fellow tradesmen) speak in less refined prose. This deliberate difference in speech draws attention to assumptions about the kind of social hierarchies that the play puts into question.[5]

If drama shares linguistic similarities with poetry and fiction, then perhaps one of its more distinctive uses of language involves its incorporation of song, which is occasionally accompanied by music and even dance. Not all dramatic works take advantage of these features, but many do. The three plays we have discussed at length in this chapter all happen to draw on music and song to varying degrees. Ophelia famously sings her sorrows in Act IV of *Hamlet*. In *A Streetcar Named Desire*, Blanche hears songs that no one else but the audience can hear. Lastly, the climactic breakthrough of the final scene of *The Piano Lesson* is triggered when Berniece finally plays the piano while singing a deeply moving song of redemption. Berniece's plea for deliverance through song is part of the "lesson" referred to in the play's title. To be sure, songs are sung in nearly every scene of *The Piano Lesson*, and are crucial in understanding the post-slavery African-American experience the play aims to represent.[6]

Another common aspect of dramatic language entails the use of **dramatic irony**, which occurs when the audience understands more about the significance or consequences of a character's actions than the character does. The situation of dramatic irony is not unlike that of the horror film in which the heroine opens a door behind which the audience knows the murderer lies in wait. Perhaps feeling the need to warn her ("Don't go in there!"), the viewer nevertheless takes a certain pleasure in knowing more than she does. In a play, dramatic irony similarly induces pleasure by heightening suspense and contributing to the play's dramatic tension. When Hamlet thrusts his swords into the curtained closet of his mother's bedroom, the audience (unlike Hamlet himself) knows it is Polonius on the receiving end of the fatal blow and not Claudius as Hamlet

---

5 For more on this, see the "Student Writing" sample at the end of this chapter.
6 The musical aspect of *The Piano Lesson* once again speaks to the importance of performance. On paper, songs can appear insignificant or unremarkable, and my students have often admitted to skimming through or simply ignoring them when reading the dramatic text. To counter this, I once played in class a video clip from the Hallmark made-for-television production of *The Piano Lesson*; the entire class was surprised (and delighted) by the way the performance of song in the clip transformed their perception of the play. In particular, students were better able to appreciate the extent to which antagonisms between characters were either suspended or even transcended through songs of common suffering and experience.

would have hoped. This desperate and hasty act ironically complicates Hamlet's desire for revenge, since it inspires the wrath of Laertes and gives Claudius an excuse to send Hamlet to England, where Claudius plans to have him executed. There is also dramatic irony in the scene that immediately precedes the hapless slaying of Polonius, wherein Hamlet forfeits his best chance to kill Claudius simply because Claudius is praying. The logic here is that murdering Claudius while he prays will send his undeserving soul to heaven. What Hamlet does not know, however, is that Claudius cannot find the right words to pray and very quickly gives up. It would, in other words, have been the perfect time to kill him.

Summary

LANGUAGE AND STYLE

- dramatic works often use stylized or "literary" language, including symbols (objects that stand for something else), metaphors (describing one thing in terms of another), and imagery (language that appeals to a person's sense of sight, smell, etc.)

- dramatic works also use language more commonly associated with poetry, such as alliteration and assonance, and may even be written in verse (i.e., language that follows specific patterns of metre and/or rhyme)

- one of drama's more distinctive uses of language involves its incorporation of song, which is occasionally accompanied by music and even dance

- dramatic irony occurs when the audience understands more about the significance or consequences of a character's actions than the character does

THEME

If someone were to ask you what *A Streetcar Named Desire* is about, you might well respond by recalling aspects of the play's setting and plot. You might say that it is about a woman named Blanche who, having suffered significant personal and financial losses, visits her sister, Stella, and Stella's husband, Stanley, in their apartment in the French Quarter of New Orleans. Her visit, you might add, is complicated by Stanley's increasingly misogynistic intolerance of Blanche's haughty affectations, and culminates in a vicious sexual attack that forces Blanche to leave her sister's home under psychiatric supervision. Suppose you were asked a follow-up question: "Okay, you've described what happens; but what is the play is *really* about?" This second question asks you to reflect on the **theme** of *A Streetcar Named Desire*. In other words, what is the overall subject of the work, and what specifically is the work saying about that subject? What kind of statement or commentary is being made?

Like many other works of drama, *Streetcar* has multiple themes that can be gleaned by analyzing the plot in conjunction with other elements of the play such as characterization and the use of imagery. Based on our previous discussion, we can see that *Streetcar* is thematically interested in gender relations: it is concerned about violence against women and about the social conditions that reinforce a woman's dependence on a man. Although Stanley is an individual character with his own personal idiosyncrasies, he also represents, on a thematic level, a powerful male force in society that is oppressive to women. What is more, his physical abuse of both Stella and Blanche throws into relief (i.e., *thematizes*) how few options some women have with respect to male oppression. On the one hand, Stella feels that she has no choice but to return to and forgive her husband after he has beaten her, while on the other hand, in lieu of a more practical alternative, Blanche responds to Stanley's violence by delving deeper into her own madness. By dramatizing these limited—even self-effacing—responses to male violence, the play implicitly dramatizes the need for more constructive opportunities for women's independence.

Blanche's mental breakdown leads us to a second major theme of *Streetcar*, namely, the failure to escape reality through fantasy. Try as she might, Blanche cannot prevent the truth about her troubled past from revealing itself to those around her. Everyone sees through her façade of emotional stability. The play represents her *exposure* in this regard through light imagery. She consistently attempts to shield her face from direct lighting as though it will somehow reveal not just her age but also something fundamental (and deeply unsettling) about her identity. "I can't stand a naked light bulb," she complains, "any more than I can a rude remark or a vulgar action" (1161). As it turns out, her fear of the "naked" light is rooted in a traumatic memory of the night her husband shot himself after being confronted about his homosexual affair with another man. From a thematic point of view, the play thus makes a complex statement about the failure of illusion to protect us from any truths we would otherwise wish to conceal.

Summary

THEME

- theme refers to the central idea or overall subject in a dramatic work

- dramatic texts may have more than one theme—e.g., *A Streetcar Named Desire* is thematically interested in gender relations and the tension between reality and fantasy

- theme often involves some kind of statement or commentary on society

DRAMATIC TYPE: TRAGEDY VS. COMEDY

Dramatic works can be categorized according to numerous types or subgenres, but by far the most common of these are **tragedy** and **comedy**. We will explore more particular differences between these two dramatic types in a moment, but first it might be useful to invoke a kind of shorthand for quickly distinguishing one type from the other. More often than not, tragedies focus on an *individual* and tend to end badly (i.e., the individual suffers profoundly and may even die). Comedies, on the other hand, focus on *groups* of individuals, and, while problems arise, things usually turn out well in the end for most characters. To put it another way, tragedies track the catastrophic consequences of *personal* actions, whereas comedies playfully invert—and may even aim to subvert (i.e., undermine)—the conventions and affairs of *social* life.

According to Aristotle, whose writings continue to influence the way we categorize literary genres, tragedy is "the imitation of a serious and complete action of some magnitude" (418). Aristotle uses the term "action" here rather than "story" partly because he is referring to a series of events *acted out* or "imitated" on stage. But tragedies could also be said to revolve characteristically around the actions of a particular character, or even a single definitive action or decision to act. In Shakespeare's *Macbeth*, for example, Macbeth decides to kill King Duncan in his sleep. This "imitation" of regicide is the play's central action. Although it takes place off stage, the action is serious (again, few things could better capture the attention of an Elizabethan audience than a regicide), and the action is also "complete" insofar as the audience observes events and conversations that lead up to Duncan's murder as well as the repercussions that follow that action. In *Hamlet*, the tragic situation is somewhat subtler since what the audience witnesses ultimately is Hamlet's *in*action, or more precisely, his decision *not* to act until it is too late. A failure to act in time or at the right moment is still an action, and in this case indecisiveness has grave consequences not only for the tragic hero, but also for the many high-ranking citizens of Denmark who die as result of Hamlet's tardy execution of vengeance.

Regardless of their differences, Macbeth and Hamlet each exhibit characteristic traits of the **tragic hero**. They are both "better than ordinary" (425), which is Aristotle's way of saying that the tragic hero possesses an elevated social status or is distinguished in some way: Macbeth is hailed as a great military general, and Hamlet is a prince. Despite being "better," they are neither wholly good nor wholly evil. While his murder of Duncan is unconscionable, Macbeth is a sympathetic and otherwise noble character, and Hamlet, as discussed above, destroys many lives on his righteous path toward vengeance. In both cases, goodness is impaired by a **tragic flaw**—or what Aristotle called the tragic hero's *hamartia* (a fatal mistake or error in judgment). Macbeth is overly ambitious and mistakenly believes that killing Duncan will make him happy (by making him king), whereas Hamlet's uncertainty prevents him from fulfilling his duty to his murdered father. According to Aristotle, the hero's tragic flaw or fatal error in judgment arouses the audience's pity and inspires fear—pity because the flaw or error inhibits the fulfillment of the hero's nobility, and fear because we sense that it will lead to the hero's destruction and possibly to the destruction of many others. The combined arousal of pity and fear produces a tension that both enthralls and unsettles the audience until they are relieved of this tension by a final **catharsis**—a purging of emotions that follows a tragedy's final **catastrophe** (i.e., its tragic outcome). For Aristotle, catharsis is acutely felt as our thoughts return to our own lives: although we are saddened by the hero's tragic fate, we are elated and grateful to have merely witnessed and not experienced that fate ourselves.

If tragedy encourages a vicarious identification with the hero's suffering and arouses the audience's fear, then comedy seeks rather to interest and amuse the audience without the uneasiness of anticipating disaster. Although the structural requirements of comedy are less stringent than those of tragedy, the telltale sign of the comedic genre is the happy ending.[7] Counter-intuitive as it may seem, comedies do not even need to be "funny"—indeed, not everyone who reads Shakespeare's comedies will find the humour in them. Rather, what typically makes a comedy is a plot structure in which an initially harmonious social order is disrupted by folly but is then restored in the final act. In this regard, comedy has a more "conservative" structure than tragedy: it works to re-establish a previous form of order, while tragedy uses catastrophe to clear the way for a new kind of order. This does not mean that comedy cannot be politically subversive. As the student writing sample at the end of this chapter endeavours to show, Shakespeare's *A Midsummer Night's Dream* faithfully follows a comic structure of order, disruption, and restoration, but it also manages to make a political statement. The play ends (as comedies tend to do) in a celebration of marriage that sanctifies social unity and reconfirms certain social values, but the mayhem that precedes this return to stability yields a *serious* (albeit subtle and indirect) critique of Elizabethan society.

Summary

DRAMATIC TYPE: TRAGEDY VS. COMEDY

- tragedy and comedy are two of the oldest and most common types of drama
  - tragedies typically focus on an individual and tend to end badly (i.e., the individual suffers profoundly and may even die)

---

7 Not every character needs to be happy in the end. While Shakespeare's *The Merchant of Venice*, for instance, ends in the happy marriage of Antonio and Portia, Shylock is far from pleased by the final turn of the play's events. He is stripped of his wealth and forced to convert from Judaism to Christianity.

Summary
DRAMATIC TYPE: TRAGEDY VS. COMEDY (continued)

- comedies, by contrast, focus on groups of individuals, and, while problems arise, things usually turn out well in the end for most characters

- the central character of a tragedy is called a tragic hero; his or her tragic flaw or hamartia (a fatal mistake or error in judgment) leads to his or her own downfall

- catharsis refers to the purging of emotions or relief that the audience feels after witnessing the text's final catastrophe (the tragic outcome)

- in comedies, an initially harmonious social order is disrupted by folly but is usually restored in the final act

READING DEMONSTRATION: *HAMLET* AND NEW HISTORICISM

For the most part, we have been discussing drama from the point of view of dramatic form—which is to say, from a formalist perspective. By way of contrast, this reading demonstration will extend our discussion of *Hamlet* by briefly considering the play from a New Historicist point of view. As discussed in Chapter 3, New Historicism aims to restore to the reading experience a sense of what Raymond Williams calls the "structure of feeling" of a text's moment in history (37). That is to say, it aspires to read literature in light of the cultural practices and frames of reference of its contemporary audiences and readerships. We mentioned in Chapter 3, for instance, that Shakespeare's portrayal of Claudius's criminal ascension to the throne in *Hamlet* effectively draws on the play's late-sixteenth-century audience's anxieties over who would succeed the aging Queen Elizabeth I. It would also have reminded that audience of previous assassination attempts on the queen's life. Indeed, Hamlet's famous observation that "Something is rotten in the state of Denmark" (1.4.90) was likely heard by some members of the audience as a veiled reference to the world just outside the walls of the Globe Theatre, where *Hamlet* was first performed. For a New Historicist critic, the play's tremendous ability to rouse feelings associated with the political uncertainty of its earliest audiences is part of what makes *Hamlet* an important work.

Hamlet effectively taps into other sources of cultural anxiety as well, including what would have been its first audiences' genuine concern over changes to long-standing religious doctrines in the early days of the Church of England. Well-known New Historicist Stephen Greenblatt provides an extended and close reading of a series of such anxieties in *Hamlet* surrounding the Christian concept of purgatory. A brief account of his argument provides a useful demonstration of what New Historicism can contribute to literary criticism. Purgatory was officially renounced as a legitimate theological concept in 1563, less than four decades before *Hamlet* was written. For those who believed in the concept both before and after its renunciation, purgatory was more than just a spiritual realm between life and death where spirits spent centuries, if not millennia, purging their souls of their mortal sins; it was also a place where spirits could be contacted through prayer and religious ritual. Purgatory was important for the living, in other words, because it facilitated their communion with the dead— enabling both a practice and a community through which the living could pray for, remember, and honour loved ones who had passed on. According to Greenblatt, the banishment of purgatory from the Church of England's official doctrine represented a significant cultural loss for many British subjects, since it meant these people could no longer openly (or at least publicly) pay tribute to their dead in a way that had been passed down through many generations.

For Greenblatt, the loss of purgatorial ritual as a practice for remembering the dead is precisely what *Hamlet* means to invoke with the ghost of King Hamlet's final request: "Remember me" (1.5.91). Even without this plea, the ghost would have triggered a common sixteenth-century perception that a ghost was just another name for a spirit of purgatory returning to settle unresolved business on earth. *Hamlet*'s ghost confirms this association (albeit without naming purgatory directly) when he identifies himself to Hamlet as "thy father's spirit, / Doomed for a certain term to walk the night, / And for the day confined to fast in the fires, / Till the foul crimes done in my days of nature / Are burnt and purged away" (1.5.9–13). The ghost's passive reference to crimes "done" while he was alive implies both his own sins and those sins committed *against* him, and would likely have reminded Elizabethan audiences of a central aspect of purgatory: the living have a responsibility to help the dead atone for their sins and to pass as quickly as possible through purgatory on their way to heaven. His father's spirit needs Hamlet to avenge his death not simply for the sake of petty vengeance, but because the sin of his own murder, though properly committed by Claudius, must be purged in order for the ghost to rest finally in peace. Without being redressed, the murder remains a kind of outstanding debt that must be repaid *by the son*.

While present-day readers can identify and even reconstruct the logic of the play's references to purgatory, such readers may not fully appreciate just how culturally charged these references likely were for Shakespeare's contemporary audience. Despite being denounced by the Church as harmfully superstitious, the idea of purgatory lingered (as superstitions tend to do) in the late-sixteenth-century cultural imagination, if only as the focal point for a series of anxieties over one's responsibilities to the dead. In light of this context, the audience's demand for vengeance (which we discussed above) is only partially responsible for the play's dramatic tension, since that demand is framed by a larger cultural tension between a need to honour and remember the dead and the loss of a traditional means of doing so. Officially deprived of purgatory within the English Church, Shakespeare's audience may well have taken vicarious pleasure in an (unnamed) *imaginary* purgatory from which King Hamlet's ghost might finally be released. That is not to say that Shakespeare is attempting to reclaim purgatory in *Hamlet* as a legitimate theological concept. Rather, his *use* of purgatory demonstrates how older systems of belief can experience a kind of afterlife in literature where feelings and emotions associated with the loss of such systems can be transformed—even purged—through dramatic catharsis.

STUDENT WRITING

The following student writing sample demonstrates how you can write an effective and engaging paper that focuses on dramatic type. Specifically, the paper examines the ways in which Shakespeare's *A Midsummer Night's Dream* both conforms to and resists the dramatic conventions of comedy. Like any good argument, however, the paper does more than just measure the play against these conventions. Rather, it offers a provocative thesis that addresses both the motives and the consequences of the play's departures from traditional form.

Choy 1

Anna Choy*
ENGL-1001/6-010
Dr. Peter Melville
Feb. 11, 2009

A Midsummer Night's Dream: A Cry for Responsible Government

Is *A Midsummer Night's Dream* the typical Elizabethan comedy? Conventional comedies depict Elizabethan views of society, particularly the belief in the cosmological order, or in other terms, the chain of being. People of the Renaissance believed in the importance of status. Each individual had a specific position in society's hierarchy, which mirrored the hierarchy they believed existed in the spiritual world. Shakespeare similarly establishes a hierarchy within the

*Essay by Anna Choy. Reprinted by permission of the author.

characters of *A Midsummer Night's Dream*, creating social order within the play. This social order is then broken, and eventually restored towards the end of the play in typical comedic fashion. Shakespeare, however, portrays authority as both the cause of disarray as well as the solution to the restoration of order, suggesting that individuals at the top of the hierarchy must act with caution and responsibility, because their actions affect the rest of the community. Although *A Midsummer Night's Dream* meets the requirements of conventional Early Modern English comedies, the play goes beyond convention, and implicitly cautions Elizabethan social hierarchy about the need for responsibility.

Shakespeare portrays the notion of a structured cosmos through both the fairy world and the human world in *A Midsummer Night's Dream*. Both the human community and the fairy community have an ordered system. Theseus is the leader of the human hierarchy, for he is the "renowned Duke" of Athens (*Midsummer* 1.1.20). He and his wife are at the top of the chain of being, or hierarchy, because of their high status. Opposite to the Duke and his wife, the character of Bottom is at the "bottom" of society, as suggested by his name. Bottom's low status is not only revealed by his name, but also by the text itself. The rest of the characters' dialogue in *A Midsummer Night's Dream* is written in verse, which Elizabethans believed to be beautiful, elevated language. Verse is the highest form of writing; therefore, Shakespeare uses verse to portray the high status of characters. Bottom and the rest of the players, however, do not speak in verse, but rather in prose. Prose is regarded as common language, and further reveals Bottom and his company as commoners, or people of low status. The spiritual world of the fairies is ordered similarly to that of Theseus' community. Oberon and Titania are King and Queen of the fairies, and parallel the rulers of Athens: Theseus and Hyppolyta. Puck, however, symbolizes the lowest rank in the fairy community, just as Bottom represents the low status of his society. Puck's low status is revealed when he does the bidding of King Oberon and refers to himself as a servant: "fear not, my lord, your servant shall do so" (*Midsummer* 2.2.269). The importance of position portrayed in both the fairy and human worlds proves that *A Midsummer Night's Dream* depicts the common beliefs of Elizabethan society; thus, the play has elements of conventional comedies.

A conservative comedy not only portrays the cosmological order, but the cosmological order is then momentarily destroyed. King Oberon overhears Helena declare her love for Demetrius. To Helena's dismay, Demetrius' response to her feelings is bitter rejection: "I love thee not, therefore pursue me not"

(*Midsummer* 2.1.189). Demetrius instead, displays his affection for Hermia, who in turn loves Lysander. In an attempt to remedy the tangled human tribulations, King Oberon orders Puck to put the juice of a magical plant on Demetrius, so that when he awakes, he will see Helena and share her affection. Oberon informs Puck that he will recognize Demetrius "by the Athenian garments he hath on" (*Midsummer* 2.2.264). Oberon's description, however, is very vague, and results in Puck placing the plant's juice on Lysander instead. When Oberon realizes Puck has crushed the "herb into Lysander's eye," he makes amends by placing the plant's potion on the correct individual: Demetrius (*Midsummer* 3.2.367). Oberon's actions only create further disarray amongst the young lovers. Lysander, instead of loving Hermia, is infatuated with Helena, who is also doted on by Demetrius. Hermia, who was initially loved by both men, is without a single suitor. The position of the lovers is completely rearranged, creating great disorder. Both Demetrius and Lysander enhance the chaos within the play when they "seek a place to fight" for Helena's affection (*Midsummer* 3.2.354). In order to thwart this battle, Oberon casts a "drooping fog as black as Acheron," preventing the suitors from seeing each other (*Midsummer* 3.2.357). The fog serves as an archetypal symbol of confusion and disorder. Cosmological disarray is a fundamental characteristic of conventional comedy.

King Oberon, the highest authority figure, is the reason for this disarray amongst the human beings. Instead of acting with responsibility when trying to solve the problems of the young lovers, he carelessly orders Puck to anoint "the Athenian's eyes / With love-juice" (*Midsummer* 3.2.36–37). By referring to Demetrius only as an "Athenian," Oberon fails to give a proper and precise description of Demetrius, which leads to Puck's error. Oberon's careless attitude towards the humans' situation results in confusion amongst the lovers. Oberon is also accountable for creating the fog, which confuses both Demetrius and Lysander, providing further evidence that Oberon is responsible for creating chaos. Oberon as the primary cause of disarray reveals the significance of responsible behaviour, for decisions of those in power affect the rest of society. *A Midsummer Night's Dream* portrays the disorder of the cosmos, which is a fundamental characteristic of comedies; nonetheless, Oberon as the source of bedlam reveals Shakespeare's desire for conscientious and reliable hierarchy.

The importance of responsibility within the hierarchy is revealed further when Oberon restores order amongst the human beings. Near the end of the play, Oberon instructs Puck to remove the plant's spell from Lysander, causing

Choy 4

Lysander to love Hermia once again, and also allowing Demetrius to dote on Helena without contempt from Lysander:

> ... gentle Puck, take this transformed scalp
> From off the head of this Athenian swain,
> That he, awaking when the other do,
> May all to Athens back again repair,
> And think no more of this night's accidents
> But as the fierce vexation of a dream.　　(4.1.57–62)

By removing the enchantment, Oberon succeeds in his attempt to "repair" the damage that was done by his carelessness. Oberon unites both Hermia and Lysander, as well as Helena and Demetrius; thus, restoring the cosmological order. In Elizabethan comedies, marriage symbolizes the return to social order; therefore, Theseus and Hippolyta's union at the end of the play further portrays the rectification of the chain of being. By making Oberon responsible for both the bedlam within the play as well as the restoration of order, Shakespeare undermines the significance of the restoration of order, and instead, puts greater emphasis on Oberon's character. Shakespeare suggests that the return to a structured society is not as significant as authority responsible for this return. The decisions of the hierarchy affect the rest of society, and can either create confusion and chaos within the community, or peace and stability. It is therefore important for authority to act responsibly in order to maintain peace and ensure cosmological order. Though *A Midsummer Night's Dream* does have the same structure of conventional comedies, it ultimately places more significance on the necessity for responsible authoritative figures.

　　A Midsummer Night's Dream was written during a period of succession anxiety. Many Elizabethans expressed immense concern over who would replace Queen Elizabeth as ruler. Shakespeare's caution for responsible leadership in *A Midsummer Night's Dream* reveals his own anxiety over the country's new leader. The necessity for good authority figures, however, is not just a Shakespearian ideal. Having responsible government is significant in today's society as well, yet with numerous political scandals, a dwindling economy, and a housing crisis, this necessity seems to be far from fulfilled. If Shakespeare was an advocate for responsible government, why should not today's society?

WORKS CITED

Shakespeare, William. *A Midsummer Night's Dream. The Norton Introduction to Literature*. Shorter 9th ed. Ed. Alison Booth, J. Paul Hunter, and Kelly J. Mays. New York: Norton, 2006. 1272–1324. Print.

WORKS CITED

Aristotle. "Poetics." *The Philosophy of Aristotle*. Trans. J.L. Creed and A.E. Wardman. New York: Penguin, 1963. Print.

Greenblatt, Stephen. *Hamlet in Purgatory*. Princeton, NJ: Princeton UP, 2001. Print.

Shakespeare, William. *Hamlet. The Norton Introduction to Literature*. Shorter 9th ed. Ed. Alison Booth, J. Paul Hunter, and Kelly J. Mays. New York: Norton, 2006. 1325–1418. Print.

Williams, Raymond. "The Analysis of Culture." *Cultural Theory and Popular Culture: A Reader*. 3rd ed. Ed. John Storey. Essex, Eng.: Pearson, 2006. 32–40. Print.

Williams, Tennessee. *A Streetcar Named Desire. The Norton Introduction to Literature*. Shorter 9th ed. Ed. Alison Booth, J. Paul Hunter, and Kelly J. Mays. New York: Norton, 2006. 1140–1203. Print.

Wilson, August. *The Piano Lesson. The Norton Introduction to Literature*. Shorter 9th ed. Ed. Alison Booth, J. Paul Hunter, and Kelly J. Mays. New York: Norton, 2006. 1205–62. Print.

Writing about Film

WHAT IS (NARRATIVE) FILM?

In contrast to "documentary" or "non-fictional" film, "narrative" film (also called "fictional" film) refers to both long and short cinematic works that tell stories in the form of a **plot** (i.e., a specific arrangement of action and events). In previous chapters, we noted how fictional prose depends on narration to convey story and plot, whereas dramatic works rely principally on dialogue (or speech) to achieve the same end. In narrative film, dialogue is likewise important, but the chief means of developing a film's plot involves the cinematic manipulation of the moving visual image—hence, the popular Hollywood industry terms *movie* and *motion picture*. Even the word *cinema* finds its origin in the Greek word for movement, *kinema*. Of course, the movement of the visual image in film is an illusion based on the inability of the human eye to perceive changes within its field of vision that occur in less than one twenty-fourth of a second. When a camera captures a continuous series of images at a "frame rate" of twenty-four frames per second (fps), the eye will not notice the stillness of individual frames when they are projected onto a screen at the same speed; we see sequential action instead. It is a trick of the eye, in other words, that allows us to enjoy the illusions of the so-called silver screen.

Many tricks of the trade have been developed since the Lumière brothers (Louis and Auguste) first brought the cinema to a paying audience in 1895. Techniques such as varied shot depths, camera angles, special effects, and **parallel action** (discussed later in this chapter) form a language unique to the cinema, one which allows film to translate a rather modest illusion of motion into the remarkably complex (and often deeply fantasy-driven) illusions of cinematic storytelling. In order to write about film, a person must first learn to identify the methods used to create these illusions and to understand their effects, for as complex as the language of cinema is, it is a language that most viewers read passively—even unconsciously. To put it another way, in order to appreciate more fully the psychological and political (or ideological) import of the cinema's medium of light and sound, one needs to keep in focus the technical manipulations of film that typically fade behind the images that move across the cinematic screen.

This chapter has a twofold purpose: (a) to provide you with critical terms necessary to write about film and (b) to help you develop your skills as an active (rather than a passive) viewer of cinema. In addition to providing explanations and examples of major filmic devices, the chapter provides a theoretical reading demonstration that considers scenes from Danny Boyle's *Trainspotting* (1996) in light of Julia Kristeva's psychoanalytic work on abjection. A brief list of suggestions for further reading appears at the end of the chapter.

A QUICK NOTE ON TAKING NOTES

One of the biggest challenges in writing about film involves the availability and frequency of your access to a film's content. Whether the film about which you want to write is still in theatres or is available on videocassette or DVD, it is essential to make brief and accurate notes during and after your viewing of the film and, if possible, to view the film more than once. In *A Short Guide to Writing about Film*, Timothy Corrigan suggests developing a "shorthand system for technical information" for your notes; for instance, the letters "cu" could be short for "close up" and "povs" could stand for "point of view shot" (26). Camera movement in a scene could likewise be represented by drawing curved or straight lines with arrows indicating direction. Your instructor will expect citations from a movie to be as accurate as quotations from a book, so you will need to take extra care in transcribing dialogue, especially if the film is not (or not yet) available on DVD or videocassette. In addition to technical aspects and dialogue, you should also incorporate into your notes whatever ideas or questions occur to you about the film while you view it. These ideas and questions may later provide a foundation for your writing topic and/or thesis, or they may even reveal to you (as you re-read your notes) how the film attempted to manipulate your feelings and played on your expectations, which will obviously be of interest to you as you build your argument.

NARRATIVE, CHARACTER, AND POINT OF VIEW

Keeping good notes during and after your viewing of a film is particularly important for reconstructing a sense of the film's story and **plot**, keeping track of its **characters**, and reflecting on its **point(s) of view** as you work your way through the writing process. These are all structural elements that film has in common with fictional prose and drama (see Chapters 5 and 6); however, while they closely associate film with literary convention, these shared elements are often transformed by the unique conditions of film production. Elia Kazan's adaptation of Tennessee Williams's *A Streetcar Named Desire* (1951) offers a good case in point. Taking advantage of the cinematic camera's *mobility* (i.e., its apparent ability to move instantaneously from one location to the next), Kazan interpolates three scenes not found in the dramatic text where the film temporarily leaves the spatial confines of the dramatic stage. The first of these scenes depicts Blanche's confused arrival on screen in the midst of a hectic and steam-filled train station, the second illustrates Stanley's hooliganism in a similarly lively and crowded bowling alley, and the third captures a violent confrontation between Stanley and Mitch in a rather large and busy factory. Together, these three very chaotic scenes add an extra dimension to *Streetcar's* plot in that they point (more directly than Williams's text does) toward the powerful forces of alienation at work in the social world that surrounds and structures the main action of the play. This use of the camera's mobility is even more transformative in a movie such as Kenneth Branagh's 1996 adaptation of *Hamlet*, where panoramic views of marching armies and sublime landscapes help Branagh to convert the political and geographic environs of Prince Hamlet's story into a kind of Hollywood spectacle.

Characterization in film occurs in much the same way as it does in drama, where personality traits are revealed primarily through speech and action—although **voiceovers** allow film to communicate additional aspects of character in a manner similar to fictional prose. Like drama and prose fiction, narrative films are populated with a range of flat (one-dimensional) and round (multi-dimensional) characters, including **protagonists** (heroes), **antagonists** (villains), and major and minor characters. Some characters may even occupy a film's central perspective—in which case, the film is said to have a *subjective* **point of view** (the vantage point from which the story is conveyed). Less common in film than in fictional prose, subjective point of view can be extreme, as in the basement scene of *The Silence of the Lambs* (1991) where the viewer experiences the illusion of seeing through Buffalo Bill's night vision goggles as he stalks Clarice through the pitch-black rooms of his cellar, or it can be more subtly conveyed through a "subjective shot" that throws the view of the camera in the same general direction as the view of a character who may or may not be in the shot him or herself. Alfred Hitchcock uses this second type of shot to great effect in *Vertigo* (1958), throughout which the viewer is called upon to participate in Scottie's voyeuristic pursuit of Madeleine. Feeling as though we are standing next to him, we simultaneously look *with* and *at* Scottie as he investigates Madeleine's curious conduct. Part of Hitchcock's interest in having us watch someone watching someone else is to call attention to the irrepressible subjective position of the viewer in an industry dominated by movies filmed primarily from an *objective* point of view—movies such as *Gone With the Wind* (1939) or *Casablanca* (1942), where the camera switches between multiple (largely remote or detached) points of view. Whether objective of subjective, point of view invariably affects the way we perceive characters in a film. Characters closer to the camera will impress us differently than those farther away. The angle at which a character is filmed (be it from below, above, or behind) may likewise determine how we view that character from a moral or psychological standpoint. When writing about film, then, it is important to consider how the story and its characters are mediated by the positioning of the camera and the field of vision it enables.

Summary

NARRATIVE, CHARACTER, AND POINT OF VIEW

- film shares many structural elements with fictional prose and drama, including plot, character, and point of view

- characterization in film occurs in much the same way as it does in drama, where personality traits are revealed primarily through speech, dialogue, and action

  - characters can be flat (one-dimensional) or round (multi-dimensional); film also uses protagonists (heroes) and antagonists (villains)

- a film can have a *subjective* point of view, when a single character occupies the film's central perspective, or it may have an *objective* point of view, when the camera switches between multiple (largely remote or detached) points of view

---

MISE-EN-SCÈNE: STAGING THE SCENE

An important critical term in film studies that refers to elements "put into a scene," **mise-en-scène** reminds us that the sets and settings of narrative film, even when they appear realistic, are necessarily *staged* to one degree or another. At one end of the mise-en-scène spectrum is a movie such as *The Wizard of Oz* (1939), whose fantastical images of the Land of Oz (not to mention its more realistic depictions of Kansas) were filmed entirely inside the artificial sound stages of the Metro-Goldwyn-Mayer (MGM) Studios in Culver City, California. Even when movie sets venture outside the contrived environments of the Hollywood studio, the artifice of the stage sometimes follows; consider, for instance, the hollow building facades of stagecoach houses and saloons of classic Hollywood Westerns. At the more realistic end of the spectrum are scenes in movies that appear to be shot amid the hustle and bustle of actual human environments such as the city. Seduced by the realism of such scenes, viewers are motivated to view activity on screen as authentic rather than as the meticulously controlled product of cinematic composition. Such is the case with scenes in Stanley Kubrick's *Eyes Wide Shut* (1999), where Dr. Harford (played by Tom Cruise) dodges both cars and people while searching desperately for a costume in Greenwich Village. As Richard Barsam observes, these scenes "[seem] natural, chaotic, even haphazard—but this illusion has been constructed as carefully as every other one in the movie," including the film's most theatrical depictions of occult sexual activity (123). The visual "noise" of the Greenwich Village scenes is choreographed in such a way that they foreground the determination and focus of Cruise's character: we "note the urgency of his quest," notes Barsam, "not the details of [his] surroundings" (123). The point is that, regardless of whether they appear fantastical or realistic, movie sets generally contain elements (such as objects, props, costumes, crowds, lighting, and weather) that are not indigenous (i.e., original) to the scene itself, but are instead mise-en-scène—deliberately put in the scene to achieve certain calculated effects. Paying attention to these elements is an important part of film criticism, especially since they often contain clues to a scene's overall meaning or purpose.

Summary

MISE-EN-SCÈNE: STAGING THE SCENE

- mise-en-scène refers to elements that are "put into a scene"
    - these include elements such as objects, props, costumes, crowds, lighting, and weather
    - the elements are not indigenous (original) to the scene itself, but are instead deliberately placed there to achieve certain calculated effects

---

CINEMATOGRAPHY: COMPOSING AND FRAMING THE SHOT

If mise-en-scène refers to what is put into a scene, then cinematography refers to the way a scene is framed and filmed by the camera. It refers, in other words, to the camera's mediation of a film's **action** (i.e., events that take place in a drama, narrative, or film). Different kinds of shots—filmed at different speeds, from different angles, with different tones—elicit different emotional and psychological responses, and thus they influence the viewer's perception of what he or she sees on the screen. Just imagine how our perception of Andy and Larry Wachowski's *The Matrix* (1999) would change were its fight scenes not mediated by variable-speed photography that shifts seamlessly between dramatic slow and accelerated motion. Think also of the remarkable opening scene of *Star Wars* (1977), where an upward-facing camera angle transforms a miniature three-foot model into Darth Vader's massive, screen-dominating Imperial Star Destroyer. And finally, we might consider the determinate effects of tone in a movie like *The Wizard of Oz*, whose spectacular shift from "black-and-white" (actually sepia tones) to brilliant three-strip Technicolor helped make Dorothy's arrival in Oz one of the most celebrated moments in Hollywood history. These shots from *The Matrix*, *Star Wars*, and *The Wizard of Oz* all demonstrate how aspects of cinematography not only mediate the viewer's engagement with the story but are also integral to each film's conversion of story into plot. In *The Matrix*, variable-speed photography is crucial in enabling the viewer to witness Neo's progressively more skillful manipulation of time and space in his quest to become "the One" who will save humanity from the Matrix. Likewise, George Lucas's clever angling of his anamorphic camera lens in *Star Wars* visually captures the desperate plight of Princess Leia's Rebel forces against an Imperial military of epic proportions. Last, but certainly not least, the contrast between Technicolor Oz and sepia-toned Kansas thematically augments *The Wizard of Oz*'s sentimental treatment of illusion versus reality.

Other equally important aspects of cinematography include a shot's depth of focus, its movement, and its distance from its subject. In terms of depth, a shot can be *shallow*, meaning that characters in the foreground remain in focus, while those in the background appear blurry; or a shot can be *deep*, meaning that characters are in focus no matter where they are. The effect of shot depth is rather straightforward: shallow focus emphasizes action in the foreground, while deep focus accentuates the importance of the background as well. Camera movement can also underscore action in significant ways: whereas camera *tracking* allows the viewer to remain close to a film's action, a *crane* shot pulls the viewer up and away in stereotypically dramatic fashion. A *pan* shot can evoke a sense of grandeur, while a *hand-held* shot typically enhances a film's sense of realism. In terms of distance, a shot can be framed within extreme proximity to its subject, as in the **close-up**, which frames the significance of particular objects or the emotional import of facial expressions, or the shot may strategically frame its subject from a distance in order to call attention to the subject's relationship with its surroundings. Like its depth of focus and its movement, a shot's distance from its subject can drastically influence the viewer's perception of a film's objects, characters, and action. So you will want to ask yourself whether (and why) the viewer sees only a part or all of a character in a scene, and whether (and why) that character is alone on screen or in view with other characters.

You might also consider *where* a character appears within the frame—is he or she near the centre or off to one side of the frame? How and where things appear on screen make up a film's composition, its framing of plot and action. Like composition in painting, composition in film is essential and must therefore be addressed when writing about film.

Summary

CINEMATOGRAPHY: COMPOSING AND FRAMING THE SHOT

- cinematography refers to the way a scene is framed and captured by the camera

- shots filmed at different speeds from different angles with different tones elicit different emotional responses and thus influence the viewer's perception of what appears on screen

- other important aspects of cinematography include

  - a shot's *depth of focus* (e.g., shallow or deep)

  - its *movement* (via tracking shots, crane shots, pan shots, hand-held shots, etc.)

  - its *distance* from its subject (e.g., the extreme proximity of the close-up, or distance shots that call attention to the subject's relationship with its surroundings)

EDITING THE IMAGE

Unlike most composition in painting, the composition of a single cinematic shot necessarily involves the shot's relation to other shots that precede and follow it. Reflecting on cinematic composition therefore requires us to think also about the way a film's sequence of moving images has been edited (i.e., assembled together). Among the most common sequences of edited shots in film are those that depict a conversation across a kitchen or restaurant table where characters eat a meal or share drinks. Such scenes are typically composed of multiple shots from different angles and at various ranges that, when spliced or "cut" together, enable contiguous alternating points of view on the same conversation. This kind of editing thus facilitates a perspective that is at least partially omniscient and may even heighten the viewer's voyeuristic pleasure: occupying several places within the same scene, the camera lets us enjoy not only the feeling of eavesdropping on a conversation but also the freedom to scrutinize, openly and at close range, each character's physical gestures and emotional responses.

It needs to be said that the pleasures and illusions made possible by this kind of editing are most effective when the viewer remains more or less unaware of the editing process. The visual culture of the twentieth and twenty-first centuries has taught the viewer of cinema to perceive edited shifts in perspective in a manner similar to the way readers of literary works read punctuation—that is to say, intuitively or unconsciously. While edited cuts organize and control the way a viewer relates to a film, they typically work to produce a rhythm that is intelligible but not conspicuous enough to distract attention away from a film's action. Writing thoughtfully about film thus requires a certain vigilance toward editing, an alertness to the silent ways that a film tries to manipulate our visual senses.

When a film cuts back and forth between two or more scenes, the viewer witnesses the illusion of **parallel action**—that is, of watching two or more events in different locations simultaneously. The procedure for constructing this illusion is called **crosscutting** or *parallel editing*. Crosscutting between parallel actions was first used (for comedic purposes) in the French film *Le cheval emballé* (1908), the opening scene of which features a delivery man running errands inside an apartment building while outside his wayward horse consumes a bag of oats that belongs to the general store of the adjacent building.[1] Since then, crosscutting has allowed filmmakers to tell increasingly complex stories. It has become a conventional way of making metaphorical comparisons between characters or actions in different situations. It is regularly used to portray actions that occur on either side of a telephone conversation, along different routes travelled to the same destination, or at opposite ends of a battlefield. Among its most dramatic and emotionally satisfying functions, however, is its ability to heighten the viewer's sense of suspense—as in the many scenes from Steven Spielberg's *Jaws* (1975) in which above-water shots of unsuspecting swimmers are crosscut with underwater shots that invoke the point of view of the film's infamous great white shark.

Related to editing is the use of **special effects**. Early filmmakers discovered that if a stationary camera was stopped and then restarted during the shooting of a scene, people in that scene could be made to appear to jump from one place to another or disappear altogether. This special effect, one of the first of its kind, was used as early as 1902 in *A Trip to the Moon*, which featured moon creatures called Selenites that exploded into dust when attacked. Another important early special effect was the invention of what Russian director Sergei Eisenstein called "dialectical montage," whereby two or more unrelated shots—such as one shot of a raised cudgel and another of a bloody face—are edited together to produce the effect of a causal relation (i.e., the cudgel is made to look as though it caused

---

1 *The Great Train Robbery* (1903) is cited as the first film to use parallel editing insofar as it depicts actions occurring in multiple locations through a series of long shots; but it cannot be said to crosscut *between* these locations as quickly as—or in the back-and-forth manner of—the opening sequence of *Le cheval emballé*.

the bloody face). Perhaps the most famous example of dialectical montage occurs in the "Odessa Steps" sequence from Eisenstein's *Battleship Potemkin* (1925): overhead shots of a baby in a carriage are crosscut with variously angled shots of the same carriage careening out of control and down the massive staircase of the Odessa Steps. The viewer cannot see the baby in the second set of shots, but the whole sequence gives the startling impression that the baby not only is still in the carriage but will also most certainly be injured when it reaches the bottom. This special effect has become a standard technique in manufacturing the illusion of danger in action films such as *Mission: Impossible* (1996) and *The Bourne Identity* (2002), or in the final scene of *Thelma & Louise* (1991), in which the titular heroines drive their 1966 Thunderbird off a cliff. Special effects have evolved dramatically since the early days of the cinema, especially with the advent of computer-generated imagery (CGI), but the premise is more or less the same—to create or alter imaginative on-screen realities by manipulating technologies available either on set or during the phases of post-production (i.e., after shooting). When writing about film, the trick is to analyze how such effects contribute to other aspects of a film, such the film's plot, theme, and metaphorical significance.

Summary

EDITING THE IMAGE

- reflecting on cinematic composition requires us to think also about the way a film's sequence of moving images has been edited

- when a film cuts back and forth between two or more scenes, the viewer witnesses the illusion of *parallel action*—that is, of watching events in different locations simultaneously

- the procedure for constructing the illusion of parallel action is called *crosscutting* or *parallel editing*

- special effects are used to create or alter imaginative on-screen realities by manipulating technologies available either on set or during the phases of post-production

READING DEMONSTRATION: *TRAINSPOTTING* AND KRISTEVAN PSYCHOANALYSIS

A good deal of psychoanalytic application in film studies falls under the category of "cine-psychoanalysis," which considers film in terms of the viewer's pleasure. One of the best-known practitioners of cine-psychoanalysis, Laura Mulvey, argues that most Hollywood films require both male and female spectators to assume a heterosexual male perspective or "gaze" in order to enjoy the cinema's two predominant sources of visual pleasure: (a) *scopophilia*, which triggers the voyeuristic fantasy of "taking other people as objects [and] subjecting them to a controlling and curious gaze" and (b) *ego identification*, which enables viewers to identify with members of the Hollywood "star system" (37). For Mulvey, this structure of cinematic pleasure alienates the female spectator and reinforces gender stereotypes.

While recommending Mulvey's article "Visual Pleasure and Narrative Cinema," this reading demonstration departs from cine-psychoanalysis by developing a Kristevan approach to the 1996 film *Trainspotting*, directed by Danny Boyle. In Julia Kristeva's psychoanalytic writings on abjection, she defines the "abject" as a culturally "jettisoned object," which is to say, an object that is "radically excluded" from the realm of a person's everyday symbolic life—for example, a corpse, or the grossly substandard living conditions of Third World poverty (2). When we are suddenly confronted by the abject (e.g., by a dead body or by images of dilapidated slum dwellings), it threatens our sense of identity and our understanding of the world around us. As Kristeva says, it "draws me toward the place where meaning collapses" (2). For Kristeva, the psychological process of "abjection" amounts to a kind of psychical defence through which the individual turns away from the abject in disgust. Nauseated by what we see, we feel a visceral need to purge ourselves of the abject in an attempt to reconstitute our own identity.

Using Kristeva's model of psychological abjection, we can propose the following thesis about *Trainspotting*: the film not only chronicles **protagonist** Mark Renton's abject encounters with the dehumanizing conditions of his own heroin addiction, it also presents a series of disturbing scenes that invite the viewer to participate in, rather than simply witness, Renton's experiences of abjection. Turning in disgust from the movie's more graphic images, in other words, the viewer endures feelings of nausea and revulsion that parallel Renton's various attempts to purge his body and his life of the "junk" of heroin addition.

The first of these graphic images occurs in a scene that takes place in "the worst toilet in Scotland." Just prior to this scene, we are shown a **montage** (i.e., a sequence of edited shots) that captures Renton's first attempt to quit heroin. We see Renton prepare for the symptoms of withdrawal by locking himself in a room that he has meticulously stocked with soup, ice cream, various prescription and over-the-counter drugs (such as Valium and paracetamol), and a series of buckets ("one . . . for urine, one for feces and one for vomitus"). The montage ends ironically with Renton breaking out of the room in search of "one final hit." In the next shot, we learn that the only heroin that his dealer has to offer comes in the form of slow-release suppositories, which Renton reluctantly accepts and inserts into his rectum. Before the suppositories have had a chance to dissolve, Renton is afflicted with diarrhea, one of the first symptoms of heroin withdrawal. Finding his way to the so-called worst toilet in Scotland, Renton evacuates his bowels before realizing that the suppositories have likewise been expelled into the appallingly unhygienic bowl. Desperate to recover the drugs, Renton thrusts his hands into the polluted water only to have his entire body magically pulled into the toilet. Beneath his own waste he discovers a vast and pristine body of water, at the bottom of which he finds the suppositories. Swimming upward toward a bright light, Renton exits the toilet bowl apparently rejuvenated and with renewed conviction: "and now," he says, "now I'm ready." According to film critic Christine L. Harold, this scene illustrates how Renton cannot simply quit heroin without confronting the abject filth of his addiction; rather, in order to transform from "junkie" to "socially acceptable" member of society, "Renton must dive head first into his own waste to encounter the abjectness of his very being" (872).

Unfortunately, the toilet scene does not represent for Renton a permanent transformation, nor is it the only scene to invoke unpleasant imagery designed to inspire the viewer's disgust. Perhaps the most disturbing scene in *Trainspotting* deals with the discovery of baby Dawn's dead body. Dawn can be seen in some of the film's earliest scenes crawling unsupervised throughout the dangerously rundown apartment where her mother routinely "shoots up." In one of these scenes, we see Dawn cooing playfully next to her mother's unconscious body with used needles, rubber tourniquets, and other abandoned drug paraphernalia carelessly strewn across the floor around her. Although these images of egregious neglect provide clues as to how or why Dawn turns up dead halfway through the film, they hardly prepare the viewer for the deeply unsettling **close-up** of Dawn as she lies lifeless in her crib, already showing noticeable signs of decay. When Sick Boy (the baby's father) demands that Renton "say something" to break the unbearable tension caused by the discovery of Dawn's body, Renton can only stare blankly at Sick Boy before managing finally to say, "I'm cooking up." In the next room, Dawn's seemingly inconsolable mother crawls over to where Renton is preparing his next dose; she holds forth a needle, rolls up her sleeve, and begs, "Cook us up a shot, Mark. I need a hit." The scene is arguably more difficult to watch than any other in the film. The baby's discoloured cadaver is nothing if not abject, and Renton's and her mother's reactions to her death are profoundly demoralizing. Dawn's death represents a new low; however, instead of inspiring transformative change, the abject propels Renton and his friends on a course of self-destruction: "our only response," Renton tells us, "was to keep on going and fuck everything, pile misery upon misery, heap it up in a spoon and dissolve it with a drop of bile, and squirt it into a stinkin' purulent vein and do it all over again." It is not until Renton nearly dies of an overdose, throughout which he consistently resembles an inert corpse, that he is finally able, with the help of his parents, to transform his identity and quit the "junk."

The film's conclusion, however, is not the happy ending that the viewer—having accompanied Renton through his course of abjection—might hope for or expect. Leaving behind all remnants of a life of addiction with a passport in one hand and a bag of cash in the other, Renton claims he is "going to change;" he plans on "cleaning up and . . . moving on, going straight and choosing life." Walking toward the camera, his grinning face blurring increasingly out of focus, Renton speaks directly to the viewer: "I'm looking forward to it already. I'm going to be just like you." Given his many **voiceovers** throughout the film that persistently satirize the empty consumerism of "sober" society, the viewer cannot help but interpret these lines as ironic. We are told he will choose *our* life, by which he means a life driven by an insatiable appetite for commodities: "the job, the family, the fucking big television, the washing machine, the car, the compact disc and electric tin opener, good health, low cholesterol, dental insurance, mortgage, starter home, leisure wear, luggage, three-piece suite, DIY, game shows, junk food, children, walks in the park, nine-to-five" and so on. As the list continues and the film fades to black, the viewer is left to ponder one of the film's difficult questions: is drug addiction the abject reflection of consumer culture? Do we see something of ourselves in the figure of the addict? Inviting the viewer to participate in Renton's experience of abjection, *Trainspotting* invites us to compare the *substance* of "healthy" and "unhealthy" forms of consumption.

WORKS CITED

Barsam, Richard. *Looking at Movies: An Introduction to Film.* 3rd ed. New York: Norton, 2009. Print.

Corrigan, Timothy. *A Short Guide to Writing about Film.* 7th ed. New York: Pearson Longman, 2009. Print.

Harold, Christine L. "The Rhetorical Function of the Abject Body: Transgressive Corporeality in *Trainspotting.*" *Journal of Advanced Composition* 20 (Fall 2000): 865–81. Print.

Kristeva, Julia. *Powers of Horror: An Essay on Subjection.* New York: Columbia UP, 1982. Print.

Mulvey, Laura. "Visual Pleasure and Narrative Cinema." *Feminism and Film.* Ed. E. Ann Kaplan. Oxford: Oxford UP, 2000. 39–47. Print.

Trainspotting. Dir. Danny Boyle. 1996. Miramax, 2004. DVD.

Part 3

Outlines, Drafts, and Revisions

In order to develop a thesis and produce a first draft of your essay, you will first need to consider many of the topics discussed in Chapters 3 through 7. Whether or not you intend to use a particular critical approach in your essay, it is still a good idea to familiarize yourself with the different schools of literary and cultural criticism outlined in Chapter 3. One of these schools might capture your interest and inspire you to write an essay in a way you might not otherwise have known was possible. Chapters 4 through 7 on literary genres and film will likewise be of interest to you before constructing an outline or writing a draft of your paper, because, presumably, the text(s) on which you want to write will belong to one or more of these genres, each of which has its own formal elements and characteristics. Acquainting yourself with these will therefore help you to brainstorm and organize your ideas in the preliminary stages of writing your essay. Chapters 4 through 7 are also useful insofar as they provide reading demonstrations and examples of student writing, so it makes sense to consult these chapters prior to "Following Through on the Writing Process."

STAGE 1: FROM THESIS TO OUTLINE

In Chapter 2, we considered different kinds of writing assignments and strategies for building a thesis out of a writing topic. This chapter will continue along those lines by reviewing the entire writing process behind the student sample essay that appears in Chapter 4, from its outline stage to the final draft. That essay corresponded to an assignment that offered multiple topics for a non-research paper. Of these, the student chose the following:

> Using specific examples from the text to support your own original thesis and argument, discuss how the *tone* and/or *speaker* of one or more poems from the textbook's sections on "Tone" and "Speaker" contribute to the overall meaning of the poem(s).

With this very broad topic in mind, the student wrote a paper on the speaker and tone of Audre Lorde's "Hanging Fire."* Before reviewing the student's work, we should read the poem:[1]

Hanging Fire

speaker's identity is quickly established → i.e., a young girl–possibly African-American like the poet herself

I am <u>fourteen</u>
and <u>my skin</u> has (betrayed) me

possible pun–i.e., exposes and undermines her

the <u>boy</u> I cannot live without

boyfriend is immature–why the line break?

still sucks his thumb
in secret

how come my knees are
always so ashy
<u>what if I die</u>
before morning

odd juxtaposition of trivial concerns and a (possibly exaggerated) fear of death

repeated at the end of every stanza →

and momma's in the bedroom
with the door closed

another juxtaposition of trivial concerns and a fear of death →

I have to learn how to dance
in time for the next party
my room is too small for me
suppose I die before graduation
they will sing sad melodies
but finally
tell the (truth about me)

what is this "truth"

speaker feels pressured by something →

There is nothing I want to do
and too much
that has to be done

odd punctuation– creates a sense of jumbled, disconnected thoughts and emotions

repetition →

and momma's in the bedroom
with the door closed

Nobody even stops to think
about my side of it

---

1 Annotations (i.e., markups) on the poem reflect issues related to the student sample's focus. Again, it is always a good idea to mark up a photocopy of a poem when writing about poetry.

*"Hanging Fire". Copyright © 1978 by Audre Lorde, from *The Collected Poems of Audre Lorde* by Audre Lorde. Used by permission of W.W. Norton & Company, Inc.

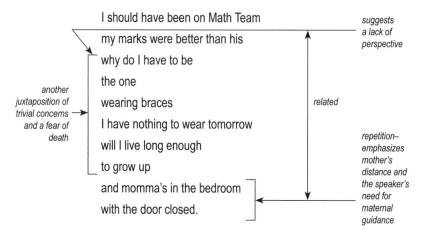

Drawn to the speaker's gloomy reflections on growing up with a neglectful mother, the student sought to explicate—and thus better understand—this poem's melancholy tone through close literary analysis. The student's earliest thesis statement consisted of the following two sentences:

> The lonely tone in which the poem is written and the youthful immaturity of the speaker combine to display the speaker's lostness without her mother. This stresses that a young person requires constructive involvement from a reliable mother figure for proper personal development.

If these sentences fail to sparkle, they nevertheless represented a good start for a student who knew there would be plenty of time to refine her thesis throughout the writing process. In the early stages of drafting your essay, it is sometimes best to focus less on perfection and more on sketching out the basic ideas of your argument. Even though she was not completely satisfied with her use of language, the student was happy that her first thesis statement successfully connected the tone of Lorde's poem with what she believed was its overall message.

After crafting an initial thesis statement, a useful next step is to create an outline of your essay that plots the essay's overall structure. Again, the point is to focus less on your use of language and more on organizing what you want to say in an effective and logical manner. To recall our metaphor of the court lawyer in Chapter 1, the outline is where you will first begin building your "case"—the *argument* you will use to support your thesis statement. Typically, lawyers build their case by organizing whatever evidence they have into a series of main points that can be easily referred to and summarized in a closing statement to the jury. Try thinking of your outline in these terms. Instead of murder weapons, forensic reports, or eyewitness testimony, your evidence will consist mainly of citations from the text and references to secondary sources. Since facts rarely speak for themselves, your outline will need to explain (if only for your own benefit) how your citations and references relate to one another and how they support your overall thesis. In other words, you will need to ask yourself what *arrangement* of the facts will make the most compelling case.

The student's outline for her essay on Audre Lorde's "Hanging Fire" arranged—and briefly summarized—its three main points as follows:

Outline for an essay on Audre Lorde's "Hanging Fire"

Introduction   Set up and state the paper's thesis:
"The lonely tone in which the poem is written and the youthful immaturity of the speaker combine to display the speaker's lostness without her mother. This stresses that a young person requires constructive involvement from a reliable mother figure for proper personal development."

1st Main Point   Discuss how the speaker identifies herself:
(a) she is young ("I am fourteen") and immature (i.e., she uses an illogical and haphazard manner of expression)
(b) she is lonely – the poem expresses a tone of detachment and abandonment – this is especially evident in her repetition of the phrase "and momma's in the bedroom / with the door closed"

2nd Main Point   (a) transition from previous main point to discuss how the speaker's loneliness and immaturity leave her feeling lost, confused, and in need of guidance
(b) the speaker's confusion and lack of direction are most obvious when she expresses her exaggerated fear of dying ("what if I die?")
(c) return to the repeated phrase about her mother's absence, which frames her fears and reinforces the importance of maternal guidance

3rd Main Point   return to the speaker's identity and discuss the importance of her being (a) a young girl, and (b) African American – i.e., how are these relevant to the poem's message about maternal guidance?

Conclusion   discuss the speaker's dissatisfaction with her mother's unavailability and recap the thesis in light of points 1, 2, and 3

We will discuss the usefulness of "transitional sentences" in the next section, but it is worth mentioning here that this well-organized outline already demonstrates how its main points will build on and reinforce one another. This strategy has multiple related benefits. First, it allows you to identify what logic, if any, motivates your argument. Second, by making your logic visible in your outline you will be better able to abide by—and *develop*—that logic throughout the writing process. And finally, it stands to reason that the more discernible your logic is, the more credible your paper will appear. After all, a reader who fails to follow your argument will most likely also fail to be convinced by your thesis.

Apart from providing a compelling structure for subsequent drafts, the outline above projects a manageable scope for the student's essay, which is an important objective for any good outline. The assignment asked the student to write a four- to five-page paper. Each of the student's three main points can be made, rather comfortably, within the space of a single page, and the introduction and conclusion would likely combine to add another full page. The outline thus forecasts an essay of approximately four pages, which would leave the student with a one-page margin to expand her argument, if necessary, during the revision stages.

STAGE 2: THE FIRST DRAFT

Once you have written your outline, you are ready to write your first draft. First drafts are meant to be "rough," so there is no need to fret over getting it right the first time. At this early stage, you are more or less trying to translate your point-form outline into a more or less comprehensible string of sentences. You should always leave yourself time to revise this first draft before submitting your paper either to the instructor or to other students (or friends) for peer review. The draft below, for instance, is good as a draft but is not really in any shape to be submitted. Although the student has already revised the language of her initial thesis so that it is less awkward and more direct, her introduction could be expanded (as it will be in later drafts) to give the reader a better sense of what the paper proposes to accomplish. A sentence or two on the method of the paper would be helpful, for instance. Nevertheless, this early version of the introduction shows much promise insofar as it manages to avoid clichés and platitudes (i.e., moralizing stereotypes), which, given the poem's subject of maternal responsibility, is no small accomplishment for a first-year introduction.

One of the more teachable aspects of this early draft pertains to the paper's interesting history with regard to the racial aspects of Lorde's poem. In addition to offering an example of how a paper develops through multiple drafts, this student's paper offers an object lesson on the difficulty that questions of race pose to literary criticism. The student exhibits a slight awkwardness—perhaps even a lack of confidence—in her handling of the poem's racial context (see the third-to-last paragraph of the draft below). She continues to struggle with this context in subsequent drafts and will even remove the discussion altogether in a future draft before returning to it in the final version. We should remind ourselves, however, that the student's difficulty with the poem's evocation of race is only fitting, since one of the functions of literature (and of Lorde's poem in particular) is to make us think twice about the way we view and inhabit the world around us.

Annotations on the essay indicate areas in need of improvement.

First Complete Rough Draft (untitled)

Audre Lorde's poem "Hanging Fire" is spoken by a lonely woman going through puberty without a mother's influence. The <u>lonely tone</u> in which the poem

awkward — is written and the speaker's lack of personal direction together express the

passive voice — poem's theme that a young person requires meaningful involvement from a

reliable mother in order to mature. ⌉ *thesis requires further elaboration*

maybe address the speaker's race, which is implied in line 2

The speaker is a fourteen-year old girl going through puberty. This is clear from the direct statements she makes about herself such as "I am fourteen" (1), indicating her youth, and "the boy I cannot live without" (3), indicating her femininity. Her immaturity is evident indirectly through the way she expresses

use more formal language

herself. She uses short, choppy phrases <u>piled on top</u> of one another in a haphazard manner. Moving though topics quickly she discusses her displeasure at being excluded from the math team, wearing braces, having nothing to wear, insecurity over growing up, and her mother's unavailability, all in one short stanza. This uninterrupted flow of exaggerated, unimportant worries indicates

avoid generalizations — a scattered thought pattern common among those going through puberty. ⌉

The girl is alone and lonely. The disjointed way she <u>throws her thoughts</u>

informal — together creates a tone of detachment and abandonment. She also repeats

the phrase "and momma's in the bedroom / with the door closed," indicating

that she wishes she had ^the^ support of her mother. Instead she faces the coldness of a closed door. The fact that she finds her mother's absence significant enough to close each stanza by expressing it underscores its importance to her. Her mention that "the boy [she] cannot live without / still sucks his thumb / in secret" (3-5) shows that even the boy she loves is incapable of supporting her through when she feels lost. She is alone in the world, trying to survive high school, confounded by the problems that plague young teens, and wishing that "momma" would open the symbolic door and help her to make sense of all the things coming at her.

awkward reference

informal

    The speaker's lack of direction gives the poem a discontented undertone, evidence of the emotional turmoil she experiences in her youth. She repeats the question "what if I die?" (8) followed by three different times in her future, all before she grows up. Each time that the speaker voices her worry concerning death, she rephrases it, but no matter the wording her insecurity about life is always evident. The poem's silence regarding anything that threatens her life suggests that her fears are unfounded and simply the result of her journey through puberty - puberty because she identifies herself as being fourteen years in line two. She has nothing to fear, thus her repetition of this illogical worry betrays her unstable emotional state.

    The speaker's concern about her own death is connected to the fact that her mother is not actively giving her guidance as she matures. These are the only two ideas repeated this clearly throughout "Hanging Fire" and they always appear in the same order in the stanza. Each reference to her own death questions if it will arrive before she becomes who she is going to be. She wonders if she'll die before she "grow[s] up" (33), which, while combined with the conclusion that "momma's in the bedroom / with the door closed" indicates that her mother's unavailability is a factor in her possible death.

requires further elaboration

explain further

needs to be recast in clearer, more direct sentences →

The youth of the speaker is necessary for the reader to remain open-minded toward the message presented. If someone already grown up spoke about the need for mothers to be involved in their children's lives it would sound more like a lecture or sermon, as though they were telling others what they should do. Someone experiencing the hardships of growing up alone is allowed

passive voice ——

to talk about their own experiences without incurring the judgment of the reader, which would detract from the poem.

The fact that the speaker is a girl is important because the expression of a female's feelings is more likely to arouse compassion than if a male expressed himself in the same way because of the dual standards for men and women that exist in many societies. A belief more common in the past but still held by

– generalizations – recast →

many today is that men should deal with their emotions in private, rather than speak them freely. The standard for women, on the other hand, is different, and

for women

it is perfectly acceptable to females to voice their emotions. A young man would have to address the belief in society that it is feminine to express emotions before he could give voice to his insecurities without being shrugged off. It is

informal ——

much simpler for a female to speak this way because it is already assumed

woman ——

that there is nothing wrong with her for doing so. For these reasons it is more effective for the speaker of "Hanging Fire" to be female so that her message is

needs to be acknowledged earlier →

taken seriously.

I believe that she is African American and believes that because her skin is black it has betrayed her by placing her in an underprivileged group of people. It is likely that the speaker has black skin because of the mention of her "ashy" knees (7), which could refer to the dry skin problem common among African Americans which causes the skin on the elbows and knees to turn "ashy" as the

needs a reference or a source ——

skin dries. This is supported by her complaint that a position on a math team was unfairly given to another. If she actually did have better marks than the boy

that got the spot [her skin color could be a reason why she was not chosen.] This   *speculative– there is no mention of the boy's race*

is all the more likely because the poem was published in 1978, right after the

Black Power Movement and Lorde herself considered herself a black feminist   *develop this reference*

(Kulii, Reuman, and Trapasso).

[The lonely tone in which the] ^The ^'s speaker ^emotional tone expresses herself] suggests that

she is not content with her mother's lack of involvement in her life. Without the

lonely way she speaks the reader could conclude that she enjoys the freedom

and independence she has. The lonely tone is necessary to inform the reader

that a mother's influence is desired and needed for a teen to "grow up".

[A second feature repeated in the poem is the unavailability of the mother.]   *sounds repetitive– recast*

She is always portrayed as being behind a closed door. What she is doing back

there seems to be something of ill-repute as it is not identified and the bedroom   *awkward*

setting alludes to a sexual encounter. But no matter what she is doing, what

is certain is that she is unavailable and that her daughter is not pleased about

this. [It is important to the daughter that she have access to her mother and is

the fact that she does not bothers her enough to close each stanza with the

sentiment.]   *unclear grammar*

This draft is not without its flaws. For one thing, its tone is perhaps too clinical when it speaks, for instance, of the so-called "thought patterns" of youth. The paper also tends to under-appreciate some of the speaker's problems, particularly when referring to the speaker's "unimportant worries." Despite these flaws, however, this first draft has much to recommend it. In particular, its paragraph structure and organization are quite good. Each paragraph begins with a strong *topic sentence*—that is, a sentence that immediately establishes the topic of the paragraph. Topic sentences tend to be direct (e.g., from the second paragraph: "The speaker is a fourteen-year old girl going through puberty"), and they keep the reader focused on the argument. They are especially effective when they facilitate a transition from the topic of the preceding paragraph, in which case the topic sentence functions simultaneously as a *transitional sentence*. The student's transitional sentences are perhaps the strongest aspect of her draft. She uses them to great effect in almost every paragraph, but the following sentence from the fifth paragraph is most exemplary: "The speaker's concern about her own death is connected to the fact that her mother is not actively giving her guidance as she matures." This sentence harnesses the topic of the previous paragraph (namely, the speaker's exaggerated fear of death) and connects that topic to the topic of a new paragraph. The transition allows the paper, in other words, to move from one point to the next in a manner that is both clear and logical.

STAGE 3: REVISING THE FIRST DRAFT

A good strategy for revising your first draft is to read it aloud to yourself. Hearing your own language may alert you to grammatical issues or "leaps" in the logic of your argument. A leap in logic occurs when a sequence of related ideas is missing a mediating element or idea that is required for other ideas in the sequence to make sense. We make leaps in logic when we assume the reader will implicitly know what we mean, when in fact the reader may need further elaboration in order to understand. Reading your paper out loud to yourself will sometimes help you hear what is missing. You might also try re-reading the text(s) you are analyzing after writing your first draft; you might discover something you missed in a previous reading that will motivate you to develop or change your argument in some way. The point of revising is obviously to improve the paper, so you should be prepared to re-read and rewrite at every stage of the writing process.

The second draft of the student essay on "Hanging Fire" represents a significant improvement from the first draft. The student's introduction is expanded to include not only the thesis but a statement on the paper's method, as well. The first draft's vague reference to "scattered thought pattern[s] common among those going through puberty" has been transformed into a thoughtful analysis of the *language* through which the speaker's "disjointed" thoughts are expressed. In this respect, the paper has matured from merely saying something about the poem to performing something much closer to literary criticism. The paper is especially effective when it cites—then directly analyzes—what it calls the poem's "ambiguous word choice" (see paragraph 9). This combination of citation and analysis is the lifeblood of literary criticism: it binds the interpretation of a poem to concrete proof in the form of textual evidence. Finally, unlike the first draft, the second draft is far more confident (and articulate) in its concluding paragraphs. See if you can detect other ways in which the second draft develops the first. (Once again, annotations indicate areas in need of continued improvement.)

Second Draft (untitled)

Audre Lorde's poem "Hanging Fire" is spoken by a lonely, young woman, experiencing the confusing hormonal changes of puberty without a mother's guidance. The lonely tone in which the poem is written, and the speaker's lack *— awkward* of personal direction, together express the poem's theme that a girl requires *teenaged — passive voice* the meaningful involvement from a reliable mother in order to mature. This paper will analyse what can be learned about the speaker from the text, identify *repetitive word choice* the theme, and analyse how the speaker's identity affects the meaning of the poem. The speaker's identity empowers the poem's message, making it palatable to the reader. *— unclear*

The most apparent information presented about the speaker is that she is a fourteen year old girl going through puberty. This is clear from the direct *— discuss the implied race of the speaker* statements she makes about herself, such as "I am fourteen" (1), indicating her youth; and "the boy I cannot live without" (3), indicating er femininity. Her adolescent immaturity is shown indirectly through the way she expresses herself. Moving though topics quickly she discusses her displeasure at being excluded from the math team, wearing braces, having nothing to wear, worry*ing* over growing up, and her mother's unavailability, all in one short stanza (24-35). These worries—all save the concern about lack of motherly involvement— are insignificant when one considers the brevity of her stage of life and their *— awkward reference* superficial nature. This uninterrupted flow of exaggerated, unimportant worries indicates an illogical thought pattern common among those going through puberty. *— avoid generalization*

The girl's lonely emotional state is expressed in different ways throughout *— passive voice* the poem. One way is through the disjointed way she compiles her thoughts.

informal

The speaker uses short, choppy phrases piled on top of one another in a haphazard manner. Each stanza contains no punctuation, save a period in closure. This causes the reader to rush through the jumbled thoughts, pausing only at the end of the collage of ideas that forms each of the speaker's sentences. This creates a lonely tone of detachment and abandonment as

requires further elaboration

each thought is cut short and abandoned before it is fully expressed.

Another expression of the speaker's loneliness is found in the repetition of the phrase "and momma's in the bedroom / with the door closed" (10-11, 23-24, 34-35). The door here acts as a symbol for an invisible barrier set up between the mother and daughter, keeping them from communicating meaningfully.

that is

Each stanza is a list of complaints concluded by the statement that "momma's in the bedroom / with the door closed". The speaker seems to see her mother's inaccessibility as the culmination of all her problems; indeed they are all amplified by their separation. The speaker laments the closed door, wishing she had the support of her mother, but instead she faces the coldness of a door she cannot, or will not, open. By closing each stanza by expressing her

awkward repetition

mother's unavailability the speaker underscores its importance to her.

A third way that the speaker shows her loneliness is through her commentary on the boy she cares for. Her mention that "the boy [she] cannot live

indicates

without / still sucks his thumb / in secret" (3-5) shows that even her boyfriend is incapable of supporting her. The repeated S sound in the last two of these lines imitates the sound of the boy sucking his thumb, adding to the immature picture she paints of the object of her affection. He, quite understandably, is

word choice

not yet mature enough to help her navigate the early teen world. This leaves the speaker to deal with her problems single-handedly, as the two people who arguably mean the most to her (her mother and boyfriend) are not offering guidance. She is alone in the world, trying to survive high school, confounded by the problems that plague young teens, and wishing that "momma" would open the door and help her to make sense of all the trials of adolescence.

The speaker is ~~insecure~~ of her ability to navigate her way to adulthood *uncertain* on her own. She repeats the question "what if I die?" (8) three times, followed by different times in the near future, up until she grows up. Each time that the *clarify* speaker voices her worry concerning death, she rephrases it, but her insecurity about life is always evident. The poem's silence regarding anything that could *are* threaten her life suggests that her fears are unfounded and simply the result of her journey through adolescence. She has nothing to fear, thus her repetition *do we really know this?* of this illogical worry betrays her unstable emotional state.

Another fact that can be deduced about the speaker is that she is African-American. She claims that "[her] skin has betrayed [her]" (2) because its colour has placed her in an unfavoured group of people. Her mention of her *develop this* "ashy knees" (5-6), refers to a dry skin problem called keritanized dehydrated disorder, which is common among African Americans and causes the skin on the elbows and knees to turn "ashy" as the skin dries (Vance). This is supported by her complaint that a position on a math team was unfairly given to another. If *SP* she actually did have better marks than the boy that got the spot her skin color could be a reason why she was not chosen. This is all the more likely because *speculative* the poem was published in 1978, right after the Black Power Movement, and because the poem's author considered herself to be a black feminist (Kulii, *develop this reference* Reuman, and Trapasso).

her
The speaker's commentary on her mother is limited to repeated reference to her mother's unavailability. She is always portrayed as being behind a closed door. The daughter does not appear to know with certainty what her mother is

doing – either that or she does not want to express what she knows is going on. The bedroom setting alludes to an illicit sexual encounter, and if the poet's intention was to convey an activity of better repute it would likely have been identified to clear up that assumption. The mother is portrayed as a bad role model, and ineffective in offering guidance to a daughter who needs and wants it. But no matter what the mother is doing, it is certain that she is inaccessible and unhelpful to her daughter in regards to her maturation.

passive voice

The speaker unveils more information about herself through her ambiguous word choice. An example of this is found when she says:

passive voice

> suppose I die before graduation
>
> they will sing sad melodies
>
> but finally
>
> tell the truth about me
>
> There is nothing I want to do (15–19).

remove period

The last two lines have two levels of meaning. The simplest interpretation is that the two ideas presented do not fit together, but the speaker has juxtaposed them in a distracted state of mind. The capitalization of the T in "there" infers the start of a new sentence, which supports the idea that these are unrelated subjects; but, the absence of a period at the end of line eighteen supports another idea. It suggests that these two lines were placed together on purpose to offer insight about the speaker through their ambiguity. When considering the lines "tell the truth about me" and "There is nothing I want to do" together it seems that the truth that mourners will finally tell about the girl is that there was nothing that she wanted to do with her life. She was without ambition or personal direction to guide her life; her death, though sad, was less disappointing because she had no purpose to her existence.

be more specific

through

is this your conclusion or hers? –be more specific

All of this information aids in understanding the speaker, which, in turn, aids in understanding her message. The main topic of "Hanging Fire" is the role of a mother in the maturation of her daughter, as is evident from speaker's repeated mention of her insecurity about her own survival to adulthood, and her mother's unavailability. This all works together to produce the message that a girl requires the meaningful involvement of a mother in order to mature. All of her problems are amplified by her mother's unavailability. This is not the role a mother should have in her daughter's life. The author's displeasure at being left alone by her mother indicates that she believes that a mother should be an active source of guidance for her child. Communication should flow freely, unhindered by closed doors separating the two, in order for there to be support. It is important to the daughter that she have access to her mother.

her message or Lorde's message?

awkward

don't confuse the speaker with the poet

The speaker's lack of direction gives the poem a discontented undertone, evidence of the emotional turmoil she experiences in her youth. The youth of the speaker is necessary for the reader to remain open minded to the message presented. If someone already grown up spoke about the need for mothers to be involved in their children's lives it would sound more like a lecture or sermon, as though they were telling others what they should do. Someone experiencing the hardships of growing up alone is allowed to talk about their own experiences without incurring the judgment of the reader, which would detract from the poem.

n / of discontent
speaker's

passive voice

passive voice

explain

The fact that the speaker is a girl is important because the expression of a female's feelings is more likely to arouse compassion than if a male expressed himself in the same way because of the dual standards for men and women that exist in many societies. A belief more common in the past but still held by many today is that men should deal with their emotions in private, rather than

–avoid generalizations

–this paragraph needs to be recast

speak them freely. The standard for women, on the other hand, is different, and it is perfectly acceptable to females to voice their emotions. A young man would have to address the belief in society that it is feminine to express emotions before he could give voice to his insecurities without being shrugged off. It is much simpler for a female to speak this way because it is already assumed that there is nothing wrong with her for doing so. For these reasons it is more effective for the speaker of "Hanging Fire" to be female so that her message is taken seriously.

avoid speaking about how the poem might have been —

The lonely tone in which the speaker expresses herself suggests that she is not content with her mother's lack of involvement in her life. Without the lonely way she speaks the reader could conclude that she enjoys the freedom and independence she has. The lonely tone is necessary to inform the reader that a mother's influence is desired and needed for a teen to "grow up". These two ideas are the only ones repeated clearly throughout the poem and they are inextricably linked to one another. It is because the daughter is alone without her mother's guidance that she has difficulties mounting the stepping stones

cliché —

that lead to maturity.

STAGE 4: PROOFREADING AND PEER REVIEW

The student prepared the above draft as her submission for a peer review exercise that was a compulsory part of the essay assignment. Peer review (i.e., presenting your work to other students for comment) is a useful tool, whether it is required by the assignment or not. It offers several advantages, not the least of which includes a fresh perspective on your paper prior to grading. Your peers will also be in the early stages of learning to write about literature, so you should always take their comments "with a grain of salt," as the saying goes. Nevertheless, their comments (if they are made, and received, in the spirit of constructive criticism) may help you to look at your paper from another angle. When we write, we are sometimes too close to our own work to see problems that are readily apparent to others. A change of perspective can certainly help. Looking critically at another student's writing can also benefit your own writing, since (a) it will give you a sense of the writing level of your peers and (b) by putting you in the position of the evaluating reader, it may enable you to better imagine your own reader (i.e., your instructor) when you return to the business of revising your paper.

The student's next draft was revised according to comments made by two other students in the class. This draft is not reproduced here because the changes made on that draft consisted mainly of minor grammatical corrections and changes in word choice. Although peer review only occasionally results in substantial suggestions for necessary revisions, it consistently helps in proofreading your paper. Peer review does not, however, absolve you from proofreading your own work. To be sure, proofreading should never be taken lightly. Careless mistakes speak to effort and can have significant consequences. Submitting a paper with a word (or worse, an author's name) misspelled in the title is like showing up for a blind date with bad breath—it makes a bad first impression. Your goal should be to present the cleanest copy of your paper possible, in both looks and content—that means no coffee stains, and doing more than running your computer's spellchecker. Use a ruler to read one line at a time if you have to, but proofread as carefully as you can. For an instructor with stacks of other papers to grade, a paper free of typos is like a breath of *fresh* air.

STAGE 5: REWORKING THE FINAL DRAFT

The one substantial revision the student made to her paper in response to the peer review consisted of eliminating her discussion of the speaker's racial identifications. Rather than attempt to rework her reading of race in Lorde's poem, the student chose to disregard this crucial aspect altogether. Fortunately, this oversight was redressed (if not fully resolved) in a final draft that responded to questions and comments made by the instructor. Re-drafting and re-submitting a paper after the instructor has given it an initial review is a common element of writing assignments in first-year English courses, and in this case it yielded an impressive result. Apart from supporting the student's return to her initial discussion on race, the instructor encouraged the student to develop her use of language—something she had already been doing throughout the essay-writing process. In particular, the final draft transforms many of the student's passive sentences (in which the subject of the sentence is *acted upon*) into active sentences (in which the subject *performs* the action). This stylistic change helped to eliminate some of the paper's inelegance and awkwardness.

The opening sentence of the final draft's second paragraph is a good case in point. In the previous draft, here is how that paragraph began:

> The most apparent information presented about the speaker is that she is a fourteen year old girl going through puberty. This is clear from the direct statements she makes about herself, such as "I am fourteen" (1), indicating her youth; and "the boy I cannot live without" (3), indicating her femininity.

In the final draft, not only are these sentences recast in an "active voice," the student's less convincing assumption about gender is replaced by a more compelling focus on race:

> Although the speaker's identity remains vague throughout the poem, we know she is young ("I am fourteen" [1]) and we can infer that she, like Lorde herself, is African-American: she complains, for instance, that "my skin has betrayed me" (2).

This revised sentence is active throughout. The previous version's passive reference to information being "presented about the speaker" (presented by whom—the poem, the speaker, the poet?) gives way to the more confident and active phrase, "we know she is young." You will also notice that the revised version rearranges the sentences of the original to give them greater impact, while at the same time it expresses the student's ideas in a more economical fashion. In other words, despite being shorter, the revised version actually says more.

The full final version of our sample essay is reproduced in the "Student Writing" section of Chapter 4 (p. 75). While it could continue to benefit from further revision, the final version represents an A-range effort. Earlier drafts of the same paper would have received anywhere from a low B (or B-) to a B+. The final draft thus demonstrates how different versions of the same essay can make more or less the same claims, but when the author "follows through" on writing process, these claims become increasingly clearer and more compelling to the reader.

Part 4

9

Documenting Your Sources and Formatting Your Paper

Whether you are writing a non-research essay that uses citations from a literary work or a research paper that also quotes from or references secondary (i.e., research) material, you will need to familiarize yourself with the documentation guidelines of the Modern Language Association (MLA). Currently the standard across North America for essays on literature, these guidelines are published in the *MLA Handbook for Writers of Research Papers*, which is periodically updated to accommodate changes in the different kinds of texts available online and in print.[1] This chapter will focus on portions of the MLA guidelines that are most relevant to writing essays about literature at an undergraduate level. You should use these guidelines whenever you want to quote the words of another text or when you need to acknowledge the source of an idea that is not your own. Failure to document these kinds of references may leave you inadvertently vulnerable to the very serious charge of plagiarism, the penalties for which can range from failure on an assignment to failure in the course, and may even lead to expulsion. Whenever you are uncertain about whether you should or should not document a source, it is best to err on the side of caution and make the reference. When it comes to avoiding plagiarism, it is always better to be safe than sorry.

The following sections cover proper methods for citing the types of references most commonly encountered when writing about the different genres of literature (including poetry, fiction, and drama) as well as various

---

1 Readily available for purchase (or through special order) at any university or college bookstore, the *MLA Handbook for Writers of Research Papers* is currently in its seventh edition (2009).

kinds of secondary sources (including books, journal articles, and electronic sources).

CITING LITERARY WORKS

I. Poetry

Poetry citations of three lines or less should appear within quotation marks in the body of your paragraph; use a forward slash with a space on each side (/) to indicate where line breaks occur:

> While claiming that she "cannot live without" him, the speaker also admits
>
> that her boyfriend "still sucks his thumb / in secret" (3–5).

This example makes two citations to three consecutive lines of the same poem: the first is a partial quotation of line 3, and the second quotes lines 4 and 5 together in their entirety. The parentheses at the end of the sentence contain a reference to line numbers, which you will have to count for yourself if the original text does not provide them. The period that closes the sentence falls after the closing parenthesis, not before it.

When citing more than three lines of poetry, you should use what is called a *block quotation* that begins on a new line, is double-spaced, and is indented one inch from the left margin of your essay:

> The speaker unveils more information about herself through her ambiguous
>
> word choice. An example of this occurs when she says:
>
>> suppose I die before graduation
>>
>> they will sing sad melodies
>>
>> but finally
>>
>> tell the truth about me
>>
>> There is nothing I want to do (15–19)

As you can see, a block quotation does not need quotation marks; the fact that it is set apart from the rest of your paragraph is sufficient to identify the passage as a quotation. No punctuation should follow the parenthetical line reference. As it happens, the final line of the above quotation does not end with any punctuation in the original text. If it did, the punctuation mark (a period, for instance) would follow the last word of the citation, not the parenthesis.

This next example involves a block quotation that reproduces lines of poetry that contain unusual spatial arrangements. As always, your goal is to be as faithful to the original as possible.

In "Death,"* William Carlos Williams uses creative line breaks and spatial arrangements to emphasize the poem's meditation on mortality and love:

> He's nothing at all
>
>   he's dead
>
> shrunken up to skin
>
> . . . .
>
> Dead
>
>   his eyes
>
> rolled up out of
>
> the light—a mockery
>
>
>   which
>
> love cannot touch—
>
>
> just bury it
>
> and hide its face
>
> for shame. (18-20, 38-46)

The most unusual spatial arrangement in this passage occurs with the placement of the word "which" in line 42, but even subtler instances (such as the spontaneous indentations in lines 19 and 39) must be preserved. The series of spaced periods (called an **ellipsis**) is not a feature of the original text, but indicates the omission of lines that, for one reason or another, the essay writer did not wish to include in the quotation. The reference to line numbers in parentheses reflects this absence by separating each line-range of cited text with a comma.

II. Fiction (and Other Prose Works)

Short quotations from fictional and other kinds of prose works are handled in a way similar to poetry citations, except that the parenthetical reference cites page numbers instead of line numbers. Also, there is no need to indicate line breaks

---

*By William Carlos Williams, from *The Collected Poems: Volume I*, 1909-1939, copyrights © 1938 by New Directions Publishing Corp. Reprinted by permission of New Directions Publishing Corp.

in a prose citation. Here is an example from an essay on *Frankenstein* that also illustrates the use of an ellipsis to signal an omission from the original text:

> Even before Felix and Agatha return to behold the monster with "horror and
>
> consternation," the old man responds to the creature's explanation of himself
>
> by exclaiming, with great alarm, "Good God! . . . Who are you?" (160).

This sentence cites two quotations from the same text, but because these quotations occur on the same page of the original text, the page reference is documented only once, at the end of the sentence. If the first quotation ("horror and consternation") had occurred on the previous page of the original text, the parenthetical reference would have read "(159, 160)." We should also note the preservation of the question mark at the end of the second quotation; it is preserved to reflect the interrogative nature of the cited passage, but a period is still required after the final parenthesis to close the sentence.

The previous example integrated the quoted text into the essay's sentence structure. Another way to incorporate a quotation into your own writing is to introduce a citation with a colon:

> Their strange encounter takes place in the most private of Victor's spaces: "a
>
> solitary chamber, or rather cell, at the top of [his] house, and separated from
>
> all other apartments by a gallery and staircase" (82).

Either method of integrating citations into your own writing is acceptable. Nevertheless, a good strategy for writing essays that are lively and engaging is to alternate between methods instead of introducing all your citations in the same way. Both methods will occasionally require you to alter the cited text to suit the grammar of your sentence or to clarify a larger context. Such changes must be framed within square brackets (e.g., "at the top of [his] house").

For long prose citations—those that would take up more than four lines if typed in the text of your essay—use a block quotation, as described in the previous section. Indented one inch from the left margin of your essay and double-spaced throughout, block quotations do not require quotation marks (unless the passage consists of dialogue). They are most often introduced with a colon, and the parenthetical page reference should appear *after* the final punctuation mark of the cited passage. Here is an example from the comparative sample paper from Chapter 5:

> Boring lectures, poison ivy, lack of fresh water, uncomfortable sleeping
>
> quarters, and cold, damp weather are all aspects of the setting that enhance
>
> both the scientists' frustration and loneliness:
>
>> They were so tired by then, twelve days into the course, and
>>
>> so dirty and overworked and strained by pretending to the

students that these things didn't matter that neither of them could

understand that they were also lonely. (Barrett 198)

In a comparative essay such as this, it may not always be clear which text you are citing; when that is the case, you need to include the author's last name in the parenthesis containing the page reference. That way, if your reader is confused, he or she can look to your Works Cited list for clarification (see "Your List of Works Cited," below). When the source of the citation is obvious, you need not include the name. The same applies to other kinds of citations, including poetry, drama, and non-fictional prose.

III. Drama

There are important differences that set quotations from a dramatic work apart from other kinds of quotations. For one thing, you need to be mindful of whether the dramatic text you are analyzing is written in verse, prose, or (as is the case with many of Shakespeare's works) a mixture of the two. Whereas short dramatic verse citations require you to indicate line breaks with a forward slash (/), short prose citations from a dramatic work do not. If you want to quote dialogue between two or more characters, use a block quotation and begin each character's speech with the character's name printed in capital letters. Here is an example from an essay on *Hamlet*:

In the graveyard exchange between Hamlet and the Clown in Act Five,

Shakespeare turns his tragic theme into material for comic relief:

HAMLET. What man dost thou dig [this grave] for?

CLOWN. For no man, sir.

HAMLET. What woman, then?

CLOWN. For none neither.

HAMLET. Who is to be buried in't?

CLOWN. One that was a woman, sir; but rest her soul,

she is dead. (5.1.99–104)

As you can see, MLA guidelines suggest placing a period after the speaker's name instead of a colon. You should also notice the proper way to set up the parenthetical reference for a classic drama like *Hamlet*: the first number (5) refers to the act in which the cited text occurs, the second number indicates the scene (1), and the number range at the end (99–104) refers to line numbers. Of course, not all dramatic texts (particularly modern ones) contain acts or scenes or numbered lines. The rule in these instances is to cite whatever is available in the same order as the above. If you think your quotation will be difficult for your reader to find—which is often the case when citing plays with unnumbered dialogue—a page reference should suffice.

When quoting a lengthy passage (such as a monologue or soliloquy) spoken by a single character, as long as that character's identity is obvious to your reader, there is no need to reprint his or her name in the block quotation. If you intend to quote only a portion of the character's speech, then you should signal missing parts with an ellipsis, as in the following:

> When accused of being a heartless opportunist, Boy Willie explains why selling the piano makes more sense than leaving it to sit unused in the parlour:
>
>> I ain't talking about selling my soul. I'm talking about trading that piece of wood for some land. Get something under your feet. Land the only thing God ain't making no more of. You can always get you another piano. . . . You can't do nothing with that piano but sit up there and look at it. (Wilson 1467)

SECONDARY SOURCES: HOW TO FIND THEM

Before considering the many ways to document references to different kinds of secondary sources, we should discuss how to find such sources. The most obvious place to begin researching a work of literature is your school library's catalogue search engine. Typing an author's last name first and first name last in a subject search field (e.g., "Cheever, John") should yield entries for every book in the library with a major focus on that author. These entries will be organized into categories such as "Cheever John biography" and "Cheever John interpretation and criticism." Depending on how many results you find, you should be able to easily peruse the titles listed in each category and click to learn more details about books that appear promising for your research purposes. When an author subject search produces more titles than you can adequately evaluate (as is often the case with major writers such as William Shakespeare or Virginia Woolf), a keyword search may be more useful in narrowing your research focus. Basic keyword searches enable you to combine keywords, such as an author's name, the title of a work of literature, and a particular subject or theme (e.g., "Woolf and 'To the Lighthouse'" or "Woolf and feminism"), whereas advanced keyword searches allow you to further refine your search by setting "optional limits" such as the type of material (print, videocassette, microfilm, etc.), date of publication range, or name of publisher.

You can expand your research horizon by executing similar searches (basic or advanced) within the reference databases available at your university or college library. These may include the *MLA International Bibliography* (which contains bibliographical records on books and journal articles related to modern languages and literatures), the *Web of Knowledge* (which includes bibliographical entries for research in the Sciences, Social Sciences, and Arts and Humanities), and *WorldCat* (which stores information on many different kinds of texts from different academic disciplines). There are many other competing reference databases, so it is best to speak with a librarian to determine which will be the most helpful for your research needs. The librarian may also instruct you on ways to locate your research texts in the library itself or through the library's online computer system.

Commercial Internet search engines (such as Google.ca or bing.com) can also aid your research efforts, but you should exercise caution when relying on information obtained online. The vast majority of online websites are not scholarly in nature. Only those that are adjudicated by experts, who evaluate the site's content according to certain academic standards, will be considered reliable within the university or college classroom. Scholarly websites typically use words like "refereed" or "peer reviewed" on their homepages and may even provide lists of university-affiliated scholars who serve on their editorial or advisory boards. An "open source" website such as *Wikipedia* features information that is regulated by registered users, but because this information is not "vetted" (i.e., reviewed and evaluated) by specialists, the website is not "peer reviewed" in the academic sense. An online journal such as *Romanticism and Victorianism on the Net (RaVoN)*, on the other hand, is considered a scholarly source since it is refereed by an international group of academic researchers in the fields of Romantic and Victorian literature and culture.

SECONDARY SOURCES: HOW TO CITE AND REFERENCE THEM

Quoting from and referencing secondary research material is very similar to citing a work of prose fiction, though there are some subtle variations that depend on the nature of the source. The following sections offer methods for documenting the most common kinds of secondary sources.

I. Books by a Single Author

If you do not mention the author's name in the sentence that contains or introduces a quotation from a book by a single author, then the author's name must be included in the parenthetical page reference:

> Coleridge's memory of his sister in "Frost at Midnight" arguably represents
>
> "an imaginary or narcissistic construct rather than a recollection of something
>
> that once existed" (Rajan 226).

Here is the same sentence with the quoted author's name mentioned in the sentence:

> Coleridge's memory of his sister in "Frost at Midnight" represents what
>
> Tilottama Rajan calls "an imaginary or narcissistic construct rather than a
>
> recollection of something that once existed" (226).

In cases where your essay quotes passages from multiple books by the same author, your parenthetical reference must also include a shortened version of the book's title. For instance, the parenthetical reference for the first citation above would read "(Rajan, *Dark* 226)" and the reference for the second would read "(*Dark* 226)." Your reader will be able to view the full title of the book—in this case, *Dark Interpreter: The Discourse of Romanticism*—in the corresponding entry of your Works Cited list (see "Preparing a List of Works Cited," below).

II. Journal Articles and Edited Collections of Essays

For single-authored articles from journals and edited collections of essays, use the same method as citing a single-authored book; if you mention the author's name in your sentence, do not include it in the parenthetical reference:

> As Gary Kelley reminds us, "Wollstonecraft's self-appointed role was to
>
> exemplify, in her texts and in the life choices that supposedly grounded
>
> them, the (female) revolutionary subject" (20).

If you quote from more than one article by the same author, include a shortened title in the final parenthesis:

> While visiting Italy, Mary and Percy Shelley grew "fascinated with
>
> *improvisatori*, performing figures, both male and female, who would
>
> extemporarily compose poems with subjects often proposed by the
>
> audience" (Vargo, "Mary Shelley" 172).

III. Sources with Multiple Authors

List the authors' names in the order they appear in the original publication:

> Godwin admired the way Rousseau "interpreted his early life so as to
>
> elucidate the foundations of his adult beliefs" (Clemit and Walker 21).

Here is the same citation with the authors' names mentioned in the sentence:

> Clemit and Walker argue that Godwin admired the way Rousseau "interpreted
> his early life so as to elucidate the foundations of his adult beliefs" (21).

When the source has more than three authors, list only the first author's last name followed by the phrase "et al." as in "(Jackson et al. 49)."

IV. Literary Anthologies and Critical Editions (Introductions, Editorial Notes, Etc.)

If you intend to quote from editorial material such as an introduction to a critical edition of a text or a footnote from a literary anthology, then you need to reference the name of the editor(s), not the literary author. You should also remember to prepare a separate entry for the editor(s) in your Works Cited list. Here is a sentence that cites Kathleen James-Cavan's introduction to the Broadview edition of Jane Austen's *Sense and Sensibility*:

> According to James-Cavan, the novel "displays a self-consciousness of its
> status as a new kind of writing, evinced by its satire of a variety of literary
> pretexts (20).

To cite an editorial footnote or endnote, affix the letter "n" and the number of the note (without spaces or intervening punctuation) to the end of the page number in parentheses:

> The story of "Young Goodman Brown" likely had a deep personal significance
> for Hawthorne, not least because "[his] own ancestors were involved in the
> persecution of witches and Quakers" (Booth, Hunter, and Mays 232n1).

V. Electronic and Online Sources

For the most part, references to electronic and online sources follow the same procedure as references to print publications. When page numbers are available, they should appear in parentheses. If the source numbers its paragraphs instead of its pages (as is increasingly the case with Internet-based journals and other online academic sources), then write the abbreviation "par." prior to the paragraph number in parentheses:

> Alan Richardson suggests that Mary Shelley's apocalyptic invention of the
> plague in *The Last Man* is rooted in "a reflex of English disgust at the colonial
> other, a disgust inextricable from commercial domination" (par. 4).

For online or electronic sources that do not provide page or paragraph numbers, refer to both the author and title of the source either in your sentence (which is preferable) or in parentheses. A combination of the two is also acceptable, as in the following:

> According to Louis Menand, the phrase "inherent vice" comes from maritime law and refers specifically to "the quality of things that makes them difficult to insure" ("Soft-Boiled: Pychon's Stoned Detective").

VI. Indirect Quotations and Noting Emphasis

It is best to cite a source directly, but when you want to quote someone else's citation of a source and cannot, for whatever reason, locate that source yourself, use the abbreviation "qtd. in" to indicate the indirect nature of the quotation. Here is an example from Chapter 1, where the quoted passage is from I.A. Richards but is found quoted in a text by F.R. Leavis:

> For Leavis, in other words, the "slow climb back" to civilized society that his colleague I.A. Richards thought was still possible began with the meticulous consideration of literary structures (qtd. in Leavis 30).

Other useful parenthetical notations include "emphasis added" and "emphasis preserved," which distinguish your own use of italics to emphasize words in a quotation from emphasis that is already present in the original text. Compare the following:

> As Jan Plug observes, the faces Coleridge hopes to see outside his classroom door "are not only familiar, they are increasingly *familiar*" (emphasis added, 31). Turning to the "half opened" door of his classroom, the young Coleridge "hoped to see the *stranger's* face, / Townsman, or aunt, or sister more beloved" (emphasis preserved, 39, 41-42).

PREPARING A LIST OF WORKS CITED[2]*

Your Works Cited list contains bibliographical entries on all texts and sources referenced in your paper. The title "Works Cited" should appear centred (without

---

[2] The organization (and some of the content) of this section is based in part on section 22-c of Jack Finnbogason and Al Valleau's *A Canadian Writer's Guide*, 4th ed. (Toronto: Nelson Education, 2010). For a full list of various Works Cited entries, see pages 108–31 of that text.

*From Finnbogason/Valleau. *A Canadian Writer's Guide*, 4E. © 2010 Nelson Education Ltd. Reproduced by permission. www.cengage.com/permissions

quotation marks or emphasis) at the top of a new page. Entries should be alphabetized according to author (or editor) surnames—or, in cases where no author or editor is provided, the first word of the title (excluding definite and indefinite articles). The first line of each entry should be flush with the left margin, while successive lines in the same entry are indented one half inch. The entire list should be double-spaced. Use italics for book titles; use quotation marks for titles that appear in larger works. For examples of Works Cited pages, see the sample essays throughout this guide, especially the research paper at the end of Chapter 2.

I. Books and Other Non-periodical Works

Book entries generally contain three pieces of bibliographical information in the following order: authorship, title, and publication details (including place, publisher, and year). MLA guidelines now suggest that you indicate the medium of the source as well (i.e., "Print," "CD," "Web," and so forth).

One author

Invert the author's first and last names. List multiple works by the same author alphabetically by title and replace the author's name in subsequent entries with three dashes and a period ("———.").

> Rajan, Tillotama. *Dark Interpreter: The Discourse of Romanticism*. Ithaca,
> NY: Cornell UP, 1980. Print.

More than one author

List authors in the order in which they appear on the title page. Only the first author's name should be inverted. (For books with more than three authors, list only the first author followed by a comma and "et al.")

> Butling, Pauline, and Susan Rudy. *Writing in Our Time: Canada's Radical
> Poetries in English (1957–2003)*. Waterloo, ON: Wilfrid Laurier UP,
> 2005. Print.

Author with an editor

Introduce the editor's name after the title with the abbreviation "Ed."

> Godwin, William. *St. Leon: A Tale of the Sixteenth Century*. Ed. William
> Brewer. Peterborough, ON: Broadview, 2006. Print.

A second or subsequent edition

If the text has more than one edition, insert the edition number (e.g., "2nd ed.") between the title and editor(s).

> Hawthorne, Nathaniel. *The Scarlet Letter; A Romance*. 2nd ed. Ed. John
> Stephen Martin. Peterborough, ON: Broadview, 2004. Print.

Translation
Introduce the translator after the title with the abbreviation "Trans."

> Kristeva, Julia. *Revolution in Poetic Language.* Trans. Margaret Waller. New
>> York: Columbia UP, 1984. Print.

Multi-volume work
If you cite just one volume of a multi-volume work, then write the volume number (e.g., "Vol. 1") after the period that follows the title, and give publication details for that volume only.

> Brown, Marshall, ed. *Romanticism: The Cambridge History of Literary*
>> *Criticism.* Vol. 5. Cambridge: Cambridge UP, 2000. Print.

When citing more than one volume, indicate the total number of volumes in the work (e.g., "2 vols.) after the period that follows the title.

> Bell, Quentin. *Virginia Woolf: A Biography.* 2 vols. London: Hogarth, 1972.
> Print.

Anthology
In cases where you cite editorial material from an anthology (i.e., introductory matter, notes, etc.), list the anthology according to the editors' names (using "et al." after the first editor if there are more than three).

> Booth, Alison, J. Paul Hunter, and Kelly Mays, eds. *The Norton Introduction*
>> *to Literature.* Shorter 9th ed. New York: Norton, 2005. Print.

Selection from an anthology
When citing a literary work from an anthology, list the entry by the author's name. A separate entry is required for different selections from the same anthology. The title of the selection appears after the author's name and is followed by the title of the anthology. Be sure to include a page range for the work cited.

> Keats, John. "Ode to a Nightingale." *The Norton Introduction to Literature.*
>> Shorter 9th ed. Ed. Alison Booth, J. Paul Hunter, and Kelly Mays. New
>> York: Norton, 2005. 843–45. Print.

II. Articles from Periodicals and Reference Works

Article entries are similar to book entries, but the order and detail of publication information is somewhat different.

Article in a journal

There is no need to include publisher names for journal articles. After the author's name and the title of the article, cite the title of the journal, the number of the volume and issue (separated by a period), and the date of publication in parentheses. The page range comes next, preceded by a colon and followed by a period.

> McWhir, Anne. "Mary Shelley's Anti-Contagionism: *The Last Man* as 'Fatal Narrative.'" *Mosaic* 35.2 (June 2002): 23-38. Print.

Article in a newspaper

Begin with the author's name; if no author is listed, then start with the article title. Cite the title of the newspaper after the article title (omitting words like the, a, and an). The date is next, followed by the edition (if applicable). The section and/or page number are last and should be cited together without spacing between them.

> Walton, Dawn. "The Inuit Cultural Matrix Reloaded." *Globe and Mail* 15 Feb. 2008, BC ed.: A3. Print.

Article in a reference work (e.g., an encyclopedia, a dictionary)

If the author's name is available, then list it first; otherwise, begin with the article title. Next, cite the title of the reference work, including the edition number (if applicable). Listing editors' names and full publication information is unnecessary; the year of publication and type of medium consulted will suffice.

> "Poetry." *The Compact Edition of the Oxford English Dictionary*. 2 vols. 1971. Print.

Review

Reviews are listed in much the same manner as articles, except that you must indicate the work being reviewed (with "Rev. of "). If the review does not have a specific title, then place "Rev. of" immediately after the review author's name.

> Coulter, Myri. "Fenced In." Rev. of *A Map of Glass*, by Jane Urquhart. *Canadian Literature: A Quarterly of Criticism and Review* 191 (Winter 2006): 122–23. Print.

III. Web Sources

When accessing books and articles online that were originally published in print, your Works Cited entries should be identical to the above examples of print sources, but instead of writing "Print" at the end of your entry, you should write "Web" followed by a period and the date on which you accessed the source. If you accessed the source through an academic service such as *JSTOR, Proquest,* or *Project Muse,* then the name of the service should appear before "Web." Use the abbreviation "n. pag." if original page numbers are not reproduced in the electronic version, and "n.p." if no publication information is available.

> Grinnell, George. "Thomas Beddoes and the Physiology of Romantic
>
> Medicine." *Studies in Romanticism* 45 (Summer 2006): 223-50.
>
> *ProQuest.* Web. 9 Sept. 2009.

URL addresses are no longer required in Works Cited entries. Nevertheless, if your instructor wants you to include the URL, place it in angled brackets (< >) at the end of your entry (i.e., after the date of access), followed by a period.

Article in an online scholarly journal

The entry for an online scholarly journal article is more or less the same as a print journal article. Instead of a page range, reference the total number of paragraphs (if numbered) with the abbreviation "pars." Remember to write "Web" instead of "Print" and include the date of access.

> Keen, Paul. "On the Highways of Literature: Herbert Croft's Unfinished
>
> Business." *Romanticism and Victorianism on the Net* 50 (May 2008): 28
>
> pars. Web. 9 Sept. 2009.

Professional website

The name of the organization takes the place of the author. Cite the title of the page in quotation marks. If the page you reference is the home page, just write "Home Page" without quotation marks.

> Human Rights Watch. "Human Rights Watch / Hellman-Hammett Grants."
>
> Human Rights Watch. Web. 22 May 2008.

Personal website

List the entry by author's name (surname first, followed by given name). Cite the title of the page containing your citation (if applicable), then the title of the entire website.

> Hutchings, Kevin. "Blake Essay." Songs of William Blake. Web. 18 Aug. 2009.

V. Other Relevant Sources (i.e., Films and Lectures)

Film, videocassette, or DVD

Begin with the title of the movie, then introduce the director(s) with the abbreviation "Dir." Next, indicate the distributor and the year of release. If you consulted the original film release, then indicate the medium as "Film."

> *No Country for Old Men.* Dir. Ethan Coen and Joel Coen. Paramount
>
> Vantage, 2007. Film.

If you consulted a videocassette or DVD of the original film, list the distributor, the year of distribution, and the medium ("Videocassette" or "DVD") after the original year of release.

> *No Country for Old Men.* Dir. Ethan Coen and Joel Coen. 2007. Paramount
>
> Vantage, 2008. DVD.

Here is an example of an educational video originally published on VHS.

> *Julia Kristeva.* Films for the Humanities, 1997. Videocassette.

Class lecture

Start with the instructor's (or speaker's) name; give the title of the lecture or unit (if available); indicate the host institution (i.e., the university or college); provide the location and date of the lecture; and state the medium (i.e., "Lecture.").

> Melville, Peter. "Simile and Metaphor." University of Winnipeg, Winnipeg,
>
> MB. 29 Sept. 2008. Lecture.

FORMATTING: WHAT YOUR PAPER SHOULD LOOK LIKE

There are plenty of student sample essays throughout this guide that can give you an idea of how your paper should be formatted. Nevertheless, the following sections cover the basics, such as paper size, proper margin settings, spacing, headings, and methods for citing titles.

I. Paper, Margins, Spacing, and Font

Print your essay on standard, good-quality 8½" × 11" (216mm × 279mm) paper, and fasten your pages with a paper clip or staple. Do not enclose the essay in any kind of binder or folder, as these are cumbersome and unnecessary. In the interest of saving paper, I allow students to submit essays that are printed on both sides of the page, but you should check with your instructor before submitting the same. Set all margins of your paper (i.e., top, bottom, right, and left) to *one inch*, keeping in mind that the margins for block quotations should be set an extra inch to the right of your left margin. Indent the first line of every new paragraph one half inch. Your paper should be double-spaced throughout, including your title, block quotations, and Works Cited list. Finally, use a reader-friendly typeface such as Times New Roman or similar, in 12 point.

II. Heading, Title, and Page Numbers

MLA guidelines suggest using a first-page heading instead of a title page. This heading should begin immediately below the top margin of your paper and should consist of four double-spaced lines (each flush with the left margin) that list details about your paper in the following order: (1) your full name, (2) your instructor's name, (3) your course code and section number, and (4) the date. Your title should be centred on the next double-spaced line, and should be descriptive of your paper's content (e.g., "The Crucial Role of a Mother: Loneliness and Insecurity in Audre Lord's "Hanging Fire"). If your title runs to more than one line, it should nevertheless remain centred and double-spaced. The first line of your first paragraph should begin on the next doubled-spaced line below your title. In a right-justified header that appears one half inch from the top of every page of your paper, type your last name and the page number. (Again, look to the sample papers in this guide for examples.)

III. Titles of Literary Works and Secondary Sources

When citing titles of literary works and secondary sources in your essay, follow the same rules you use when citing titles in your Works Cited list. Use italics for the titles of longer works (including books, novels, novellas, plays, films, and long poems). For shorter works such as short stories, shorter poems, journal articles, and book chapters, use double quotation marks. When a title occurs within a title, do the following:

Longer work title within a shorter work's title
Preserve the italics of the long title (e.g., "Mirror Images and Otherness in Mary Shelley's *Frankenstein*").

Longer work title within a longer work's title
Reverse the italics of the cited title (e.g., *Approaches to Teaching Shelley's* Frankenstein).

Shorter work title within a shorter work's title
Use single quotation marks for the cited title (e.g., "The Rhetoric of Secrecy: Figures of the Self in 'Frost at Midnight'").

Shorter work title within a longer work's title
Preserve the double quotation marks of the cited title (e.g., *"Young Goodman Brown" and Other Stories*).

Glossary of Critical Terms

The following glossary contains only a select list of critical and literary terms. There are a number of more comprehensive glossaries available online and in print. A list of some better-known print editions follows the terms below.

ACT: A major division in a dramatic work, often subdivided into scenes that are held together by setting and unity of action.

ACTION: Events that take place in a drama, narrative, or film; the flow from one event to the next in a series of events.

ALLEGORY: A narrative, in prose or verse, in which there exists a second layer of meaning beneath the "literal" interpretation of the text. Often didactic, allegory functions as an extended metaphor in which characters, places, and things signify abstract ideas.

ALLITERATION: A poetic device that involves the repetition of sounds, usually consonants, in a sequence of words.

ALLUSION: An indirect reference to a literary, mythological, or historical figure or event; often refers to a well-known theme or story in a particular literary tradition.

AMBIGUITY: Language that expresses multiple meanings or a diverse range of emotions or attitudes.

ANTAGONIST: A character in drama or narrative whose purpose is to oppose the protagonist.

ARCHETYPE: An image, character, theme, or narrative that is common in one or more literary traditions.

ASSONANCE: A poetic device that involves the repetition of vowel sounds in a sequence of words.

BLANK VERSE: A poetic term that refers to any unrhymed verse but is typically used to describe unrhymed iambic pentameter.

CANON: The collection of widely recognized "major" works and "classic" authors that make up a given culture's literary history.

CATASTROPHE: The dénouement that follows the climax in a tragedy; usually involves the suffering and/or ruin of the tragic hero.

CATHARSIS: An element of tragedy through which the audience's emotions are effectively "purged" or "purified" at the end of the play. This final feeling of relief is a response to the feelings of fear and pity that the tragedy evokes in its audience.

CHARACTER (Flat vs. Round): A person in a narrative or dramatic text. A "flat" character is a simple, predictable, one-dimensional character often made to represent a single idea. A "round" character is a complex, multi-dimensional, unpredictable character whose actions and motivations resemble those of a real person.

CHARACTERIZATION: The way characters are represented in a literary work.

CLIMAX: A moment of great tension or intensity in a literary work. In drama, the climax usually follows the rising action and precedes the falling action, and it often coincides with the "crisis."

CLOSE-UP: A cinematic shot in which the distance between a person's face and the camera is very short; close-ups can also feature an object or another part of a person's body.

COMEDY: A literary genre that depicts the everyday lives of common people, usually in simple vernacular, and ends happily for the main characters. The purpose of the comedy is to entertain and amuse the audience.

COMIC RELIEF: The use of humour in a serious work to relieve some kind of tension; often used in tragedy.

CONCLUSION: The end of a fictional story, when the central conflict is typically resolved; also called "resolution."

CONFLICT: A confrontation between characters in a narrative work; a character's struggle against forces in the plot that are beyond his or her control.

CONNOTATION: The associations that a particular word conjures up in the mind of the reader; the secondary or subliminal feelings or ideas that are not directly linked to the word's literal meaning.

CONSONANCE: A poetic device that involves the repetition of the final consonant in a series of words or lines of verse.

COUPLET: Two lines of rhymed verse that are paired together and often share the same metre.

CRISIS: The turning point in a plot, determining the outcome of the events to follow.

CROSSCUTTING: A film editing technique that cuts, in a back-and-forth manner, between action occurring in two or more locations.

DÉNOUEMENT: A dramatic element through which the plot's conflict is resolved.

DIALOGUE: Conversation between characters in a literary text.

DICTION: An author's or character's word choice.

DRAMA: A literary work written for performance in front of an audience.

DRAMATIC IRONY: A situation, in a drama, in which the audience gains knowledge that a particular character is lacking.

DRAMATURGY: A theatre (and cinema) term that refers to directorial decisions about stage and costume design, lighting and sound effects, character movement and action on stage, acting style, and so on.

ELLIPSIS: A sequence of spaced periods that denotes the omission of a particular word or words.

ENJAMBMENT: When a phrase or sentence in poetry does not end with a grammatical break at the end of a line, but carries over onto the next line.

EPIC: A long, narrative poem, written in a formal style, that documents and celebrates the actions of a hero whose fate is tied to that of a race or nation.

EPISODE: The literary depiction of one event in a series of events that are connected by plot or by subject matter.

EYE RHYME: When two words share similar spelling but are pronounced differently (e.g., "spook" and "book").

EXPOSITION: The part of a story that introduces readers to the story's setting, situation, and main characters.

FALLING ACTION: Events that follow the climax or crisis in a dramatic or narrative text.

FICTION: A prose narrative wherein the characters and events are imagined or created by the author.

FIGURATIVE LANGUAGE: Language that refers to a meaning that is other than or exceeds the literal meaning.

FIRST-PERSON NARRATIVE: A narrative in which the narrator assumes the "I" (i.e., subjective) point of view and recounts his or her story accordingly.

FIXED FORM: Refers to genres of poetry in which a series of rules govern metre and rhyme.

FLASHBACK: When characters reflect on or recall events that occur prior to the beginning of the narrative.

FOIL: A character whose attitudes and actions contrast with those of the protagonist. The foil character thus emphasizes certain qualities of the protagonist that he or she lacks.

FOOT: A poetic unit made up of a group of syllables; syllables in a foot are either stressed or unstressed.

FOREGROUND: Refers to events, objects, or actions in a narrative that are emphasized or made prominent over other elements of the same narrative.

FORESHADOWING: A literary device used by an author to suggest events or themes that will be evident later in the work.

FREE VERSE: Verse that does not conform to traditional poetic conventions of rhyme and metre.

HALF RHYME: When the final consonants of two particular words rhyme, but not the vowel sounds.

HERO, HEROINE: The protagonist in a narrative or drama, often of noble birth, who is both morally and physically superior to the other characters. Typically the hero/heroine will overcome adversity and demonstrate courage in the face of great danger.

HEROIC COUPLET: A pair of rhyming iambic lines, frequently used in epic poems and heroic dramas.

HYPERBOLE: A figure of speech that involves exaggerating something in order to emphasize a point.

IAMBIC PENTAMETER: A line of poetry composed of ten syllables; these syllables are grouped into five rhythmic sequences (or "feet") in which an unstressed syllable is followed by a stressed syllable.

IMAGE: A pictorial representation of something through language; the representation of an object that engages one or more of the senses.

IMAGERY: Language that appeals to the senses.

INTERNAL RHYME: When two or more words rhyme within a single line of poetry.

IRONY: The recognizable contradiction between appearance and reality.

LIMITED OMNISCIENCE The point of view of a character or narrator who has a limited knowledge of the events and actions in the story.

LINE BREAK: The end of a line of poetry.

METAPHOR: A figure of speech in which a thing, idea, or action is represented as something different from, but analogous to it.

METRE: The pattern of stressed and unstressed syllables in a line of poetry.

MISE-EN-SCÈNE: A cinematic term that refers to elements that are deliberately put into a scene prior to filming; also refers to theatrical elements used on the dramatic stage.

MONOLOGUE: A long, uninterrupted narrative or speech given by a single character.

MONTAGE: A series of related images that emphasize a particular theme or idea through repetition.

NARRATION: The act of telling or retelling a story.

NARRATIVE: A story, involving characters and events, that is told by one or more narrators.

NARRATOR: The speaker who recounts a narrative; may or may not be one of the characters in the story.

NOVEL: A long narrative of fictional prose.

NOVELLA: A work of fictional prose that is longer than a short story but shorter than a novel.

OBJECTIVE NARRATOR: A narrator who withholds judgment of the events that he or she is describing.

OCTAVE: A group of eight lines of poetry that follow an *abbaabba* rhyme scheme. In an Italian or Petrarchan sonnet, the octave precedes the sestet.

OMNISCIENT NARRATOR: An all-knowing, all-seeing narrator who has access to the details of the story and the inner thoughts of the characters.

ONOMATOPOEIA: The use of words that sound like the objects they denote.

OPEN FORM: A type of poetry that does not follow the traditional conventions of rhyme and metre; often called "free verse."

PARALLEL ACTION: A cinematic device that occurs when two or more lines of action in a film are crosscut together and thus appear to happen simultaneously.

PASTORAL: A poem that glorifies natural landscapes and rural settings.

PERSONA: The identity that is assumed by a writer, speaker, or narrator of a given text.

PERSONIFICATION: A poetic device through which human qualities and characteristics are attributed to non-human entities.

PETRARCHAN SONNET: A poetic form of fourteen lines that is divided into an octave and a sestet; also called an "Italian sonnet." It usually follows an *abbaabba cdecde* rhyme scheme.

PLOT: The action and events in a narrative that significantly alter or affect the character's lives and capture the reader's interest.

POETRY: A literary genre that follows a pattern of rhythm or metre so as to emphasize particular sounds, images, and ideas.

POINT OF VIEW: The vantage point from which a story or poem is conveyed.

PROSE: Writing that does not follow a specific pattern of rhythm or metre.

PROTAGONIST: The main character in a narrative.

QUATRAIN: A stanza of four lines.

RHYME: The repetition of particular sounds within words.

RHYTHM: The duration and stress of syllables in poetry or prose.

RISING ACTION: The part of a narrative or play that precedes the climax.

SCANSION: Analyzing metre in verse; dividing verse into metrical feet.

SCENE: A segment in a narrative, dramatic, or cinematic work that is held together by setting and unity of action.

SESTET: In an Italian sonnet, the final six lines that follow the octave; there, their rhyme scheme is usually *cdecde*.

SETTING: The time and place in which a narrative unfolds.

SHAKESPEAREAN SONNET: A poem made up of fourteen lines—three quatrains and a couplet—and written in iambic pentameter. The sonnet follows an *abab cdcd efef gg* rhyme scheme. Also called an "English sonnet."

SHORT STORY: A work of fictional prose that, because it is minimal in duration, usually has only one or two characters and typically pursues one central idea, event, or conflict.

SIMILE: A direct comparison using "like" or "as."

SOLILOQUY: In a dramatic work, a single character's speech in which the character expresses his or her thoughts and feeling to the audience.

SONNET: A poem consisting of fourteen lines, usually written in iambic pentameter.

SPEAKER: In poetry, the persona of the point of view through which the poem is expressed.

SPECIAL EFFECTS: Effects produced by a filmmaker's manipulation of technologies available either on set or during the phases of post-production (i.e., after shooting).

STAGE DIRECTIONS: The italicized instructions in a dramatic text that indicate how the events of the play are supposed to take place on stage.

STANZA: Lines in poetry that are grouped together and typically share a similar rhyme scheme and metre.

STEREOTYPE: A preconceived notion of a particular person, group of people, or thing that gains significance through repetition.

SUBPLOT: A series of events that coincide with the main plot, in a drama or narrative.

SYMBOL (SYMBOLISM): An object that stands for something else. Symbolism is the use of objects to convey emotions or ideas.

TERCET: A stanza or section of a poem consisting of three lines.

THEME: The central idea in a literary work.

THESIS: A statement or summary of the main ideas and arguments in an academic essay.

THIRD-PERSON NARRATIVE: A narrative told from the perspective of someone who is not a character in the story; the third-person narrator observes and comments on the events of the text.

TONE: The mood of a literary work; an author's (or speaker's) perceived attitude toward the reader or the text.

TRAGEDY: A dramatic work that represents the downfall of the protagonist.

TRAGIC FLAW: The protagonist's weakness that brings about his or her downfall in a tragedy.

TRAGIC HERO: The protagonist in a work of tragedy, who is neither completely good nor completely evil but evokes the audience's pity and terror. The tragic hero's central weakness (or tragic flaw) is partially or wholly responsible for his or her downfall.

UNRELIABLE NARRATOR: A narrator whose perspective is distorted in some way.

VERSE: Writing, most often poetry, that adheres to some structure or pattern of rhythm and metre.

VOICEOVER: A term that describes a voice that is superimposed over a cinematic image or scene.

SUGGESTED FURTHER READING

Abrams, M.H., and Geoffrey Harpham. *A Glossary of Literary Terms*. 9th ed. Boston: Cengage Wadsworth, 2009. Print.

Baldick, Chris. *The Concise Oxford Dictionary of Literary Terms*. 2nd ed. Oxford: Oxford UP, 2001. Print.

Hamilton, Sharon. *Essential Literary Terms: A Brief Norton Guide with Exercises*. New York: Norton, 2006. Print.

Kennedy, X.J., et al. *Handbook of Literary Terms: Literature, Language, Theory*. New York: Longman, 2004. Print.

Murfin, Ross C., and Supryia M. Ray. *The Bedford Glossary of Critical and Literary Terms*. 3rd ed. Boston: Bedford/St. Martin's, 2009. Print.

Index

A

Achebe, Chinua, 41
Acker, Kathy, 4
action, 84, 128, 174
acts, 109, 174
actual readers, 42–43
Adorno, Theodor, 46
aesthetics, 3
allegory, 94, 111–112, 174
alliteration, 6, 67, 174
allusion, 66, 112, 174
Althusser, Louis, 38, 46
ambiguity, 66, 174
amphibrach, 69
amphimacer, 69
anapest, 69
Anderson, Gil, 71–72
Animal Farm (Orwell), 8
antagonists, 90, 106, 126, 174
anthologies, 166, 169
archetype, 59, 174
arena stage, 110–111
Aristotle, 37
Arnold, Matthew, 2
articles. *See also* sources
    in journals, 170
    in newspapers, 170
    in online scholarly
      journals, 171
    from periodicals, 169–170
    in reference works, 170
assonance, 67, 111–112, 174
Atwood, Margaret, 92

Austen, Jane, 88
author with an editor, citation for
    book by, 168

B

Barrett, Andrea, 92, 97–102
Barsam, Richard, 128
Barthes, Roland, 38, 39
Battleship Potemkin (1925), 132
Beauvoir, Simone de, 47
Benjamin, Walter, 46
Beowulf, 24
*Between Men: English Literature and
    Male Homosocial Desire* (Sedgwick),
    49–50
Bhabha, Homi K., 52
biographical references, 29
blank verse, 71, 175
block quotations, 159
books, citing, 168–169
Booth, Wayne, 42
Bourne Identity, The (2002), 132
Boyle, Danny, 133
Branagh, Kenneth, 126
Brecht, Bertolt, 46
Browning, Robert, 61
Burns, Robert, 5–6, 59
Butler, Judith, 47, 49
Byron, Lord, 65

C

camera tracking, 129
canon, 4–5, 175

Carroll, Lewis, 7–8
Casablanca (1942), 127
catastrophe, 116, 175
catharsis, 108, 116, 175
Césaire, Aimé, 16–17
characterization
    definition of, 175
    in drama, 105–107
    fictional, 89–91
    in film, 126
    in poetry, 61
characters, 89, 104, 105–107,
    125–127, 175
Cheever, John, 84–86, 87–89
cinema, 124
cinematography, 128–130
cine-psychoanalysis, 132–133
citations, 159–165
    drama, 162–165
    fiction, 160–162
    poetry, 159–160
    prose works, 160–162
Cixous, Hélène, 47
class lecture, 172
climax, 86, 175
close-up, 175
Coleridge, Samuel Taylor, 21, 71
comedy, 9, 115–116, 175
comic relief, 107, 175
commentary, 27
comparative paper, 27–28
composition, 58
computer-generated imagery (CGI), 132
conclusion, 86, 109, 175
concrete poetry, 58
conflict, 86, 108, 175
connotation, 74, 175
Conrad, Joseph, 41
consonance, 67, 175
Corrigan, Timothy, 125
"Country Husband, The" (Cheever),
    84–86, 87–89
couplet, 66, 175
Course in General Linguistics (Saussure), 39
crane shot, 129

creative entry, 26
crisis, 176
critical editions, 166
critical entry, 26
critical race theory, 51–53
critical references, 30
criticism, 36–53
    critical race theory, 51–53
    feminist, 46–48
    formalism, 36–38
    gender, 48–50
    Marxist, 45–46
    New Criticism, 36–38
    New Historicist, 50–51
    postcolonial, 51–53
    poststructuralist, 40–41
    psychoanalytic, 43–45
    reader-response, 42–43
    structuralist, 38–40
crosscutting, 131, 176
Cruise, Tom, 128
cultural determinism, 49
cultural materialism, 46, 50
culture, 2

D

dactyl, 69
deconstruction, 40–41
deconstructionist feminism, 47
dénouement, 86, 176
Derrida, Jacques, 40
dialectical montage, 131–132
dialogue poem, 61
diction, 61, 73, 176
différance, 40
Don Juan (Byron), 65
Donne, John, 7
drafts, 142–155. *See also* writing
    assignments
    first, 142–147
    peer review, 153–154
    proofreading, 153–154
    revising, 147–153
    reworking, 154–155

drama, 104–122
    characterization, 105–107
    characters, 105–107
    comedy, 115–117
    definition of, 176
    vs. fiction, 104
    language and style, 111–113
    plot, 108–110
    quotations from, 162–163
    reading demonstration, 117–119
    stage, 110–111
    structure, 108–110
    theme, 113–114
    tragedy, 115–117
dramatic irony, 112–113, 176
dramatic text, 105
dramaturgy, 105, 176
DVDs, citing, 171–172

E

Eagleton, Terry, 46
écriture féminine, 44, 48
editing (film), 130–132
ego identification, 133
Eisenstein, Sergei, 131
electronic sources, 166–167. *See also*
    sources
Eliot, T.S., 7
ellipsis, 160, 176
emphasis, 167
Empire of the Senseless (Acker), 4
English sonnet, 70, 179
enjambment, 176
epic, 176
episode, 27, 84–85, 176
essays, edited collection of, 165
explication, 27
exposition, 86, 109, 176
eye rhyme, 176
Eyes Wide Shut (1999), 128

F

falling action, 86, 109, 176
"Fears in Solitude" (Coleridge), 21
Feminine Mystique, The (Friedan), 47

feminism, 46–48, 95–97
feminist criticism, 46–48
feminist writers, 44–45
fiction, 83–102
    characterization in, 89–91
    citations, 160–162
    definition of, 83, 176
    vs. drama, 104
    narration, 87–89
    plot, 84–87
    point of view, 87–89
    quotations from, 160–162
    reading demonstration, 95–97
    setting, 91–93
    short fiction, 95–97
    symbolism, 93–95
    theme, 93–95
fictional characterization, 89–91
figurative language, 63, 176
film, 124–135
    character, 125–127
    cinematography, 128–130
    cine-psychoanalysis, 132–133
    cited work, 171–172
    editing, 130–132
    first draft, 142–147
    mise-en-scène, 127–128
    narrative, 125–127
    note-taking, 125
    overview, 124–125
    point of view, 125–127
    reading demonstration, 132–135
Finnegans Wake (Joyce), 6
first draft
    revising, 147–153
    writing, 142–147
first-person narrative, 87, 176
Fish, Stanley, 43
fixed form, 68, 70, 176
flashback, 84–85, 176
flat character, 175
foil, 177
font, 172
foot, 68, 177
Forbidden Planet, The (Wilcox), 16–17

foreground, 177
foreshadowing, 85, 177
formalism, 36–38
formatting, 172–173
    font, 172
    heading, 173
    margins, 172
    page numbers, 173
    paper, 172
    secondary sources, 173
    spacing, 172
    titles, 173
Foucault, Michel, 49
"fourth wall", 110–111
Frankenstein (Shelley), 19, 22
Fraser, Clara, 47
free verse, 177
Freud, Sigmund, 43–44
Freytag, Gustav, 85
Friedan, Betty, 47
"Frost at Midnight" (Coleridge), 21, 71

G

Gardner, John, 24
Gates, Henry Louis, Jr., 52–53
gender criticism, 48–50
Gender Trouble: Feminism and the
    Subversion of Identity (Butler), 49
"Gentlemen Take Polaroids" (Anderson),
    71–72
Ginsberg, Allen, 8
Globe and Mail, The, 83
Gone With the Wind (1939), 127
Govier, Katherine, 95–97
Gramsci, Antonio, 46
Greenblatt, Stephen, 50–51, 117–118
Grendel (Gardner), 24
gynocriticism, 48, 95–97

H

half rhyme, 68, 177
hamartia, 115
Hamlet, 9
    characterization in, 106
    dramatic language in, 112–113
    New Historicism and, 117–119

plot, 108
    tragic situation in, 115
hand-held shot, 129
Handmaid's Tale, The (Atwood), 92
"Hanging Fire" (Lorde), 74–78
Hardy, Thomas, 61
Hawthorne, Nathaniel, 94
Hayward, Steven, 92
heading, 173
Heart of Darkness (Conrad), 41
hegemony, 46
hero, 90, 177
heroic couplet, 68, 177
heroine, 90, 177
historical references, 29
history, 7–8
Hitchcock, Alfred, 126
hooks, bell (Gloria Jean Watkins), 52–53
Horkheimer, Max, 46
hyperbole, 74, 177

I

iamb, 69
iambic pentameter, 68, 177
ideology, 45
imagery, 72, 111–112, 177
images, 27, 177
implied readers, 42–43
"In a Station at the Metro" (Pound), 4
In Search of Lost Time (Proust), 84
indirect quotations, 167
internal rhyme, 68, 177
Irigaray, Luce, 44, 47, 48
irony, 177
Iser, Wolfgang, 42–43
Italian, The (Radcliffe), 23
Italian sonnet, 70, 178

J

Jakobson, Roman, 37
Jameson, Fredric, 46
Jaws (1975), 132
Johnson, Barbara, 41, 47
journal articles, 165
journal entries, 26–27
Joyce, James, 6

K

Kazan, Elia, 126
Keats, John, 24–25, 60, 62–63, 64, 65, 66,
    79–82
Kristeva, Julia, 44, 47, 48, 132–135
Kubrick, Stanley, 128

L

Lacan, Jacques, 44–45
language, 111–113
Le cheval emballé (1908), 131
"Leaving the Motel" (Snodgrass),
    14, 25
Leavis, F.R., 3
Lévi-Strauss, Claude, 38
limited omniscience, 88, 177
line break, 71–72, 177
"literary", definition of, 5
literary anthologies, 166
literary language, 5–6
literature, 2–5
    affective power of, 9
    culture and, 2
    definitions of, 5
    historicity of, 7–8
    literary language, 5–6
    politics of, 3, 8–9
    properties of, 5–10
"Littoral Zone, The" (Barrett), 92,
    97–102
Lorde, Audre, 74–78
Lucas, George, 129
Lukács, Georg, 45, 84
Lumière, Auguste, 124
Lumière, Louise, 124

M

Macbeth, 22, 115–116
Man, Paul de, 41
Mare, Walter de la, 73–74
margins, 172
Marlowe, Christopher, 7
Marx, Karl, 45
Marxist criticism, 45–46
Marxist feminism, 47
Matrix, The (1999), 129

McGann, Jerome, 51
metaphor, 15, 64–65, 104, 177
methodological references, 29–30
metre, 68–69, 111–112, 177
Midsummer Night's Dream, A, 9, 112,
    116, 119–122
Miller, Henry, 4
Miller, J. Hillis, 41
Millet, Kate, 47, 95
"Mirror" (Plath), 59–60
mise-en-scène, 127–128, 177
Mission Impossible (1996), 132
"A Modest Proposal" (Swift), 8
monologue, 178
montage, 178
Morrison, Toni, 52
Munro, Alice, 90–91
multiple authors, 165–166
multi-volume work, 169
Mulvey, Laura, 132–133

N

Narayan, Uma, 47
narration, 83, 87–89, 178
narrative, 84, 125–127, 178
narrators, 83, 87. See also fiction
    definition of, 178
    limited omniscience, 88
    objective, 89, 178
    omniscient, 88, 178
    unreliable, 88, 180
New Criticism, 36–38, 73–74
New Criticism, The (Ransom), 38
New Historicism, 8, 46, 50–51,
    117–119
non-comparative paper, 27–28
non-research essays, 27–28
non-thesis, 23–24
novellas, 84, 178
novels, 84, 178
"Nuns Fret Not" (Wordsworth),
    70–71

O

objective narrator, 89, 178
octave, 70, 178

"Ode to Nightingale" (Keats), 79–82
    allusion in, 66
    ambiguity in, 66
    metaphor in, 64
    personification in, 66
    setting in, 62–63
    simile in, 65
    speaker in, 60
Oedipus Rex, 43
omniscient narrator, 88, 178
online sources, 166–167
onomatopoeia, 178
open form, 70–71, 178
Orwell, George, 8
outline, 138–142
Oxford English Dictionary, 5, 58

P

page numbers, 173
"A Pair of Tickets" (Tan), 92,
    97–102
pan shot, 129
paper, 172
parallel action, 124, 131, 178
parallel editing, 131
pastoral, 178
pastoral setting, 63
pathos, 9
peer review, 153–154
persona, 59, 178
personal website, 171
personification, 60, 66, 178
Petrarchan sonnet, 70, 178
Piano Lesson, The (Wilson), 30–35,
    108–109, 111, 112
Plath, Sylvia, 59–60
Playing in the Dark: Whiteness
    and the Literary Imagination
    (Morrison), 52
plays, *see also* Drama, 105
plot
    definition of, 178
    in drama, 104, 108–110
    in fiction, 84–87
    in film, 124

poems, 59–72
    figurative language, 64–67
    form and structure, 70–72
    interpretation of, 15–16
    prosody in, 67–70
    setting of, 62–63
    situation in, 62–63
    speaker, 59–62
poetic language, 64–67
    allusion, 66
    ambiguity, 66
    metaphor, 64–65
    personification, 66
    simile, 65
    symbol, 66
Poetics (Aristotle), 36–38
poetry, 58–82
    blank verse, 71
    citations, 159–160
    definitions of, 58, 178
    fixed form, 70
    New Criticism and, 73–74
    open form, 70–71
    overview, 58–59
    sonnet, 70
point of view
    definition of, 178
    in fiction, 87–89
    in film, 125–127
    in poetry, 59
politics of literature, 3
postcolonial criticism, 51–53
postcolonial feminism, 47
poststructuralist criticism, 40–41
Pound, Ezra, 4
preferred reading, 41
Pride and Prejudice (Austen), 88
professional website, 171
proletariat, 45
proofreading, 153–154
Propp, Vladimir, 38
proscenium stage, 110–111
prose, 58, 83, 160–162, 178
prosody, 67–70
protagonist, 90, 106–107, 126, 179

Proust, Marcel, 84
psychoanalytic criticism, 43–45
psychoanalytic feminism, 47

Q
quatrain, 70, 179
queer theory, 47, 48–50
quotations, 159–165
    drama, 162–165
    fiction, 160–162
    poetry, 159–160
    prose works, 160–162

R
Radcliffe, Anne, 23
Rakow, Lana F., 46
Ransom, John Crowe, 38
reader-response criticism, 42–43
realism, 45
"A Red, Red Rose" (Burns), 59
references, 29–30
reflection papers, 26–27
research essays, 29–30
research paper, 30–35
resolution, 109
response papers, 26–27
reviews, 170
Rhetoric of Fiction, The (Booth), 42
rhyme, 68, 111–112, 179
rhythm, 6, 68, 179
Rich, Adrienne, 47
rising action, 86, 109, 179
Romeo and Juliet, 64–65
round character, 175
Rubin, Gayle, 47
"Ruined Maid, The" (Hardy), 61
Russian Formalism, 37–38

S
Said, Edward, 52
Saussure, Ferdinand de, 39
scansion, 68, 179
scenes, 27, 109, 179
scopophilia, 133
second or subsequent edition, 168

secondary sources, 163–167
    books by single author, 164–165
    critical editions, 165–166
    edited collection of essays, 165
    electronic and online sources,
      166–167
    emphasis, 167
    indirect quotations, 167
    journal articles, 165
    literary anthologies, 165–166
    sources with multiple authors,
      165–166
    titles, 173
Secret Mitzvah of Lucio Burke, The
    (Hayward), 92
Sedgwick, Eve Kosofsky, 47, 49–50
sestet, 70, 179
setting, 91–93, 104, 179
Sexual Politics (Millet), 47
Shakespeare, William, 7
    Hamlet, 9, 106, 108, 111–113, 115,
      117–119
    Macbeth, 22
    Midsummer Night's Dream, A, 9,
      112, 116, 119–122
    Romeo and Juliet, 64–65
    Tempest, The, 16–17
Shakespearean sonnet, 70, 179
Shelley, Mary, 19
short fiction, 95–97
Short Guide to Writing about Film, A
    (Carrigan), 125
short stories, 84, 179
Showalter, Elaine, 48
signification, 39
signifiers, 39, 40–41
Signifying Monkey, The (Gates), 52
Silence of the Lambs, The, 126
simile, 6, 65, 179
Snodgrass, W.D., 14, 25
socialist feminism, 47
"Sociology" (Govier), 95–97
soliloquy, 106, 179
"Soliloquy of the Spanish Cloister"
    (Browning), 61

Sonnet 12, 68
sonnets, 70, 179
Sophocles, 43
sources, 158–172
    books by single author, 164–165
    critical editions, 165–166
    drama, 162–163
    edited collection of essays, 165
    electronic and online sources,
      166–167
    emphasis, 167
    fiction, 160–162
    indirect quotations, 167
    journal articles, 165
    literary anthologies, 165–166
    literary works, 159–163
    with multiple authors, 165–166
    poetry, 159–160
    prose works, 160–162
    secondary, 163–167
    titles, 173
spacing, 172
speaker, 59–62, 179
special effects, 131, 179
Spivak, Gayatri Chakravorty, 47, 52
spondee, 69
stage, 110–111
stage directions, 179
stanza, 63, 179
Star Wars (1977), 129
stereotypes, 91, 107, 179
stock characters, 107
Streetcar Named Desire, A (Williams),
    105–106, 111, 112, 113–114, 126
strong thesis, 25
structuralist activity, 39
structuralist criticism, 38–40
structure, 108–110
student writing, 20–22
    drama, 119–122
    fiction, 97–102
    poetry, 74–78
subplot, 109, 179
superstructure, 45

Swift, Jonathan, 8
symbolic order, 44
symbolism, 93–95, 179
symbols, 15, 27, 66, 104, 109, 179

T

Tan, Amy, 92, 97–102
Technicolor, 129
Tempest, A (Césaire), 16–17
Tempest, The (Shakespeare), 16–17
tercet, 70, 180
Thelma & Louise (1991), 132
theme, 93–95, 113–114, 180
thesis, 22–26
    definition of, 180
    non-thesis, 23–24
    strong, 25
    weak, 24–25
    in writing process, 138–142
third-person narrative, 87, 180
thrust stage, 110–111
Tin Flute, The (Roy), 92
titles, 173
tone, 61, 180
topic sentence, 146
topics, 16–18
tragedy, 9, 37, 115–116, 180
tragic flaw, 115, 180
tragic hero, 115, 180
Trainspotting (1996), 132–135
transitional sentence, 147
translation, 169
Trip to the Moon, A (1902), 131
trochee, 69

U

unreliable narrator, 88, 180

V

variable-speed photography, 129
verse, 180
Vertigo, 126
videocassette, 171–172
voiceover, 180

W

Wachowski, Andy, 129
Wachowski, Larry, 129
Watkins, Gloria Jean (bell hooks), 52–53
weak thesis, 24–25
web sources, 170–171
"When We Dead Awaken: Writing as
　Re-Vision" (Rich), 47
Who Do You Think You Are?
　(Munro), 90–91
Wilcox, Fred M., 16–17
Williams, Raymond, 46
Williams, Tennessee, 105–106, 111
Wilson, August, 30–35, 108–109, 111
Wizard of Oz, The (1939), 127, 129
Wollstonecraft, Mary, 47
women writers, 5
Women's Liberation Movement, 47
Woolf, Virginia, 47
Wordsworth, William, 60, 70–71
Works Cited list, 167–172
　anthologies, 169
　articles from periodicals, 169–170
　articles in journals, 170
　articles in newspapers, 170
　articles in online scholarly journals,
　　171
　articles in reference works, 170
　author with an editor, 168
　books, 168–169
　class lecture, 172
　DVD, 171–172
　film, 171–172
　more than one author, 168
　multi-volume work, 169

　non-periodical works, 168
　one author, 168
　personal website, 171
　professional website, 171
　reviews, 170
　second or subsequent edition, 168
　selection from anthologies, 169
　translation, 169
　videocassette, 171–172
　web sources, 170–171
writing assignments, 13–16. *See also*
　drafts
　journal entries, 26–27
　non-research essays, 27–28
　research essays, 29–30
　response papers, 26–27
　student writing, 20–22
　thesis, 22–26
　with topics, 16–18
　without topics, 18–20
writing process, 138–155
　peer review, 153–154
　proofreading, 153–154
　revising first draft, 147–153
　reworking final draft, 154–155
　from thesis to outline, 138–142
writing topics, 16–18

Y

Yearsley, Ann, 8
"Young Goodman Browne"
　(Hawthorne), 94

Z

Žižek, Slavoj, 44